Collaborations

Collaborations

Anthropology in a Neoliberal Age

Edited by Emma Heffernan, Fiona Murphy
and Jonathan Skinner

Routledge
Taylor & Francis Group

LONDON AND NEW YORK

This edition published 2021
by Routledge
2 Park Square, Milton Park, Abingdon, Oxon, OX14 4RN

and by Routledge
52 Vanderbilt Avenue, New York, NY 10017

Routledge is an imprint of the Taylor & Francis Group, an informa business

British Library Cataloguing-in-Publication Data
A catalogue record for this book is available from the British Library

Library of Congress Cataloging-in-Publication Data
A catalog record has been requested for this book

ISBN: 978-1-3500-0226-5 (hbk)
ISBN: 978-1-0001-8514-0 (ebk)

Typeset by RefineCatch Limited, Bungay, Suffolk

Cover Design: Adriana Brioso
Cover image © Cara Brophy, 2016

Contents

Figures

Tables

Notes on Contributors

Anne Sigfrid Grønseth is professor in social anthropology at Lillehammer University College, Norway.

Tracey Heatherington is associate professor of anthropology at University of Wisconsin-Milwaukee, USA.

Emma Heffernan is an anthropologist and nurse currently working in clinical research in Dublin, Ireland.

Carolyn Hough is associate professor of anthropology at Augustana College, Illinois, USA.

Colin Irwin is a research fellow at the University of Liverpool, UK.

Adam Kaul is professor of anthropology, sociology and social welfare at Augustana College, Illinois, USA.

Laura Korčulanin is a design anthropologist, water toilet advocate, lecturer and artivist based in Lisbon, Portugal.

Philipp Lottholz is a research assistant at the University of Reading, UK.

Scott MacLochlainn is an anthropologist at Georg-August-Universität Göttingen, Germany.

Fiona Murphy is an anthropologist and a research fellow at the Senator George J. Mitchell Institute for Global Peace, Security and Justice, Queen's University Belfast, Northern Ireland.

Cris Shore is professor of social anthropology at the University of Auckland and guest professor of public management at the Stockholm Centre for Organizational Research, Sweden.

Jonathan Skinner is a reader in anthropology at the University of Roehampton, UK.

Eli Støa is professor in housing at the Faculty of Architecture and Fine Arts at the Norwegian University of Science and Technology, Norway.

Alisse Waterston is an anthropologist and Presidential Scholar and Professor at the John Jay College of Criminal Justice of the City University of New York (CUNY), New York, USA.

Foreword

Jonathan Skinner

This volume originates from the conference panel 'Symbiotic Anthropologies: Theoretical Commensalities and Methodological Mutualisms' at the 2015 annual conference of the Association of Social Anthropologists of the UK and Commonwealth held at the University of Exeter. We had been struck by this conference theme established for the event and sought to examine how anthropology engages with the academic and non-academic worlds; how it is positioned as a discipline viz. the other; how interdisciplinary, collaborative, symbiotic anthropologists and their work are and what manner of strengths and difficulties, tensions and advantages there are to these engagements. As a concentrated engagement with contemporary anthropology, the conference ranged from collaboration across disciplinary boundaries to the cross-pollination of theory and practice for anthropologists, activists, consultants and the like (ASA 2015). Interstitial, liminal, 'betwixt and between', anthropology is a hub or 'trading zone' (Galison 2010; see also Skinner, this volume) subject area. That makes it precarious as it straddles social worlds. But that does not mean that it has to be non-committal. It can be 'militant' (Scheper-Hughes 1995) and radical just as much as it is relativistic (cf. Geertz 1984) or neutral (Firth 1981). This volume considers just some of these positions and leanings from leading anthropologists.

For the ASA conference organizers (for which we must thank Samantha Hurn, Ann Kelly, Tom Rice, Katharine Tyler, Hannah Rumble and Andrea Butcher and the ASA Committee then under the auspices of Veronica Strang), 'symbiotic anthropologies' represented 'those occasions and relationships when in response to institutional pressures, or ethnographic demands, we are forced, obliged or fortunate enough to depend upon others for our institutional survival, or our theoretical and methodological innovations' (ASA 2015). For them, symbiosis is a natural double-edged sword. More prosaically, they describe anthropology as a discipline with a 'conjunctive – and at times parasitic – sensibility' (ASA 2015) as it works with other people but in so doing relies upon them and the relationship with them cultivated during fieldwork. Symbiosis is typically a relationship of mutual benefit, living together like lichen or gut flora in the biological world. Anthropologist Robert Layton (2009: 248) draws equivalences between symbiosis, parasitism and predation in a range of species, including 'human society'. In the social world – a 'social symbiosis', as coined by Nadel (1949) working with and among the Nupe of Nigeria – it is a relationship of support and reliance, and occasionally necessity. Breusers, Nederlof and van Rheenen (2000) note symbiotic exchange relationships between farmers and herders in Burkina Faso as a more contemporary example. These relations might have a syncretic dimension as out of the mutualism something special develops. This can range from voodoo to the interview as exemplified by Desmangles (1990: 476) in Haiti and Sparkes (1997) writing about the relationship building between interviewer and interviewee. Writing in *Current Anthropology*, Veronica Strang (990) suggests that anthropologists should develop 'positive symbiotic relationships' with indigenous communities they work with, acknowledging co-authorship for their theories as well as the ethnographies that arise. This possible 'happy coincidence' (Strang) is characterized as idealistic 'multicultural symbiosis' by Escárcega (2006: 994), especially when power/knowledge relations tend towards the more parasitic than symbiant (cf. Fairhead 2006: 995).

Our preference, then, is for an examination of a 'collaborative anthropology'. This presupposes a desire to work together rather than assume a necessity in the relationship. This volume considers the complexities, creativities and complicities of these new collaborative forms and posits that such collaborations are key to the long-term sustainability of anthropology as a discipline. We ask to what extent is collaborative anthropology ultimately sustainable? What are its relations, boundaries, motives and merits, and the associated fallout, debris, ethics and problems? This edited collection contains an international and expert set of theoretical, methodological and empirical papers from the ASA conference as well as specially commissioned contributions that explore the natures, nurtures and necessities of such collaborative anthropologies. Key to this volume is the way in which it shows how anthropologists contribute to contemporary problems and issues in society, whether in academia or in the community – if such a pure and applied division can be maintained; recall Sue Wright, writing in Benthall's *The Future of Anthropology* (1995: 67), lamenting the treatment of anthropologically trained practitioners working in contract environments outside of the university as 'no-longer anthropologists'.

Collaboration has become the key to survival in this austere age of self-justification by social media and disciplinary justification by research audits and exercises. It has increasingly become a topic of examination in anthropology, especially with the new journal *Collaborative Anthropologies* conceived and edited by east coast American anthropologist Luke Eric Lassiter since 2008. The journal supports dialogue across subfields and related disciplines and recognizes 'the complexity' of relations between researchers, practitioners, interlocutors and disciplines (*Collaborative Anthropologies* 2019). It is typically engaged, participatory and activist in orientation. Collaborative anthropology is described as a meaningful approach with mentors in the field (Kistler 2015); it can be community-based participatory action research (Schensul, Berg and Williamson 2008); it is also about collaborating in the co-production of ethnographic knowledge from fieldwork to text – 'side by side', as Les Field advocates (2008). This is more than a response to 1980s 'writing culture' critiques on representation and ethnographic writing. The 'collaborative turn' (Haviland 2016: 17) is found in Haviland's recent collaborative arts-based photographic work with the Chiapas or among the Jalaris Aboriginal Corporation of Western Australia, which are examples of 'co-creativity' (2016: 153; see also Haviland 2014) where the anthropologist works with, alongside, and sometimes for, their collaborators. These are team approaches to document voices and generate new artwork. They are attempts to work on a level playing field, combatting the 'asymmetries' (Clerke and Hopwood 2014) and power differences of the research relationship.

Before establishing the *Collaborative Anthropologies* journal, Lassiter (1998, 2001, 2005a, 2005b) published extensively on the nature of collaboration in anthropology, specifically in collaborative ethnography, using focus groups, indigenous readers and co-writers in developing his/their work. For Lassiter, collaboration is 'working together', a practice intrinsic to ethnography. However, foregrounding the collaborative aspect of ethnography '*deliberately* and *explicitly* emphasizes collaboration at every point in the ethnographic process' (Lassiter 2005c, author's emphases). This is the unveiling of anthropology's building blocks. It is 'inherently advocative' (2005a: 84) in its positioning of the ethnographic work and traces a lineage back prior to postmodern and feminist debates on the representation of culture, way back to early Americanist ethnography at the turn of the twentieth century. It was only with the solidification of the discipline that anthropology presented a more 'scientific', objective and single authored stance. More recently, Lassiter (2005a: 94) notes anthropology's disciplinary goals have shifted: 'The goals of anthropology seem to be shifting as the discipline's practitioners, academic and applied, establish themselves in streams of practice more relevant, more public, and more accessible to a diversity of constituencies.'

Lassiter seeks to instil collaboration in ethnographic work, with obvious effect upon the wider discipline. For Lassiter (2005a: 93), ethnography should grasp at 'the trope of collaboration' and keep it as one of the discipline's defining motifs. This retains a humane, dialogic, multi-authored, layered collaborative ethnography that has had many passes through the fieldsite as best practice. The concern, here, in this volume about collaborative anthropology, is how to understand these disciplinary turns, its stasis, advantages, difficulties, pressures, tensions, and the implications for the future of anthropology and its practitioners. We recognize and admire collaborative ethnography, but concentrate on an examination of collaborative anthropology. What has prompted those shifts Lassiter identifies and where are they leading us? This book gives examples and testimony of contemporary anthropology in academia and in practice on topics from university and disciplinary restructuring to peace negotiations to prostitution, well-being to international business. The examples show the collaborative and interdisciplinary value of anthropology as a tool with which to examine complex and urgent societal issues, how to work with people and across institutions. The case studies also warn of the difficulties that lie down some new directions. Taken together, we show collaboration itself as a concept within the discipline of anthropology and how it is operationalized within very different contexts, in different styles and voices, with different understandings and intensions of collaboration, what collaboration brings to other disciplines and in turn what other disciplines bring to anthropology. In the neoliberal university where impact agendas are now foremost and the value of the humanities and social sciences are being eroded, we argue that collaboration is one of the more fruitful avenues to securing the position of anthropology in what can be described as an insecure space.

Writing in his article in *Social Anthropology/Anthropologie Sociale*, 'Anthropology in and of the Academy: Globalization, Assessment and our Field's Future', Don Brenneis (2009) reflects on his position as journal editor and the changing face – nay, mask – of the academic landscape. Education has become a commodity for privatization, and we quite literally and theoretically live within a new 'knowledge economy', he demurs. Moreover, he writes, '[t]he contemporary context is both complex and challenging, with already ongoing processes of centralisation, standardisation and transformation deeply inflected by the current economic situation' (Brenneis 2009: 262); mix in the perils and pandemics of the Anthropocene and you get Pinney's (2012: 393) 'gentle Apocalypse'. This is a sign of the times and what Shore and Wright recently label 'the death of the public university' (Shore and Wright 2016, 2017), commonly identified as a change in the tertiary institution of the last thirty years with the rise of an academic capitalism from fees for students to commercial spinouts for staff and intellectual property for the university itself. This transition is lamented as an aspect of 'neoliberalisation' (Shore and Wright 2016: 47) that stresses private wealth over common good. For them it has the following key reform features: state disinvestment, regimes of competitiveness and audit, administrative bloat under the rise of an 'Administeriat', new entrepreneurial income streams, and a reorientation towards private investment over and instead of public good (Shore and Wright 2017). Citing Zapatista rhetorics on globalization and the new Fourth World War against capitalism, Martin Mills goes further, dramatizing the conflict by suggesting a dystopian shift taking place around him when he writes:

> What we see in universities today is exactly that: a new battleground for the nature of who we truly are as scholars, academics and students, as the logic of scholarship is transformed, apparently, into the remorseless logic of business. As we stand in our seminar rooms and lecture halls, the world seems to shift around us. When once academics and students were united, at least in principle, in the shared pursuit of scholarship and understanding, we are now divided from one another in the very quality of our personhood within a larger economic game.
>
> 2017: 47–8

At the time of writing, Mills had been supporting the Reclaim the University campaign at Aberdeen University (Mills 2016) with a manifesto part-instigated by Professor of Anthropology Tim Ingold (Ingold 2016). The aim was – and continues to be – to reform universities beset by new business regimes and to press for a return to more communal and civic-minded university missions (Anon. 2016). To not support such political stances, to not give one's solidarity, is to face the charge of collusion – or rather complicity, as Shore and Davidson (2014) prefer, or worse, to be guilty of the charge of 'gadfly turned horse' by one of our editors, Fiona Murphy (2018): exploitative academics retaining an elitist position by abusing 'the precariat of academia' – the casualized academic labourer, often lacking tenure and facing 'academic assholery' (Dunn 2018) from their line managers. We are fortunate to have contributions in this volume not only from Fiona Murphy and Cris Shore, but also Tracey Heatherington, one of the editors of the journal issues of ANUAC (La rivista dell'Associazione Nazionale Universitaria Antropologi Culturali) that published some of Mills and Shore and Wright's position on the neoliberal university.

Returning to the work of linguistic anthropologist Don Brenneis, this neoliberal governmentality of accountability and audit has a distinct turn of phrase and an impetus that can be used to generate new collaborative dialogues and ways of coming together. We can learn from these changes, develop an understanding of the new language games at play, and ultimately come to reshape the discourses. Peer review is one example of finding a voice from the scale of journal article to department rating. Interdisciplinary funding and the shifts in research bodies and councils is another where anthropology can work as the traditional 'bridgehead of communication' (Overing 1985: 3) or, as Ingold (2018: 119) recently phrased it, our anthropology matters as a holistic study of 'the entwinement of aspects of life'. Anthropology is collaborative at its comparative ethnographic heart. It is holistic in outlook and contextual in practice. This is a more optimistic perspective on the present and the condition of the neoliberal academic, one where we are less buffeted by deterministic approaches to life, proxies for our selfish genes (cf. Wolf-Meyer and Collins 2013), the bullshit jobs, bullshit tasks or bullshit anthropologies that are around us, to further coin Marxist anarchist activist establishment LSE Professor of Anthropology David Graeber's (2013, 2018) recently minted expression. An equally polemical, if more informed, view on our neoliberal condition comes from David Harvey, geographer-turned-distinguished Professor of Anthropology at the City University of New York. For him,

> Neoliberalization is in the first instance a theory of political economic practices that proposes that human well-being can best be advanced by liberating individual entrepreneurial freedoms and skills within an institutional framework characterized by strong private property rights, free markets, and free trade.
>
> Harvey 2005: 2

In short, for old-fashioned Marxist Harvey, neoliberalism is political policy writ large upon the state landscape. It is 'the financialisation of everything' (2005: 33), a rapacious 'anarchy of the market' and 'chaos of individual interests' (2005: 82). This business version of the risk society calculus stresses the entrepreneurial more than the social democratic, and individual freedoms over social justice. For us, it is linked with the expansion of higher education, its massification in the UK and further afield. Free from market regulation, capital and labour divorce from each other with, we might say, the academic precariat standing in – quite literally 'subbing' – for the traditional proletariat. Academics alienated by austerity (a policy shift from 'fiscal stimulus to fiscal consolidation' [Wren-Lewis, undated: 18]) bridle at their difficult and sometimes demeaning circumstances. In this volume we hear of their resilience and resistance. We learn how anthropology is and can be a conduit for creative translation and innovative collaborative practice. Just like the anthropologists, anthropology is a resilient modern discipline for all its twentieth-century late origins. It has an important place in this diverse and fracturing world of ours.

Introduction

Emma Heffernan, Fiona Murphy and Jonathan Skinner

Towards a collaborative anthropology in a neoliberal age?

The notion of collaboration has long preoccupied the anthropological imagination. In recent years, however, with the growth of the neoliberal university, collaborative orientations have assumed a different hue. Notions such as collaboration, multidisciplinarity (even interdisciplinarity), public engagement and impact sit to the forefront of many discussions on how anthropology can refashion its presence in the university and broader society. This is one of the main threads throughout this collection and sets the scene for how a collaborative anthropology has been newly constituted in a neoliberal age. The thinking behind this volume was inspired in part by a number of conversations we had on the challenges of collaborative and interdisciplinary work for anthropologists.

Together, as three editors, we start from the perspective of a collaboration emerging from different kinds of anthropologies and different career trajectories and personal positionalities. Lead editor Emma Heffernan is currently working in clinical research in a number of Dublin hospitals. She completed her PhD in anthropology at Maynooth University in 2011 and a Master's in public health at University College Dublin in 2013. Emma is also a Registered General Nurse. Her research interests include social exclusion, global health, social and cultural determinants of health and illness, sexuality, social epidemiology, public health and clinical research.

Emma is joined by Fiona Murphy, an anthropologist who has worked across scholarly, industry and policy spaces. Fiona is, at the time of writing, a research fellow in the Senator George J. Mitchell Institute for Global Peace, Security, and Justice, Queen's University Belfast. She specializes in indigenous politics and movements, refugees and mobility studies, and sustainability. She has done fieldwork in Australia, Ireland, France and Turkey. Her work has led to collaborative research with colleagues in marketing, sociology, political science and law. As an anthropologist and advocate, Fiona blogs and reviews online for *Allegra: A Virtual Lab of Legal Anthropology Blog, Open Democracy, The Conversation UK* and for the *LSE Review of Books*.

Writing with Emma and Fiona, Jonathan Skinner is an anthropologist at the University of Roehampton, a member of CRESIDA (Centre for Research in Evolutionary, Social and Inter-Disciplinary Anthropology) in the Department of Life Sciences. After a traditional period of social anthropological fieldwork investigating postcolonial expressions of identity on the British island of Montserrat, he turned to more applied development work, following a volcanic eruption on the island, in terms especially of tourism regeneration. This interest and concern led to his editing the journal *Anthropology in Action* (2001–7). While still working in tourism and heritage studies, he also has active interests in the anthropology of dance as an avid social dancer inquisitive about teaching and learning practices (principally salsa and tango) and social inclusion and well-being (migrants, the elderly).

Together, the three co-editors have different perspectives on but a similar particular interest in how such interdisciplinary working relationships, particularly in an industry context, can be supported or troubled by ethical, even moral clashes. Hence the development of the panel 'Symbiotic Anthropologies' led by questions such as: 'To what extent is anthropology collaborative, colonizing, symbiotic and ultimately sustainable? What are its relations, boundaries, motives and merits, and the associated fallout, debris, ethics and problems?' In our quest to answer some of these questions we developed this volume from a range of chapters that explore the natures, nurtures and necessities of collaborative and symbiotic anthropologies.

One of the defining features of this collection is that we critique the very many permutations of a collaborative anthropology, reflecting on both the positive and negative impact of collaboration. In so doing, we also examine the genealogy of what we consider to be collaboration in a range of anthropological subdisciplines. This collection has contributions from precarious early to mid-career anthropologists as well as permanent/tenured anthropologists up to professorial level. To some degree, their starkly different views on collaboration reflect not just their specific subdisciplinary approaches, but also their career trajectories, often evolving very differently with the growth of neoliberalism and precarious work. Many new issues present to the precarious in the neoliberal university, and collaboration in this context often requires a different approach. Nonetheless, there is an important conversation in this book between the precarious and the tenured that underlines what, regardless of our positions and place in the neoliberal university, we can learn from one another. Such a collaboration, as one of the editors, Fiona Murphy, argues in her chapter, is necessary to reinvent ourselves and our relationships with one another in the neoliberal university.

As outlined in the Foreword, the neoliberal university has brought the conditions of the 'market' to education systems globally and so has corrupted education as a public good, particularly striking in countries such as the UK, the United States and Australia. As the site from which we write, even the space which forces us to 'be' scholars in a very particular capacity, its logics require problematization and critique, both modes of analysis which the neoliberal university often attempts to shut down. Indeed, many of the contributors herein seek to situate the particularities of collaboration in the contemporary university within the frame of neoliberalism.

Much of this conversation takes the form of both autoethnographic and autobiographical reflections, with contributors considering the specific forms their own collaborations have assumed in quite different settings. This approach leads to a rich theoretical discussion that explores the many disciplinary conflicts on how collaboration should be undertaken in anthropology today. The volume is thus a collective reflection that links trends towards collaboration and the denigration of the social sciences in the neoliberal university in order to interrogate the role of collaboration in moving our discipline forward. We present this conversation as one cognisant of the paradoxes of collaboration in a neoliberal context, as an orientation inextricably linked to (sometimes even dependent on) the demands of neoliberalism itself. However, our discussions undergird a premise which seeks the broader communication of the value of anthropology in a world of intersecting crises. Many of the collaborations delineated in this collection have issues of rights and social justice at their heart, calling thus for stronger notions of reciprocity, accountability, transparency and public responsibility to be more centred in our discipline. This book, therefore, challenges readers to adopt a more nuanced approach to understanding and thinking about the role of collaboration in anthropological endeavours.

While many scholars suggest that anthropology is collaborative by its very nature, we, however, set out the complexities of different collaborative pathways within a number of the expert or subdisciplinary parts of anthropology to encourage an agonistic reading of collaboration. The notion of collaboration has a long and complex history within the discipline of anthropology (in fact too long to rehearse herein); this extends even to the ways in which collaboration is defined and in terms of where and with whom it takes place. It is a premise that has underpinned much debate, and, as the Foreword highlights, a number of dedicated spaces such as the journal *Collaborative Anthropologies* have evolved into a kind of repository for collaborative anthropological work. It is therein that well-known figures such as Carolyn Fluehr-Lobban (1991; 2003) have argued that collaborative anthropological research is in fact 'ethically conscious' research. Fluehr-Lobban's stance on collaborative anthropologies is one we echo in this book – ultimately, an anthropology that pushes against traditional, hierarchical Boasian forms of anthropology (with very particular notions of collaboration). In its confronting of such traditions and hierarchies, it is also engaging a new and different machinery – that of neoliberalism, the challenges of which are widely documented in a number of the contributions herein. In breaking with a notion of collaboration grounded in imperial legacies, an anthropology bedfellow of the colonial enterprise, we push our collection into a space of discontinuity, interdisciplinarity and multidisciplinarity.

Ultimately, the collaborations herein engender spaces conversant with new contexts and approaches, making way for a shapeshifting collaborative anthropology deeply cognisant of the power relations, hierarchies and subversions embedded within the discipline, between disciplines and in wider societal engagements. As such, this is a call for more horizontal collaborations that sit in contrast to erstwhile anthropologies. Key to our reflections is the call for anthropology to reckon more strongly with decolonizing its theories, approaches and engagements through collaboration. This shift towards a decolonial anthropology is important to this collection, as it connects to our articulation of what a collaborative anthropology should look like. Central to this dynamic is the role of critique in fashioning a more reflexive yet dialogic collaborative anthropology. A collaborative anthropology anchored in thick description, situated histories and narrative as well as critique can be yielding for all participants.

Transformative collaborations

At its core, we believe anthropology to be collaborative, in its methods and theoretical orientations. It is a discipline which has contributed immeasurably to other expert areas, including but not limited to medicine, business, psychology and health. However, as a discipline born in imperial eras and engaged through colonial times, some of its history of collaboration continues to cast a dark shadow. The discipline has faced many crises, from controversy in El Dorado to support for the military-industrial complex with the Human Terrain Project in the United States. Indeed, since the watershed crisis of representation, anthropologists have continually questioned our approaches and methods in an attempt to remake and decolonize anthropology.

This collection emerges at a time when anthropology has witnessed its most recent crisis. An open access, young but high-ranking journal named *HAU* became the subject of much controversy and debate regarding its treatment of its staff. Much of this debate took place in social media realms, with some arguing that it was anthropology's #metoo moment. One of the striking aspects of this debate was the accusation that the journal played a role in reproducing an elitist anthropology built on old boys' networks and colonizing theoretical approaches. Further, the debate highlighted the divisions between precarious anthropologists and permanent/tenured anthropologists and called for more of an awareness of how the neoliberal university and publishing industry impact early to mid-career anthropologists in their everyday working lives. Large association conferences, such as the European Association of Social Anthropologists and the American Association of Anthropologists, undertook dedicated panels in their 2018 events in Stockholm and San Diego respectively to debate the issues that this crisis had provoked. This volume, however, attempts to shed such negative associations by demarking a new space of collaboration where anthropologists are aware of the ethical, moral and political impetus but also the limitations of their collaborative approaches.

Collaboration in this book takes place in multiple ways: within fieldwork; between anthropologist and research participants/collaborators; between academic anthropologists and applied spaces such as health and industry (to name but two); in the use of fieldwork data and in writing; between different disciplines and, indeed, between the precarious and those with security of tenure. Whether a business or a medical anthropologist, a dance anthropologist or an environmental expert, the challenges of collaborating with disciplines or experts beyond one's own space can overlap but can also be quite singular. As such, by design, we do not reach an overall conclusion or hypothesis on how collaboration should be undertaken by anthropologists; rather, we point to the very many ways anthropology can embrace a collaborative spirit more openly while remaining wary of its challenges. In editing this collection, we did not strive for a singular analysis of how collaboration is constituted in the discipline; to do so would have been limiting and a great disservice to the diverse, collaborative approaches within the discipline. However, to capture all such approaches would be beyond the limits of one collection and so we take the approach of examining subdisciplinary orientations through the lens of both 'Anthropology and Academia' and 'Anthropology in/of Practice'. While we divide the collection in this manner, we do not adhere to a philosophy of academics 'think' while practitioners 'do'; the division is merely to highlight the complementarities and dialogues between such spaces. This collection is ultimately exploratory in nature, aiming to provide an opening for debates on collaboration in what are the ever-increasing exigencies of neoliberalism today.

In the many spaces in which anthropologists work today, the question of how to collaborate – and even 'why' – features large. In the distinctive conditions of the neoliberal university and vagaries of economic globalization, anthropologists have to find new ways of working. The particularities of collaborating in these settings requires a deeper sense of moral responsibility and action with respect to one's research participants, subject matter, colleagues and the broader public. All of the contributors in this book have substantively different approaches and interpretations of what a collaborative anthropology should look like. But one of the key lines of debate in this book is how a collaborative, engaged anthropology which sits beyond the confines and limits of the neoliberal university can better serve the discipline in an age where anthropology as well as other social sciences come so frequently under attack. The contributors are anthropologists drawn from different subdisciplines, some based in universities, others working as practitioners from diverse geographic regions including Ireland, the UK, the United States, New Zealand, Slovenia, Germany and Norway. Their expertise is eclectic and relates anthropology to medicine, psychology, criminology, religion, business, dance and the body, environmentalism and sustainability, neoliberalism, peace and conflict studies, education and migration. Many of the contributors have developed a public engaged anthropological writing for varied publics, as experts in policy, as writers contributing to journalistic and fiction genres. This is reflected in the style of the different contributions from the Foreword to the Introduction, to the various chapters. Individual chapters question the role collaboration has played in their authors' anthropological practice, the lessons they have learned from such collaborations, including the moral and ethical limits to their practice, and future approaches to developing collaborations in the context of neoliberalism. The emphasis herein is on what anthropology can both gain and give through collaboration. As such, we call for a collaborative anthropology that is underpinned by reciprocity and a moral and ethical engagement – in short, a collaborative anthropology that must be transformative for all of its participants.

Collectively, the authors in this collection speak to the importance of understanding new regimes of responsibility and accountability in our collaborative practices, thus remaking our spaces of engagement. Such awareness is situated within the knowledge that collaboration in today's neoliberal contexts can be generative of dangerous hierarchies and prejudices, particularly in collaborations with neocolonial entities. Many of our contributors, in their reflection on such challenges, delimit the spaces of possibility for a collaborative anthropology, flagging the ethical tensions of limiting and challenging precarious neoliberal conditions. In our collective call for collaboration, we emphasize the role of accountability, responsibility, reciprocity, advocacy and an anthropology that works 'with' and 'alongside', not 'on', research participants. As such, many of the authors in this collection see themselves as collaborative translators of ontological and cultural differences. In a world witness to global and intersecting crises, where alterity is the subject and object of growing populism and radicalism, we see a collaborative anthropology as playing a critical role in translating such epistemological and ontological differences. The contributors in this volume strongly reflect (in both their sensibilities and writing) what it means to take collaborative research seriously, as participants, translators and advocates.

Structure of the volume

The volume is divided heuristically into two sections: 'Anthropology and Academia' and 'Anthropology in/of Practice'. This is heuristic in the sense that anthropologists working within universities and without universities 'practise' anthropology, whether in an applied fashion or not. Many of the contributions fall into the different categories of public, engaged, activist, advocate, applied, advocate and academic. While some scholars argue for a clear demarcation between such categories, many of our contributions in their collaborative spirit cross, even transgress, what can be at times rather facile divisions. The division we present herein thus represents the focus of the chapters in this collection rather than a larger commentary on how such categories have evolved or exist. In the first section, anthropologists are commenting and critiquing on their workplace university environments, whether US liberal arts college, modern campus university, business school or commercialized/capitalized global university. Here we read examples of the difficulties of operating as an anthropologist in traditional and modern university settings, how nimble academics have become to keep up with the recalibrations of the postmodern neoliberal education landscape. Academic capitalism, precarity, austerity, neoliberalism are the challenges faced by academics under pressure. We learn of their negotiations, collaborations, dreams, desires and despairs. In the second section, 'Anthropology in/of Practice', the focus is more on the work of anthropology and anthropologists in the community, from healthcare to peace making. This is applied work that shares anthropological interpretations with broader audiences and collaborators. Many of the contributors in this section move or have moved between university and applied worlds, and often work across both spaces.

Part 1: Anthropology and Academia

This book challenges notions of how a collaborative anthropology should be fashioned to the backdrop of neoliberalism. It also questions and reflects on the role of the collaborating anthropologist in the neoliberal university. In this section of the book, we include reflections, many autoethnographic, on the experiences of anthropologists who work in diverse settings beyond traditional anthropology departments. Therefore, in order to frame the context of this book – that of anthropology in the neoliberal university – we open with the ambitious attempt of Cris Shore to document how anthropology departments are faring in neoliberal universities using the particular case study of New Zealand. Shore's chapter, entitled 'Symbiotic or Parasitic? Universities, Academic Capitalism and the Global Knowledge Economy', evinces how changes in the political economy of higher education, including cuts in public spending, rising student fees, the privileging of STEM (science, technology, engineering, mathematics) subjects over the arts and humanities, and the proliferation of new regimes of audit and accountability, pose challenges for anthropology as well as the future of the university itself. By analysing the discourse of contemporary university management, Shore brings together a number of his research interests, particularly the way that universities, like many other public and private sector organizations, are being transformed by new regimes of audit and accountability and the growing emphasis on demonstrating 'impact', 'relevance' and 'external stakeholder' engagement – or what is sometimes suggestively termed the university's 'third mission'.

Shore thus presents an erudite critique of the ways in which the focus within the neoliberal university on engagement and impact has placed pressure on academics to be more entrepreneurial, to focus on 'impact', and to engage more proactively with business in order to generate new revenue streams and foster a more commercially oriented 'innovation ecosystem'. This has produced a notion of 'third mission' activities and a forging of a 'triple helix' of university–industry–

government relations which now underpins much of the funding of higher education in places such as the UK, Australia and New Zealand. Shore questions what such partnerships between public universities and private financial interests are doing to anthropology and academia more generally. These are the broader collaborations within the neoliberal university that anthropologists must suffer the costs of. Having to work in environments created through discourses of investment, commercialization and entrepreneurship, anthropology has become a target of attack in a number of jurisdictions. Shore asks the important question of whether these new relationships that are being forged between universities and academic capitalism can be described as symbiotic or parasitic, thereby framing the broader dynamics and challenges within which this volume is situated.

In Chapter 2, 'Leave a Light On For Us: The Future of a Collaborative Anthropology in the Neoliberal University', Fiona Murphy unpacks her professional trajectory and CV as a female precarious anthropologist working in and between a number of different disciplines in the neoliberal university. She does so in order to point to the challenges of collaboration for the precarious in the neoliberal university. In mapping her career trajectory, Murphy documents how the experience of precarity led to her working in a number of different kinds of space, including in a business school, and later, with policy makers, in what was a completely new direction for her. What undergirds Murphy's chapter is a theorization of collaboration as often being 'choiceless' in the career pathways of the precarious in the neoliberal university where demands of engagement and impact feature large. These are often the parasitic collaborations which reflect Shore's concerns about how the neoliberal university is impacting anthropological practice. However, there are positives, and Murphy argues that precarious anthropologists are often more flexible, fluid and broader in their skill sets which, to some degree, will have an impact on how the future anthropologies are shaped.

The volume proceeds with Chapter 3 by Jonathan Skinner: 'Most Humanistic, Most Scientific: Experiencing Anthropology in the Humanities and Life Sciences'. Using examples and disciplinary debates from dance anthropology and the anthropology of tourism, Skinner looks at the positioning and repositioning of anthropology and its subdisciplines in the education sector. The chapter is autoethnographic and autobiographical in orientation, with examples and experiences of teaching and learning anthropology in the social and behavioural sciences, in the humanities, and in the life sciences. In each capacity, and in each university, anthropology has been delivered differently: as part of a wide social and behavioural sciences team, as a core social anthropological discipline, and as a joint bio-social programme with integrated team teaching. Spanning the arts, humanities, sciences and social sciences, anthropology struggles with recognition and yet affords us multiple alternative perspectives and unique and critical insights from other disciplines. So why, in an age of austerity and accountability, does anthropology seem caught in a struggle with its institutional and public positioning and yet with which it is well formed to engage? After a comprehensive positioning of anthropology in the humanities and life sciences, this chapter goes on to address the complex politics of the discipline and its subdisciplines as one of the possible reasons for its plight.

Chapter 4, 'Polyphony for the Ivory Tower Blues: Critical Pedagogies in Graduate Professional Development', is Tracey Heatherington's evocative title for an examination of how disciplines are (re)produced – and reduced – in neoliberal conditions of austerity and competition – an 'entrepreneurial subjectivity' in academia, as Heatherington coins. Heatherington's chapter examines the implicit collaborative articulations that reproduce not only the discipline of anthropology, but also its institutional contexts. As the academy goes through a phase of contraction, many sing 'the ivory tower blues' as they note declining opportunities for new PhDs to gain secure jobs as teachers and researchers. The 'best model' of student professionalization has accordingly shifted to emphasize the transferable skills needed to become flexible and resilient, whether inside or outside centres of higher education. Drawing on the experience of 'applying anthropology' to an administrative role in graduate education, Heatherington considers how anthropology's analytical insights into the changing university system might inform our practices of graduate student training, both within and beyond our field. The metaphor of 'polyphony' describes an approach to 'preparing future faculty and professionals' that fosters a critical awareness of neoliberal transformations in the academy, and reaffirms the role of universities as centres of democratic participation. In similar vein to points cited by Shore and Skinner, she suggests that conditions of scarce resources in the university sector necessitate a kinship and community response. We must reimagine ourselves and work with our graduate students to prepare them with career skills, interdisciplinary thinking and an 'alt-ac' career of non-faculty academic jobs, Heatherington presses. Her account of working conditions at the University of Wisconsin Milwaukee (UWM) echoes, too, Skinner's experiences at Queen's University Belfast, although, as Associate Dean of the Graduate School, Heatherington is able to introduce and support a raft of graduate training programmes stressing new dimensions of skill, understanding and creativity in students that do not fall into the 'self-help' category of self-professionalization narrative. They are able to bring together staff, alumni, donors and community members to work on harmonies and counterpoints in their work. This group approach to training establishes a 'polyphonic' dialogue about the vision, purpose and orientation of graduate degrees. It encourages community-engaged scholarship, breaks down traditional town/gown divides, and fosters a renewed sense of community. This is an interdisciplinary collaborative practice, knowledge transfer across academic and public fields that, as Heatherington celebrates, is truly transformative. It is collaboration that recalibrates the academy.

In Chapter 5 'Symbiosis or Entrepreneurialism? Ambivalent Anthropologies in the Age of the (Neo)Liberal Arts', authors Carolyn Hough and Adam Kaul analyse the ambiguous position of anthropologists in not just a neoliberal era but in what they refer to as a (neo)liberal arts and sciences institution, namely their Augustana College in Rock Island, Illinois. Responding to contingencies and constantly changing directions in order to coordinate with others is what they deem necessary for establishing anthropological symbioses in the midst of the neoliberal era of higher education. Their chapter's ambivalent approach to such symbioses is the result of contradictory goals for reaching out beyond anthropological boundaries. On the one hand, neoliberalism forces a particular kind of creative connectivity, which, in the late-capitalist regime, is branded 'entrepreneurialism'. On the other, they write from a small, selective liberal arts institution where the goal is deep interdisciplinarity and epistemological syntheses. In this sense, symbiosis is not forced upon them so much as it is the point of what they do. A goal of this chapter is to ask the question: when is the discipline of anthropology being forced into entrepreneurialism and when is it being allowed to create symbioses? In response, they attempt, in the midst of the crisis, to find a symbiotic space, ambivalent, contingent and nuanced, between neoliberal corporatism and a romantic ideal of the liberal arts.

Here, the 'entrepreneurial subjectivity' broached by Heatherington is also countered by anthropologists who invest in their subject the possibility to introduce an ambivalence in what they see as an increasingly uncertain polarized and bleak socio-economic situation played out in higher education as well as wider society. The subtlety and nuance of a people's discipline appears to be at odds with the neoliberal telos seen (quite literally) and chosen (administratively) about the campus: the one advocating risk management through individual self-mastery, and educational decision making based on lay notions of market values, encouraged by a liberal distribution of flags and banners promoting college values (from 'Accountability' to 'Care' and 'Responsibility'); the other in the value of understanding cultural diversity, in advocating multiculturalism, tolerance and the pursuit of an active engaged citizenship. It is a campus contrast of social worth versus personal wealth. Hough and Kaul's anthropology is caught up in this desire for liberal arts interdisciplinarity, intellectual capital and epistemological syntheses, but the reality is one of education as a capitalist exchange value system with college being used to ensure professional development and employment security. The banners show how the educational landscape is being bureaucratized. Further, with extensive 'Viking Scorecard' programmes to tally student employment activities while at college, Hough and Kaul note how the neoliberal student subjects are self-regulating themselves, Foucauldian bodies disciplined by economic fears, future-proofing and 'credentializing' themselves against any potential credit crunch ahead of them. While the college attempts to reframe faculty and student identities, the college is itself affected by Illinois state politics and budget cuts, just as the state is subject to federal financial controls. Here, then, is an immediate example of neoliberal corporatism percolating down from the nation to the classroom, from the capital to the campus.

Chapter 6 by Alisse Waterston, entitled 'Matters of Anthropology and Social Justice: Reflections on Collaborations', is situated, like Hough and Kaul's, in the US context. Waterston takes as her starting point Didier Fassin's call for a moral anthropology that includes a critical reflection on the discipline's 'engagement in the world with the ultimate intention to make it better' (2012: 3). In the epistemological dimensions of this critical reflection, Waterston, in autoethnographic vein, acknowledges the moral commitments and ethical positions that shape her world view as an anthropologist and direct the shape of her 'engagement in the world'. Politics, history and political economy are never far from those commitments and positions. Through the lens of critical reflexivity, she explores and translates her raw experiences in three domains of her anthropological engagement – the classroom, writing and publishing, and in a professional society of anthropologists – to consider the creative dimensions of 'collaboration'. In each of these domains, she has, like Skinner and indeed, Hough and Kaul, 'delivered anthropology differently': as part of an interdisciplinary undergraduate internship programme focused on social justice and social change; in relation to the production of an edited volume featuring the work of non-anthropologist 'indigenous' scholars and activists; and as president of the American Anthropological Association. In the context of the contemporary neoliberal world and considering the location of anthropology within it, Waterston examines her experiences for what they suggest about the possibilities and impossibilities of collaboration for a 'good, right, just or altruistic' critical anthropology, for meaningful engagement and for the sustainability of the discipline.

Part 2: Anthropology in/of Practice

In the second part of the book, we shift focus to examine more engaged and applied collaborative projects across a number of different contexts. While the strictures of the neoliberal university also impact the anthropologists in this section, it is not the main focus of their discussions. Rather, in this section, they reflect and critique their various collaborations to engender new insights into the shape and form of a contemporary collaborative anthropology.

We begin with Chapter 7, Laura Korčulanin's 'Anthropology, Art and Design as Collaborative Agents of Change for a Sustainable Future: The *Give a Shit* Project as Case Study'. In this novel, engaged piece of work, Korčulanin shows the importance of collaboration of anthropology and design being seen as a 'change agent' towards a more environmentally sustainable future society. Using her *Give a Shit* project as an example, she demonstrates an innovative model of collaboration between anthropological research: ethnography and design thinking as useful and pertinent tools for co-creation and engagement with society as well as an important framework for industry, business, architecture, design and arts, among others. Through an analysis of *Give a Shit*, Korčulanin demonstrates the engagement of different disciplines in providing a solution to the existing Western systems of toilet design and in offering an innovative, creative, collaborative response to sustainability challenges. Korčulanin's project highlights the inventiveness inherent in many collaborations, and brings a very creative dialogue into play in this volume.

In Chapter 8, we continue this engagement with design and architecture but shift focus to the issue of refugees and well-being in Norway. Anne Sigfrid Grønseth and Eli Støa's 'Anthropology and Architecture: Motives and Ethics in Creating Knowledge' explores how anthropology can relate to and collaborate with architectural approaches with a focus on motives, merits and ethics in the mutual process of knowledge creation. From engaging in an interdisciplinary research project that investigated the effect of the physical environment on life quality of asylum seeker reception centres in Norway, they discuss how anthropology can contribute to open the field of research to acknowledge a complexity, which may channel between the physical structures and the experiences of lived life. Combining anthropological and architectural approaches, the study conducted short-time field visits to selected reception centres focusing on observations, informal talks with staff and a few asylum seekers, together with photographic documentation of aesthetic and spatial features, combined with a web survey documenting the physical structures and placement of the asylum reception centres. This project recognizes and explores how the processes of 'othering' are both mental and spatial. The research presents original empirical material feeding into a controversial and heated political debate concerning immigration policy, housing quality, integration and well-being in Norway.

In Chapter 9, 'Collaboration in Crisis: Towards a Holistic Approach to Health and Social Care Supports for Vulnerable Populations', Emma Heffernan writes about how the high unemployment and emigration that defined the 1980s and much of the early 1990s – the dawn of the 'Celtic Tiger' – was a time of huge social and economic change in Ireland. This period saw an increase in social mobility and expansion of the middle classes; however, a significant section of the population did not benefit from this newfound success. In 2008, Ireland experienced its worst economic and labour market crisis since the foundation of the state, which had a profound impact on the standard of living among Irish households. Currently 1.3 million people in Ireland are experiencing deprivation, a figure that has almost doubled since 2008. Using ethnographic data collected during her PhD fieldwork, Heffernan examines the lives and experiences of one of the most vulnerable populations in Irish society who, even at the peak of the boom, were struggling to survive – homeless, drug-using women involved in street-based prostitution in Dublin's inner city. As Ireland moved from a moment of prosperity to austerity, cuts to public and social services impacted on the risk-taking activities of these women, further entrenching their vulnerability and social exclusion. This chapter calls for a social determinants of health approach to developing appropriate policies and interventions to alleviate consistent and intergenerational poverty and structural violence. State agencies, NGOs across the entire gamut of sectors, from housing to social welfare, education and health and social care, must work collaboratively to develop more appropriate, person-centred interventions.

'Anthropology and Peace Making' is the title of Chapter 10 by Colin Irwin. Irwin gives us a particularly international example of an applied anthropology of conflict resolution that ranges from early fieldwork among the Inuit, informed by sociobiology, to the development and diplomatic deployment of peace polls to identify potential areas of compromise and negotiation between conflicted parties. In this chapter Irwin brings together insights from the biological, linguistic and cultural subdisciplines of anthropology to demonstrate the explanatory strengths of the discipline from a human nature perspective. With a focus on human group conflict and conflict resolution, he uses the ethnographies of hunter-gatherers to examine the sociobiological origins of in-group and out-group behaviour to suggest it is a persistent human trait that always has to be culturally managed. From his own studies of the Inuit, who, for survival reasons in the harsh Arctic environment, had to eliminate the costly behaviour known in most cultures as 'war', he illustrates the effectiveness of comparative linguistic analyses. Then, by employing the reflexive methods of emic and etic ethnographic description, he is able to apply the Inuit trait of consensus decision making to contemporary conflicts in Northern Ireland and elsewhere. Inevitably the results of these attempts at conflict resolution among contemporary populations are mixed, depending on the power relationships and interests of the parties to the conflicts. But the insights from such emic and etic analysis of the parties' perceptions of a conflict should always be helpful to those who seek peace through compromise. Irwin's work is highly international, ranging from conflict mediation and resolution in Northern Ireland to Sri Lanka, Egypt and Syria. This work links applied anthropology with peace studies. It is notable in its trajectory and development from postgraduate research in the Arctic to career in peace making living and working in and from Belfast, Northern Ireland. This chapter engages across the sciences from anthropology to sociobiology, evolutionary psychology to political science, with its research into group conflict in humans and whether or not it has a genetic predisposition. Working globally, Irwin is able to caution us and to counter his thesis that it does have an influence through enculturation into consensus decision making and repeatedly reminding us of the need to be ever vigilant as to our self-destructive potential.

Irwin's contribution is followed by Chapter 11, Philipp Lottholz's 'More Than a Matter of Proportion: A Critical Consideration of Anthropology's Role in Peace and Conflict Studies'. This penultimate chapter takes a more disciplinary stance on the contribution anthropology can make to peace and conflict studies. Fine-grained ethnography allows us to understand local social actors; it gives them voices that are typically muted by more hegemonically driven disciplinary perspectives such as political science and international relations – disciplines criticized by Lottholz as essentializing and (proto)positivist. Lottholz works in the (post-conflict) transition countries of Kyrgyzstan and Tajikistan. His focus is on the everyday reality of the citizen subject, in their daily ambiguities and in their internalization and reproduction of discourses and ideologies of peace. A symbiotic anthropology of peace and conflict is a transdisciplinary approach to understanding ordinary/everyday and professional/governmental community security and order making in society. In Tajikistan we hear of discourses of peacefulness (*tinji*) as a conflict fatigue with former civil war. Life is less post-conflict in Kyrgyzstan, where the global discourses on Islamic radicalism and securitization are being continually internalized in community security practices. The result is an ongoing tussle between state and civil actors, some feeling excluded and marginalized either by the lack of prohibition on the movement and access by perceived dangerous 'missionaries' radicalizing and contaminating the environment, or by the lack of understanding of violent extremism and how it is and can be countered in society. Lottholz argues for a reframing by rephrasing of stance from Islamic radicalism to non-traditional faith. This is the non-essentializing and non-hegemonic peace studies inflected by anthropology.

Finally, Scott MacLochlainn brings our focus to the notion of being an anthropological witness to collaboration in the field in the last chapter in the book: Chapter 12, 'For Christ and State: Collaboration and the Individual in Duterte's Philippines'. In this chapter, MacLochlainn interrogates the term 'collaboration' and frames it within the terms of affiliation. He does so by way of a discussion of Christian subjectivity in the Philippines, by highlighting the collaborative nature of Christian affiliation, and in particular the role of partial, or nominal affiliation ('in name only'), before briefly discussing Christian responses to the nature of state governance in the Philippines since 2016. Not only does Christianity arguably form the most marked point of entry and institutional repository of ethical thinking/authority in the Philippines, the prominent roles of affiliation and intention within contemporary modes of Christian discourse arguably have something to say about the broader remit of collaboration and the forms of subjectivity that it constitutes. While for many, there is something of a straight line to be drawn between Christian subjectivity and neoliberalism, MacLochlainn is not so concerned here in replaying such a narrative. Undoubtedly, Christian ontologies are in many ways ideally suited to, and historically implicated in, neoliberal contexts. Briefly stated, this argument holds that the form of individualism constituted by Christianity – individuals, and not communities, are saved – together with a type of ethics and governance that focuses on the improvement of self, begin to look very similar to a classic neoliberal subject. But his main concern in this chapter is rather to highlight how within the dividing line of explicitly articulated beliefs and the lived life – being Christian – exists a space in which the individual is much more of a collaborative project than it might seem. That is, for all of the focus placed on the relationship between the Christian self and God, there are many more people and things involved in producing and maintaining that relationship. Situated within the modes of interaction between anthropology and Christianity, as well as among Christians themselves, he briefly highlights (1) how the dividing line between Christianity as a lived system of beliefs and ethics and Christianity as an explicit and formalized (and ritualized) discourse on that belief and ethics, results in notably partial and nominal types of affiliation, and (2) how much collaboration and communal work is invested in Christian contexts in which the individual is notably prominent.

In sum, the contributors in this volume advocate for a collaborative anthropology fashioned anew. As editors, we too call for a collaborative anthropology/gies that sit(s) apart from the unsuccessful or difficult collaborations of the past. It is this break with times past that is critical to the sustainability and evolution of anthropology in the digital era. Our approach ultimately echoes Tsing et al.'s (2017) call for meaningful 'symbiotic relations' between anthropologists on different career trajectories and also with our interlocutors and research foci. To close this introduction, we reiterate that this is a collection grounded in the symbiotics of 'theoretical commensalities and methodological mutualisms' with a view to generating a collaborative anthropology that holds the potential to be transformative for the discipline more broadly. Crucially, collaboration in our view is critical to the discipline's survival and renewal in what are challenging times especially for the humanities and social sciences in the neoliberal university. As Fiona Murphy's contribution argues, following Rolfe (2013), perhaps working in parallel to the neoliberal university in the form of a 'paraversity' (Rolfe 2013) may well be the most suitable site to sustain these kinds of collaborative anthropologies. Ultimately, as the chapters in this volume evince, this is happening in such a wide variety of contexts that it can only mean that we are in a period where anthropology is being revitalized and seen as valuable in both theoretical, and practical and applied ways. This is a collaborative anthropology that reflects and refracts, engages and converses, reciprocates and advocates; it is an anthropology for the future.

References

ASA (2015), 'Symbiotic Anthropologies: Theoretical Commensalities and Methodological Mutualisms: Theme'. Available online: https://www.theasa.org/conferences/asa15/theme.html (accessed 28 December 2018).

Brenneis, D. (2009), 'Anthropology in and of the Academy: Globalization, Assessment and Our Field's Future', *Social Anthropology/Anthropologie Sociale*, 17 (3): 261–75.

Breusers, M., S. Nederlof and T. van Rheenen (1998), 'Conflict or Symbiosis? Disentangling Farmer Herdsman Relations: The Mossi and Fulbe of the Central Plateau, Burkina Faso', *Journal of Modern African Studies*, 36 (3): 357–81.

Clerke, T. and N. Hopwood (2014), *Doing Ethnography in Teams: A Case Study of Asymmetries in Collaborative Research*, London: Springer.

Collaborative Anthropologies (2019) 'About the Journal', University of Nebraska Press. Available online: http://unp-bookworm.unl.edu/product/Collaborative-Anthropologies,673970.aspx (accessed 3 January 2019).

Desmangles, L. (1990), 'The Maroon Republics and Religious Diversity in Colonial Haiti', *Anthropos*, 85 (4/6): 475–82.

Dunn, E. C. (2018), 'The Problem with Assholes'. Available online: http://publicanthropologist.cmi.no/2018/06/20/the-problem-with-assholes/ (accessed 10 January 2019).

Escárcega, S. (2006), 'Comment on "A Happy Coincidence? Symbiosis and Synthesis in Anthropological and Indigenous Knowledges"', *Current Anthropology*, 47 (6): 993–4.

Fairhead, J. (2006), 'Comment on "A Happy Coincidence? Symbiosis and Synthesis in Anthropological and Indigenous Knowledges"', *Current Anthropology*, 47 (6): 994–5.

Field, L. (2008) '"Side by Side or Facing One Another": Writing and Collaborative Ethnography in Comparative Perspective', *Collaborative Anthropologies*, 1: 32–50.

Firth, R. (1981), 'Engagement and Detachment: Reflections on Applying Social Anthropology to Social Affairs', *Human Organization*, 40 (3): 193–201.

Fluehr-Lobban, C. (2008), 'Collaborative Anthropology as Twenty-first-Century Ethical Anthropology', *Collaborative Anthropologies*, 1: 175–82.

Galison, P. (2010), 'Trading with the Enemy', in M. Gorman (ed.), *Trading Zones and Interactional Expertise: Creating New Kinds of Collaboration*, 25–52, London: Massachusetts Institute of Technology.

Geertz, C. (1984), 'Anti Anti-Relativism', *American Anthropologist*, 86 (2): 263–78.

Graeber, D. (2013), 'On the Phenomenon of Bullshit Jobs: A Work Rant', *STRIKE*, 2, August 2013. Available online: https://strikemag.org/bullshit-jobs/ (accessed 17 December 2018).

Graeber, D. (2018), *Bullshit Jobs: A Theory*, London: Penguin Books.

Harvey, D. (2005), *A Brief History of Neoliberalism*, Oxford: Oxford University Press.

Haviland, M. (2014), 'The Challenge of Cross-Cultural Creativity', in I. McLean (ed.), *Transculturation and Indigenous Contemporary Art*, 117–135, Cambridge: Cambridge Scholars Publishing.

Haviland, M. (2016), *Side by Side? Community Art and the Challenge of Co-Creativity*, London: Taylor & Francis.

Ingold, T. (2016), 'Reclaiming the University of Aberdeen', Council for the Defence of British Universities. Available online: http://cdbu.org.uk/reclaiming-the-university-of-aberdeen/ (accessed 13 January 2019).

Ingold, T. (2018), *Anthropology: Why It Matters*, Cambridge: Polity Press.

Kistler, A. (2015) 'Meaningful Relationships: Collaborative Anthropology and Mentors from the Field', *Collaborative Anthropologies*, 7(2): 1–24.

Lassiter, L. (1998), *The Power of Kiowa Song: A Collaborative Ethnography*, Tucson, AZ: University of Arizona Press.

Lassiter, L. (2001), 'From "Reading over the Shoulders of Natives" to "Reading Alongside Natives", Literally: Toward a Collaborative and Reciprocal Ethnography', *Journal of Anthropological Research*, 57: 137–49.

Lassiter, L. (2005a), 'Collaborative Ethnography and Public Anthropology', *Current Anthropology*, 46 (1): 83–106.

Lassiter, E. (2005b), *The Chicago Guide to Collaborative Ethnography*, Chicago, IL: University of Chicago Press.

Lassiter, E. (2005c), 'An excerpt from *The Chicago Guide to Collaborative Ethnography*'. Available online: https://www.press.uchicago.edu/Misc/Chicago/468909.html (accessed 7 January 2019) (amended from the original).

Layton, R. (2009), 'Cultural Variation and Social Complexity: A Comment on Nettle's "Beyond Nature versus Culture"', *The Journal of the Royal Anthropological Institute*, 15 (2): 247–9.

Mills, M. (2016), 'Reclaiming Our University – Dr Martin Mills, Aberdeen University [including Q&A]', Democracy TV. Available online: https://www.youtube.com/ watch?v=f9BwcVCAENY (accessed 10 January 2019).

Mills, M. (2017), '"A Strange Modernity": On the Contradictions of the Neoliberal University', in T. Heatherington and F. Zerilli (eds), *Special Issue: Anthropologists Witnessing and Reshaping the Neoliberal Academy*, Forum, *Anuac*, 6 (1): 47–52.

Murphy, F. (2018). 'When Gadflies Become Horses: On the Unlikelihood of Ethical Critique from the Academy', *FocaalBlog*. Available online: https://www.focaalblog. com/2018/06/28/fiona-murphy-when-gadflies-become-horses/ (accessed 12 December 2018).

Nadel, S. (1949), 'The "Gani" Ritual of Nupe: A Study in Social Symbiosis', *Africa: Journal of the International African Institute*, 19 (3): 177–86.

Overing, J. (1985), 'Introduction', in J. Overing (ed.), *Reason and Morality*, 1–29, London: Tavistock Publications.

Pinney, C. (2012), 'Anthropology in the New Millennium', in R. Fardon, O. Harris, T. Marchand, C. Shore, V. Strang, R. Wilson and M. Nuttall (eds), *The SAGE Handbook of Social Anthropology*, 393–9, Thousand Oaks: Sage Publications.

Rolfe, G. (2013), *The University in Dissent*, Abingdon: SRHE and Routledge.

Schensul, J., J. Marlene and K. Williamson (2008), 'Challenging Hegemonies: Advancing Collaboration in Community-Based Participatory Action Research', *Collaborative Anthropologies*, 1: 102–37.

Scheper-Hughes, N. (1995), 'The Primacy of the Ethical: Propositions for a Militant Anthropology', *Current Anthropology*, 36 (3): 409–40.

Shore, C. and M. Davidson (2014), 'Beyond Collusion and Resistance: Academic–Management Relations Within the Neoliberal', *Learning and Teaching*, 7 (1): 12–28.

Shore, C. and S. Wright (2016), 'Neoliberalisation and the "Death of the Public University"', in T. Heatherington and F. Zerilli (eds), *Special Issue: Anthropologists in/ of the Neoliberal Academy*, Forum, *Anuac*, 5 (1): 46–50.

Shore, C. and S. Wright (2017), 'Introduction – Privatizing the Public University: Key Trends, Countertrends and Alternatives', in S. Wright and C. Shore (eds), *Death of the Public University? Uncertain Futures for Higher Education in the Knowledge Economy*, 1–27, Oxford: Berghahn.

Sparkes, A. (1997), 'An Elite Body, Illness, and the Fragmentation of Self: A Collaborative Exploration', *Auto/Biography*, 1(2/3): 27–37.

Strang, V. (2006), 'A Happy Coincidence?: Symbiosis and Synthesis in Anthropological and Indigenous Knowledges', *Current Anthropology*, 47 (6): 981–1000.

'"The Manifesto": Reclaiming the University Campaign Website' (2016). Available online: https://reclaimingouruniversity.wordpress.com/ (accessed 13 January 2019).

Tsing, A., H. Swanson, E. Gan and N. Bubandt (2017), *Arts of Living on a Damaged Planet: Ghosts and Monsters of the Anthropocene,* Minneapolis, MN: University of Minnesota Press.

Wolf-Meyer, M. and S. Collins (2013), 'Parasitic and Symbiotic: The Ambivalence of Necessity', *Semiotic Review 1: Parasites*, June 2013. Available online: https://www.semioticreview.com/ojs/index.php/sr/article/view/29/28 (accessed 20 December 2018).

Wren Lewis, S. (undated), 'A General Theory of Austerity', paper hosted on Royal Irish Academy website. Available online: https://www.ria.ie/sites/default/files/chapter_1_1.pdf (accessed 1 December 2018).

Wright, S. (1995), 'Anthropology: Still the Uncomfortable Discipline', in A. Ahmed and C. Shore (eds), *The Future of Anthropology: Its Relevance to the Contemporary World*, 65–93, London: Athlone Press.

Part One

Anthropology and Academia

1

Symbiotic or Parasitic? Universities, Academic Capitalism and the Global Knowledge Economy

Cris Shore

Introduction: University reform – an economic or ecological project?

This chapter originated from a panel at the 2015 Association of Social Anthropologists' conference in Exeter, whose organizing theme was anthropology and the idea of 'symbiosis'. During the conference, many speakers talked enthusiastically about ecology and symbiosis as a framework for advancing a more environmentally engaged anthropology that recognizes the challenges of the Anthropocene and takes seriously multiple ontologies and multispecies ethnography. Influenced in large part by the work of Anna Tsing (2009, 2011) and other environmental anthropologists, symbiosis was referred to repeatedly in terms of 'landscapes', 'ecosystems', 'synthesis' and 'multi-species mutualism'. Overall, it seemed, the language of ecology and sustainability was a discourse to be welcomed and embraced as something that could lead to fertile and productive exchanges (or 'methodological mutualisms') between anthropology and the natural sciences.

The conference title of 'symbiotic anthropologies' made me think about my own research on the neoliberal restructuring of higher education and the New Public Management reforms that have swept through universities over the past two decades. Here too there is much talk about the need for universities to develop closer 'symbiotic' relations with industry, nurture 'innovation ecosystems' and a 'culture of entrepreneurialism' and become more financially 'sustainable'. This ecological turn in both the framing of university governance and anthropological theory also remined me of earlier feminist analyses of the

politics of language and the power of metaphor. Some three decades ago Emily
Martin wrote an article in the influential feminist journal *Signs* about the way
biology textbooks reproduce stereotypical male/female roles (the 'passive female
egg versus the active male sperm' and so forth). One of her key arguments
concerned the seductive power of science, and the often invisible work that
scientific metaphors perform when describing (and thereby creating) social
reality. The challenge, she concluded, 'is to wake up those sleeping metaphors' by
becoming aware of their implications so that we 'rob them of their power to
naturalize our social conventions about gender' (Martin 1991: 501). Similar
arguments could equally be applied to those metaphors that frame policy
thinking about higher education reform and university futures. As several
conference speakers argued, borrowing concepts across disciplines opens up
interesting new possibilities for academic research and thinking. But this process
can also have negative effects, particularly when used instrumentally for
managerial purposes.

Taking up Emily Martin's challenge, I want to explore the assumptions behind
these blended ecological metaphors, the way they are used by university
managers and policy makers, and the implications of this discursive framing for
the future of the public university. As I hope to show, biological idioms and
organic analogies have acquired a new saliency as mobilizing metaphors in the
discourse and practices of university reform. For some authors, this ecological
turn offers a way to rethink the university in more holistic and non-instrumental
ways that integrate academic teaching, learning and research with closer ties to
communities and society (Wright 2016). However, this relational understanding
of the university as a networked, socially embedded institution that is intimately
connected with its wider habitat is a very different model to that envisaged in
current higher education policy reforms.

By analysing the discourse of contemporary university management, I also
want to bring together a number of my own research interests over the past two
decades, particularly the way that universities, like many other public and private
sector organizations, are being transformed by new regimes of audit and
accountability (Strathern 2000; Shore and Wright 2000) and the growing
emphasis on demonstrating 'impact', 'relevance' and 'external stakeholder'
engagement – or what is sometimes suggestively termed the university's 'third
mission' (Etzkowitz 2008; Shore and McLauchlan 2012). The University of
Auckland, where I conducted ethnographic fieldwork for fourteen years, is a
good case in point. Here too there is frequent discussion among the university's
senior management team and government ministers about the need to make

higher education more responsive to industry and employers. Successive governments of all political persuasions have advanced the idea that universities should become 'engines for economic growth' that will drive New Zealand forward in the competitive knowledge economy. These market metaphors typically frame management narratives on the purpose of the university and its future. However, the strategy for achieving this vision of a high-value knowledge economy is increasingly seen as one in which universities become networked into a new ecology involving applied science, industry, finance capital, government and other key stakeholders.

This chapter is therefore a contribution to an 'anthropology of universities' and, more specifically, the transformation of the public university as an institution in an age characterized by the increasing neoliberalization of the world's economies and societies. I start from the premise that universities are good sites for 'studying up' and for engaging in the more reflexive kind of 'public anthropology' (Borofsky 2019) or 'anthropology at home'. Given that universities are the primary sites where anthropology as a discipline is reproduced, it seems pertinent to consider how the changing conditions of academic existence are influencing disciplinary knowledge and practice. In this sense, universities also provide exemplary locations for exploring the effects of globalization, neoliberalization and New Public Management on key institutions of Western societies, the institutional logics, rationalities of governance and new forms of contractualized relationships that these processes are helping to introduce into the workplace, and the new kinds of subjects that these processes are creating.

How, therefore, are universities being networked into this new economy (or 'ecology') of knowledge production and what are the implications of these reforms for the future of the public university as an institution? Some of these questions have been explored elsewhere (see Shore and Wright 2017). In addressing these questions, I also want to reflect on what anthropology can bring to the study of higher education reform and the connections between universities and society. First, however, let me introduce my argument with two brief ethnographic vignettes which provide some empirical evidence and context for the analysis that follows.

Celebrating entrepreneurship at the University of Auckland

It is Thursday night and the lecture theatre – one of the largest in the Business School – is packed. Over five hundred people, including students, academics and *university managers, are eagerly awaiting the start of this Grand Prize Giving and the announcement of the NZ$100,000 'Spark Challenge' award. There is an excited buzz of conversation as the Masters of Ceremony James Penn and Spark CEO Alina Varoy walk to the rostrum to welcome the speakers and introduce the evening's events. Varoy explains that Spark's mission is to 'develop a spirit of enterprise and a culture of innovation at the University of Auckland'. Indeed, the programme had already created over 100 start-up ventures, raised NZ$180 million and was 'stimulating a wave of individual transformations' by bringing together graduates with 'entrepreneurial mindsets', scientists and engineers interested in learning the pathways to commercialization, and high-profile corporate, government and 'social good pioneers'.*

Following this welcome, the MCs introduced the evening's keynote speaker, Alexei Dunayev, the young and charismatic CEO and co-founder of the award-winning ('Top Tech Startup New Zealand' 2013, and 'Best Startup Silicon Valley' 2014) company called 'Transcribe Me'. Dunayev was a confident and inspirational speaker who recounted the story of how he had taken his company from a fledgling start-up to a successful global venture. Casually dressed and pacing energetically up and down the auditorium with microphone in hand, his talk was full of words of wisdom and advice to the aspiring young entrepreneurs in the auditorium, with memorable one-liners like 'entrepreneurship is a discipline, a mindset, and a direction to make something that hasn't existed before'. These ideas were supposedly epitomized in the work of the thirteen shortlisted finalists for the Spark Prize, whose innovations included 'TeamSelecta', a sports management technology for managers who want an easier way to select teams by rating players from the sidelines; 'Autonomous Aerial Asset Monitoring', a 'real time asset management system' that uses unmanned aerial vehicles to automate certain farming tasks; 'UVsense', a UV sensor and wearable app that helps people determine how much time they should spend in the sun to attain sufficient vitamin D without risking sunburn; and 'Avatar Anonymous', a business technology that uses 'innovative virtual reality techniques to deliver accessible, affordable and sustainable behaviour change modules for global markets' in commercializable areas of health management, including 'weight loss, smoking cessation or physical activity' (UoA 2013).

As I sat reflecting on the evening, what struck me most about this 'Cultivating Entrepreneurship' ceremony was its evangelical, almost cult-like character. The atmosphere in the lecture theatre recalled a charismatic church sermon or a Billy Graham crusade. Like many evangelical meetings, the Spark Prize ceremony combines prophets and proselytism with messages that are future-orientated and full of promises and warnings. As the Dean of the Business School told reporters at the Spark Awards the following year, 'MIT has identified the University of Auckland and the innovation ecosystem built around it as one of the top half dozen in the world', but to 'carry New Zealand forward' it was also necessary to 'grow technology-based innovation in its traditional industries' (Whittred 2014).

Two years later it looked like the university's strategy to forge 'entrepreneurial mindsets' had borne fruit. This was excitedly captured on the university's news website under the headline 'Most innovative university in Australia'. As the UniNews reporter excitedly proclaimed: 'The University of Auckland has been ranked as the most innovative university in New Zealand and Australia in the inaugural Reuters Top 75: Asia's Most Innovative Universities rankings. In the newly-launched rankings, the University of Auckland was placed 27th, ahead of the leading Australian universities. No other New Zealand university was ranked in the top 75. The ranking is a further endorsement of the University's ongoing investment and recognition of innovation and entrepreneurship excellence ... Through UniServices, its commercialization company, the University already has a high level of connectivity between its researchers and businesses, both nationally and internationally ... We are committed to fostering this entrepreneurial culture within the University, driving the growth of new high-value business, and strengthening our traditional industries through innovation' (UniNews 2016).

The idea of cultivating an 'entrepreneurial culture' and 'innovation system' within universities has paralleled other major changes in the political economy of the higher education system, following the raft of neoliberal-inspired reforms of the past two decades. These reforms began during the 1980s with the withdrawal of state support for universities and were largely pioneered in the UK by Thatcher's Conservative government but continued under the Blair Labour administration. Behind this public disinvestment in universities lay a new and altogether more individualistic understanding of higher education. A university degree was no longer seen as a public good, as education for citizenship and personal growth, or as a necessary national measure for raising human capital and creating a more educated and skilled workforce. Rather, it was now treated as a personal and private investment in one's individual career. In the UK, this vision was firmly entrenched in the *Brown Report* of 2010. Perversely titled *Securing a Sustainable Future for Higher Education* (another illustration of the appropriation of ecological terms), Brown argued that individual students, not the state, should bear the costs of university education. As a result, university fees were increased from some £3,000 to £9,000, while state funding fell from £3.5 billion to just under £700 million: effectively an 80 per cent cut, and 100 per cent in areas such as the arts, humanities and social sciences – areas that government viewed as having no economic utility (Vernon 2010).

This had a number of effects on the political economy of higher education, as students and their parents have been forced to pay for education through the kinds of debt-financing arrangements that most governments now regard as far too risky and dangerous for themselves. While the level of national debt is considered so ruinous that it requires emergency austerity measures, students in England and Wales are being actively encouraged to take out loans based upon imagined future incomes, gambling that the loan will eventually pay off by enhancing their future job prospects and earning power. This so-called 'graduate premium' was typically used to frame loans as a more 'progressive' way to fund higher education. However, these loans have effectively become a form of sub-prime mortgage for education. They are also guaranteed by the state. As a result, and somewhat perversely, higher education in England and Wales was reorganized around the same kinds of financial speculation that produced the financial crash of 2008 (Vernon 2010). Yet universities did not follow the expected market logic and differentiate their fees according to demand; instead they all charged the maximum fees allowable. Ten years later, the former minister for higher education David Willets (now Lord Willets) admitted his government had got its calculations wrong. 'We expected competition on the price of tuition fees and that was a mistake.' As he explained to a BBC reporter, this was 'because students weren't paying up-front; they weren't understanding the basics of the system' (Jeffreys 2019). Because the amount they paid back was dependent on their earnings, these loans were not really perceived as loans. In fact, many students considered it unlikely they would ever earn enough to meet the threshold for repayment. Replacing student grants with loans also appealed to government ministers because, thanks to creative accounting, these loans were not included on the government's budget sheet, although this has now been called into question.

While Britain has been at the forefront of experiments in the neoliberal restructuring of higher education, these trends are far from unique to the UK. In Australasia, Europe and across the Americas, students and academics have been protesting against similar processes: rising fees; growing levels of student debt; the massive expansion of university management and administration, particularly around measuring the quality and 'excellence' of research and teaching provision; a desperate search for new income streams from high-fee-paying overseas students (what in New Zealand and Australia is called 'export education') or online consumers; and the increasing casualization and precariousness of academic labour, as new staff are placed on short-term and insecure contracts, often with draconian or unachievable performance targets (Grove 2015; Wright and Shore 2017). Another effect has been the explicit privileging of the sciences, technology, engineering and mathematics (the so-called STEM subjects) over the arts and humanities. At the same time, the infamous systems designed to measure research outputs and audit teaching quality, which were supposed to hold universities to account for their use of public money by encouraging greater productivity and economy (by teaching larger classes and hyperactive journal publications), have now been refashioned around the idea of utility and what is termed 'impact'.

It is against this background that we can begin to understand why innovation, entrepreneurship and sustainability have acquired such significance as contemporary 'keywords' (Williams 1977) in the lexicon of government and management. Following the dictates of financial expediency, and in line with the new idea that commercializing university research is itself a form of 'public good' (Shore and McLauchlan 2012), universities have embarked on various strategies to generate new revenue streams. These range from commercializing their own intellectual property through patents, licences and spin-out companies, to developing partnerships with industry and fund-raising from alumni. In Britain and the United States, this trajectory is so well advanced that the 'death of the public university' as an ideal appears to be almost complete, particularly with respect to the humanities and social sciences (Colini 2009; Wright and Shore 2017). Similar processes are well underway in other countries as managerial hierarchies and commercial objectives come to dominate the entire scope of the university's affairs. In the past, university vice-chancellors and rectors would often justify their preoccupation with commercialization as a necessary expedient to enable the university to continue investing in, or subsidizing, its traditional teaching and research activities. Today, commercialization has increasingly become an end in itself – a measure of a university's status and prestige and part of its reputational capital. Universities seemingly everywhere have now found themselves recast, discursively and structurally, as transnational corporations operating in a global knowledge economy, rather than public institutions with a social and critical mission.

University futures and the rise of the 'third mission'

A key element of this transformation – and what is most interesting in terms of shifting connections between higher education and society – is the reconceptualization of universities as sites tasked with a 'third mission'. If teaching and research were the first two missions of the university, universities are now expected to engage directly with external actors and publics beyond academia, including policy makers, civil society and partners from industry and the business sector (Nedeva 2008). While the term 'third mission' is most often used in the UK and Europe, it is well captured in other now commonly used terms such as 'knowledge transfer', 'translational research', 'knowledge exchange', 'impact', 'technology transfer' and 'relevance to end-users' (see Molas-Gallart et al. 2002). This new role is closely linked to the politics of accountability with regards to funding mechanisms (Shore and Wright 2000). As a result of the financial pressures outlined above, universities are increasingly expected to rely on external funding, while the public funding that remains is redirected towards 'impact' and 'investment'. The original idea behind the term 'third mission' also included community and social engagement and educational outreach activities involving wider publics (Cooper 2009; Douglas 2012). In New Zealand, however, the concept is defined more narrowly. Here 'external engagement' refers almost exclusively to activities related to the commercialization of university capabilities (teaching, research, infrastructure and other assets), usually through contract research, conferences, events management, consultancy, commercial teaching programmes, incubation services, the generation of spin-off companies, and various forms of partnership with business (Molas-Gallart and Castro-Martinez 2007: 322; Robertson and Kitagawa 2011). As one senior university research office manager and former New Zealand Ministry of Education official summed it up:

> It's no longer research, it's innovation. It's no longer a grant, it's an investment. Research is yesterday's term. Innovation is a euphemism for business assistance. Research funding from government is now a contract and they see it as an investment and they are seeking a return (for the nation) on that investment. It's no longer about you, it's a team activity. It's not an exploration, it's about making a difference, it's not about research outputs, it's about societal impacts.
>
> Smart 2013

These expectations have required universities to take on an increasingly entrepreneurial subjectivity, identifying markets, engaging with financial investors, and becoming hawkers of their own academic goods as a condition of their basic survival – although as we saw in the ethnographic vignette above, some university leaders appear eager to adopt and cultivate this new kind of entrepreneurial subjectivity. As well as being welcomed by some universities, these developments are also far from new or recent phenomena. Rather, they represent a continuation of the trajectories identified long ago through now well-known analyses of the 'entrepreneurial university' (Marginson and Consadine 2000), the 'university of excellence' (Readings 1996) and 'academic capitalism' (Slaughter and Rhoades 2004). What is new, however, is the degree to which these third mission activities and logics have become institutionalized and dominant in many universities.

In the past, it was left-wing intellectuals who dominated the debate about the crisis of higher education (Lyotard 1994; Giroux and Myrsiades 2001; Evans 2014). Today, the debate is being driven much more by think-tanks and interest groups on the right of the political spectrum. Over the past ten years there has been a flood of reports and books about the future of the public university, most of them warning of dire times ahead. Predictions have included nothing short of a 'revolution' in higher education (Bokor 2012), an 'avalanche of change [that will] sweep the system away' (Barber et al. 2013), a 'tsunami' (Hennessy, quoted in Auletta 2012), and a 'disruptive innovation ... allowing both for-profit and traditional not-for-profit institutions to rethink the entire higher education model' (Christiansen and Eyring 2011). These accounts often purport to be diagnostics of what is to come, yet they also act as powerful drivers for bringing about the transformations they predict.

A good example of this is the 2012 Ernst and Young report on Australian higher education entitled *University of the Future* (Bokor 2012). Suggestively subtitled 'A thousand year old industry on the cusp of profound change', this asserts that '[t]he current Australian university model – a broad-based teaching and research institution, with a large base of assets and back office – will prove unviable in all but a few cases' (2012: 4). This predicts that private providers will 'carve out' new opportunities, that for higher education providers 'exciting times are ahead – and challenges too' (Bokor 2012: 4). It argues that universities – as 'one of the main drivers of Australia's economic future as a key source of the talent, insight, new ideas and intellectual property required to build a high-performing knowledge economy' – are failing (2012: 26). Its message to university leaders and policy makers is that they should assess whether their current model is 'future proof', and, if not, determine where and how to play in the future' (2012: 28).

The *Avalanche is Coming* report, authored by Michael Barber (2013) and his team and published by the UK's Institute of Public Policy Research, presents an equally apocalyptic picture, this time drawing on metaphors of impending environmental disaster. Traditional models of higher education, they say, are 'broken'. The new global era, which is characterized by 'accelerated innovation', 'wearable computing', 'driverless cars' and 'biotech revolutions', poses a growing threat to universities (2013: 2); 'communications technologies and MOOCs are severing the relationship between higher education and place'; students are increasingly mobile, courses can now be streamed via MOOCs and 'the student consumer is king' (2013: 10). However, the next five decades could be a 'golden age for higher education' if governments 'seize the initiative and act ambitiously. If not, an avalanche of change will sweep the system away' (2013: 5). The solution that Barber and his colleagues propose is to 'unbundle' universities in order to release their value chain. What Barber means by this is that the various functions of the university should be disassembled and outsourced to external providers. The report lists ten such components of a university: research, degree-awarding powers, faculty staffing, students, governance and administration, curricula, teaching, learning, assessment, and the student experience. Barber proposes that these be 'outsourced to private providers who can provide these services more cheaply and efficiently' (2013: 54). The report goes on to argue that in future there will be five alternative, yet coexisting models of the university:

1. The elite university, which, with its global brand, strong endowments and stellar track record, will win the lion's share of prestigious research grants.
2. The mass university, which will act as higher education provider to the growing global mass middle class (and others).
3. The niche university, modelled on the United States' liberal arts college, will comprise private, for-profit institutions that cater for the more arts-focused middle-class elite.
4. The local university, a mid- to lower-tier institution that exists primarily to serve the local or regional economy.
5. The 'lifelong learning mechanism', a non-university institution with degree-accrediting powers.

Translating policy into practice: The UK Higher Education White Paper

Many of the ideas contained in the Barber report were taken up and developed by the British Conservative government in its 2016 UK White Paper entitled *Success as a Knowledge Economy: Teaching Excellence, Social Mobility and Student Choice* (BIS 2016). Like previous government white papers, this began with the claim that British universities are failing to deliver the necessary skills and competences necessary to compete in the global knowledge economy because of 'insufficient competition and a lack of informed choice' (BIS 2016: 8). Courses based on the traditional three-year undergraduate model, it argued, are 'inflexible', while graduate employment outcomes are uneven, and employers are 'suffering skills shortages, especially in high skilled STEM areas' (ibid.). The solution it proposed to these problems entailed opening up higher education to competition from the private sector, which would 'deliver better outcomes and value for students, employers and the taxpayers who underwrite the system' (ibid.). 'Competition between providers in any market', it declared, 'incentivizes them to raise their game, offering consumers a greater choice of more innovative and better quality products and services at lower cost. Higher education is no exception' (ibid.).

Central to the White Paper's vision of reform was a series of changes that would enable external, for-profit providers to acquire degree-awarding powers ('DAPs'), a measure designed to break the 'monopoly' that universities currently maintain over this area. New providers would be granted access to state student loans and would also be allowed to charge the maximum tuition fees. The White Paper also proposed eliminating the size threshold required for applications to have university status, allowing for the creation of much smaller institutions. To deliver these objectives, the government proposed creating a powerful new regulatory agency, the Office for Students (OfS), a 'consumer focused market regulator' (2016: 16) that would have new statutory powers and an extended remit to police the regime for quality and standards across all registered HE providers, including protecting academic freedom and institutional autonomy (2016: 56). Described as a 'Non-Departmental Public Body' at 'arms' length from government' (2016:16), the OfS would distribute grants, award university status and have power to enter premises with a warrant. The 2016 Higher Education Bill also proposed transferring the authority to grant degree-awarding powers and university titles from the Privy Council to the new Office for Students.

Other proposals in the White Paper included measures aimed at:

1. Promoting stronger links between the auditing of teaching quality through the new Teaching Excellence Framework (or TEF) and tuition fees. Universities that met standards in 2017–18 and 2018–19 would be allowed inflation increases in tuition fees, ahead of the introduction of differentiated caps in 2019–20, while providers whose TEF levels fell would be required to lower their student fees.

2. Assessing universities according to their performance on student satisfaction, retention and graduate employment, and other metrics yet to be developed.
3. Introducing measures to enable students to access detailed information on graduate earnings by individual degree course. This will be provided using HMRC (Her Majesty's Revenue and Customs) tax data, rather than information on graduate destinations provided by the universities themselves.
4. Publishing headline results on graduate earnings each year, with detailed breakdowns by subject and institution.

In short, the White Paper was a blueprint for fundamentally redrawing the relationship between universities, the state, students and research. Its aim was to unbundle the university's core functions so that these could be outsourced and rebundled by new, for-profit providers. It also sought to create an ever-tighter coupling of performance measures, state surveillance and marketization. Like the earlier Ernst and Young and Barber reports, it portrayed the traditional university as outmoded, unsustainable and an impediment to success. Its policy prescriptions were couched in the language of risk, environmental hazards and urgency ('university leaders must take "urgent action" to "future-proof" their institutions or face disaster'). It also hailed the moral superiority of the free market model as the natural way to drive up quality, increase transparency and empower students through choice. Competition and privatization are depicted as the only viable pathway to long-term sustainability, better value for money and the weaning of higher education from dependence on the state.

University–industry–government collaboration: The 'triple helix' model

If the UK White Paper provides one example of how the university third mission is being translated into practice, another is the 'triple helix' model, which portrays higher education, government and industry as part of a closely connected and mutually beneficial innovation system. Developed by Etzkowitz and Leydesdorff (1997), the triple helix model suggests a much more complex and collaborative framework for capitalizing innovation than previous 'technology push' and 'demand pull' models (Collier and Gray 2010: 8). The triple helix emerges as the knowledge economy gains precedence and universities come to be understood as central economic actors for their regions or nations. Etzkowitz and Leydesdorff (2000: 110) termed this the 'second academic revolution' – the first academic revolution having occurred in the late nineteenth century when universities added research to their teaching mission. Etzkowitz links the emergence of the triple helix to the shifting nature of the global economy when science 'emerged as an alternative engine of economic growth to the classic triumvirate of land, labor and capital' (Etzkowitz 2003: 109). Following this third revolution, industry and universities are both able and compelled to work together due to 'a convergence of methodological and epistemological aims and norms between academy (industrialization of science) and industry (scientification of industry)' (Etzkowitz and Viale 2010: 600). For these authors, the third mission is an inevitable result of society's latest 'great transformation' (2010: 595) and its shift to a knowledge economy.

Whereas the UK White Paper aimed to reform universities by increasing competition and enabling external providers to capture and commercialize their resources, the premise behind the triple helix model is that academia, industry and government should work more collaboratively to ensure that knowledge generated in publicly funded research institutions ends up in the marketplace, drives innovation and promotes national prosperity: a symbiosis between the state, science and enterprise that works for the mutual benefit of society. This model draws even more heavily on biological metaphors and imagery, most notably in its evocation of DNA and the double helix – the basis of life itself.

In New Zealand, these ideas have been given a further twist through the popular notion of 'NZ Inc'. This phrase, which was borrowed from the term 'Japan Inc', is often used by New Zealand governments to promote the idea that everyone should 'pull together' to enhance national competitiveness. Echoing Japan's successful corporatist approach to post-war economic reconstruction, NZ Inc was part of a wider state project to harness economic nationalism and jingoism in order to more effectively target strategic export markets. During the 1980s, this strategy was institutionalized through the publicly funded, privately governed New Zealand Trade Development Board (NZTDB). It was subsequently used to promote New Zealand tourism and the organization of a national science system. Given higher education's importance to the knowledge economy, it was arguably only a matter of time before this 'NZ Inc' approach would also be applied to universities as instruments for developing innovation, promoting entrepreneurship and expanding the returns from 'export education'.

The third mission in New Zealand: Universities and 'innovation ecosystems'

Between 2013 and 2015, I was part of an interdisciplinary research project to investigate how the third mission was being organized, implemented and performed in each of New Zealand's eight universities. In New Zealand, as we discovered, the third mission has taken a very similar trajectory to that of the UK and has largely been co-opted into government projects for economic nationalism of the NZ Inc kind outlined above. This top-down and state-led approach was typically justified on the grounds that New Zealand, as a 'small country' situated at the bottom of the world, far from its main markets and totally dependent on external trade for its survival, has no option but to act in a strategically corporatist manner to marshal its resources (Shore 2017). A striking aspect of New Zealand higher education since the 1980s has been the close functional relationship between universities, the state and projects for national development. Even during its most radical neoliberal phase, the state has frequently intervened to promote national development through supporting business growth with research and development funding, training investment and export incentives. Another notable feature of this period is the concerted efforts of successive governments to 'brand' New Zealand as a small yet innovative developed economy. Universities have become increasingly central to this vision of economic development: as trainers of human capital; as nodes of innovation in medicine, engineering, science and technology; as conduits between New Zealand and a global economy; and as the commercialization interface between innovative ideas and discoveries and a business world ready to take these to a global market. As a result, New Zealand's universities are increasingly funded in relation to their potential contribution to economic development and are continually subject to internal reorganizations to meet that driver. Beyond calls for more 'translational' research, they also face pressure for 'relevance' in their teaching programmes and, since the early 1990s, demands by government that they deliver a 'return on investment' (ROI).

Our research highlighted several areas where the commercialization of the university appears most advanced. One of these was the rise of technology transfer offices (TTOs), which was something that every university now had, although these were mostly small entities with just a handful of employees. The exception was Auckland UniServices Ltd, the University of Auckland's research commercialization unit which, with over 700 employees and clients in over 45 countries, is the largest entity of its kind in Australasia. All of these commercialization units told a similar story about 'breaking new ground', unleashing 'untapped potential', connecting researchers with investors and creating new start-ups. Most of them echoed the narrative about the failure of the traditional university, the promise of science and technology, and the need to commercialize their university's intellectual property.

Our study found that the University of Auckland, New Zealand's largest university, was also the most commercially oriented. This was reflected not only in the influence UniServices exerted over the university and in the way the university's hiring and investment policy priorities are often skewed toward UniServices' financial and commercial objectives (see Lewis and Shore 2017), it was also manifest in the way the university's vice-chancellor and senior leadership team measured success and defined the purpose of the university in terms of innovation, entrepreneurship and commercialization. A particularly novel aspect of this entrepreneurial turn, however, was the way that this commercialization agenda was folded into a discourse of symbiosis and the idea of universities as entities embedded within a regional and national 'innovation ecosystem'. While the 'innovation ecosystem' concept is not unique to New Zealand, the way it has been used for economic and nationalist ends in New Zealand is particularly novel.

'Innovation ecosystem' is an idea that numerous international organizations have embraced, including the US National Science Foundation and the EU's 'Horizon 2020' research programme.[1] However, what that term actually means is often unclear. As Deborah Jackson (2011) explains, whereas a biological ecosystem involves complex relationships between living organisms and habitats in ways that sustain equilibrium, an innovation ecosystem is modelled on the idea of 'the economic rather than the energy dynamics' of the relationships between actors and entities 'whose functional goal is to enable technology development and innovation' (Jackson 2011: 2). These actors and entities include:

> material resources (funds, equipment, facilities, etc.) and the human capital (students, faculty, staff, industry researchers, industry representatives, etc.) that make up the institutional entities participating in the ecosystem (e.g. the universities, colleges of engineering, business schools, business firms, venture capitalists (VC), industry- university research institutes, federal or industrial supported Centers of Excellence, and state and/or local economic development and business assistance organizations, funding agencies, policy makers, etc.). The innovation ecosystem comprises two distinct, but largely separated economies, the knowledge economy, which is driven by fundamental research, and the commercial economy, which is driven by the marketplace.
>
> Jackson 2011: 2

In the case of Auckland UniServices, that innovation ecosystem includes the Business School's 'Spark' programme for fostering entrepreneurs, its postgraduate degrees in Commercialization and Entrepreneurship and Bioscience Enterprises, and its 'Return on Science' (ROS) research commercialization programme, whose aim is 'to turn raw research into commercial outcomes' by connecting 'world leading' academics and entrepreneurs with 'venture capitalists, commercialisation R & D specialists, experts from Fortune 500 companies and company start up specialists' (UniServices 2016). According to UniServices, this 'award-winning' programme produced a 438 per cent ROI on technologies invested in 2013 (UniServices 2016). The University of Auckland Business School (2016) claims it has successfully grown an 'entrepreneurial ecosystem', one that 'fosters a spirit of enterprise and innovation – a mind-set grounded in a structure of flexible, adaptive and mutually-reinforcing elements'. The Business School defines its key objective as 'economic transformation and the creation of wealth in New Zealand', a task which it says it achieves by creating productive synergies between postgraduate researchers and industry scientists (Whitcher 2013).

In 2013, UniServices devoted an entire issue of its magazine *Evolve* to the topic of how to develop such 'entrepreneurial ecosystems'. Under the headline, 'Evolving Ecosystem Delivers on Government Biotech Vision', it asks, rhetorically:

> How do you define a university in 2013? The world's best are moving rapidly away from the 'ivory tower' notions of yesteryear, where elevated learning was a pure pursuit that stood apart from the commercial business imperatives of the 'real' world. Today, leading universities such as Cambridge, the University of California in San Francisco and The University of Auckland are embracing a very different model – a fusion of exceptional learning and industry engagement. These are the only three universities in the world using this model and for New Zealand it means delivering on a government vision for fuelling national economic growth through a vibrant, innovative biotechnology industry.
>
> UniServices 2013

At the heart of this model is the idea that innovation and entrepreneurship can be successfully nurtured by co-locating researchers with industry experts and venture capitalists in order to form dynamic 'biotech clusters'. Auckland University's Institute for Innovation in Bioscience (IIB) epitomized this approach. In 2013, it had secured eight companies based around clusters in agritech, health technology and food and nutrition. As its former director, Joerg Kistler explained: 'We have big open spaces and open plan laboratories' so that postgraduate students and industry scientists can share practical technical knowledge (UniServices 2013). This architectural set-up was designed to create an ecosystem 'where knowledge transfer can flourish' and where 'business savvy scientists' are created:

> The building layout is designed for maximum interaction: 10,000m2 of research space, room for 400 scientists, one main entrance and one cafeteria. Joerg calls this 'maximising the water cooler effect'. A biotech networking hub is formed ... forging partnerships between multi-national companies and The University of Auckland, enticing companies to New Zealand, bonding industry and academia even more closely.
>
> UniServices 2013

The idea here is that entrepreneurship is a 'mind-set' that can be acquired through a process akin to osmosis, with industry scientists, postgraduate researchers and commercialization experts rubbing shoulders together and transferring their knowledge and skills in a shared confined arena. Together, these elements combine to form the University of Auckland Entrepreneurial Ecosystem, which, we read, the Massachusetts Institute of Technology Skoltech Initiative Report has identified 'as one of the top five "emerging leaders in entrepreneurship" from around the world' and expects to become a 'major international entrepreneurial and innovation powerhouses in the decades ahead' (Auckland UniServices 2016).

Again, universities forging links with business is nothing new. But what is novel is the extent to which these relationships have been institutionalized and the influence they now exert over academia. In the past, cultivating entrepreneurship and commercializing academic knowledge were considered peripheral activities and secondary to the university's core business of teaching, research and scholarship. Today, cultivating links with business and the pursuit of new income streams is increasingly viewed as the university's main business. Entrepreneurialism, innovation and competitiveness are the key qualities required of the aspiring young researcher seeking to establish a career in a 'world ranked' university. As a senior research office director summed up, in the modern 'world ranked' university, 'innovation has replaced the idea of research – and grants are considered "investments" that require financial returns'.

Conclusion: University–business links – symbiotic or parasitic?

Reading the literature produced by UniServices and the Auckland University Business School, one could be forgiven for thinking that the institution in question is a private, for-profit enterprise, rather than a public university with a social mission and charitable status. That is because boundaries between these alternative visions of the university have become increasingly blurred in recent years. In the case of the UK, the main driver behind recent higher education reforms has been the government's attempt to 'open up' universities to enable their assets to be exploited by predatory external providers. The 'unbundling' called for by Sir Michael Barber and his colleagues is code for a new form of asset stripping, but it also represents a major gamble with the future of the university (McGettigan 2013). This is what David Harvey (2004) has elsewhere termed 'accumulation by dispossession' and it is a model best exemplified in the University of Phoenix in the United States (Hotson 2011).

By contrast, higher education reform and the rise of the third mission in New Zealand have taken a very different trajectory. Despite the country's reputation for being a laboratory for neoliberal policy reform, the privatization of New Zealand's universities is not a policy priority as there is no real free market alternative to state-funded universities or research in New Zealand. Instead, the government has sought to mobilize universities, industry and venture capitalists towards a shared project of economic nationalism. The logics of innovation, commercialization and entrepreneurship have been folded into a discourse of ecosystems, symbiotic partnerships and sustainability. These concepts and keywords have created a powerful assemblage of metaphors and ideas that have helped reshape the relationship between universities, industry and the state. In true corporatist fashion, these constituencies have been brought together for the purposes of wealth creation and national development – and for the higher goal of promoting an 'NZ Inc approach' to higher education and research. Yet while the language of 'innovation ecosystems' and symbiosis may fit this corporatist vision of university futures, the practice is more akin to casino capitalism than corporatization (McGettigan 2013; Levin and Greenwood 2016). It is significant that the vice-chancellor of Auckland University is also chair of UniServices, yet even more significant that neither the minister for higher education nor the university's governing council sees any conflict of interest or contradictions in these roles being combined. How, one might ask, can a public institution with charitable status and a social mission legitimately harbour an enterprise geared explicitly to academic capitalism and the commercialization of university research? One answer, perhaps, is that this is achieved by creating an internal state of exception (Agamben 2005). Like the offshore tax haven or gambling casino, UniServices operates as a space symbolically and functionally set apart from the rest of the university, where different rules and norms apply (Shore and McLauchlan 2012).

The new forms of university research and practice I have described in this chapter represent a very different understanding of the university's mission and meaning to that epitomized by the traditional public university model, or what UniServices dismissed as the 'ivory tower notion of yesteryear'. With its claims about relevance, forging synergies between science, industry and academia, producing better returns on investment for the nation, and driving the knowledge economy, it might be argued that this emphasis on 'innovation ecosystems' represents a break with the past and the outline of a better way to organize universities in the future: a model that perhaps provides an answer to, or even goes beyond, critiques of academic capitalism.

That would be the optimistic conclusion to draw. A more realistic interpretation, however, is that what we see in New Zealand is the extent to which commercialization and the third mission are redefining and displacing the university's other missions, and in the process, changing research priorities, hiring practices and what counts as valid knowledge. In short, the university is being reimagined – and reinvented – around a new set of discourses, norms and practices associated with the third mission and its associated notions of 'impact', 'relevance', wealth creation and 'return on investment'. Critics often rail against the 'corporatization' of the university, but in New Zealand and probably many other countries, universities appear to be doing this themselves: reorganizing themselves in order to mirror business corporations – or more accurately, what they believe to be practices of business corporations. These processes are changing the way that universities are organized, but they are also changing academic subjectivities as the new priorities and conditions of employment become normalized and embodied in policy. In New Zealand, the language of innovation, entrepreneurialism and commercialization has been rendered more acceptable by its conflation with concepts from ecology and environmentalism. Ecosystems, resilience and synergy are terms that have all been appropriated and reframed in ways designed to make commercialization seem both natural and ethical. Few of those involved in the project to advance the university third mission seem to question whether these university–business relations are 'symbiotic' rather than predatory or parasitic. To echo Emily Martin (1991), we need to 'wake up those sleeping metaphors', not only to rob them of their power to 'naturalize our social conventions about the world' but, more importantly, to protect those worlds from the predatory economic and financial interests that the third mission is unleashing. Given the close 'symbiotic relationship' between the university and the reproduction of anthropology as a discipline, this challenge is particularly pressing.

Note

1   As the European Commission explains, a key aim of its 'Research, Development and Innovation' strategy is to 'strengthen the local innovation ecosystem as stronger local public sector demand for innovative solutions attracts additional investments into the region and helps to prevent relocation of innovative companies to other parts of the world' (European Commission 2014: 99).

References

Agamben, G. (2005), *State of Exception* (trans. K. Attell), Chicago: University of Chicago Press.

Auckland UniServices Ltd. (2013), 'Evolving Ecosystem Delivers on Government Biotech Vision', *Evolve*, 5. Available online: http://www.uniservices.co.nz/about/evolve/evolve-issue-5/evolving-ecosystems (accessed December 2016).

Auckland UniServices Ltd. (2016), 'Capability Overview: The University of Auckland and UniServices Entrepreneurial Ecosystems', Auckland: University of Auckland. Available online: http://www.uniservices.co.nz/about/uniservices (accessed January 2017).

Auletta, K. (2012), 'Get Rich U', *New Yorker*, 30 April. Available online: http://www.newyorker.com/magazine/2012/04/30/get-rich-u

Barber, M., K. Donnelly and S. Rizvi (2013), *An Avalanche is Coming: Higher Education and the Revolution Ahead*, London: Institute for Public Policy Research.

BIS (Department of Business, Innovation and Skills) (2016), *Success as a Knowledge Economy: Teaching Excellence, Social Mobility and Student Choice*, Higher Education White Paper, May, London: Her Majesty's Stationery Office.

Bokor, J. (2012), 'University of the Future: A thousand year old industry on the cusp of profound change', Ernst and Young Report, Australia: Ernst and Young.

Collier, A. and B. Gray (2010), 'The Commercialisation of University Innovations: A Qualitative Analysis of the New Zealand Situation', Research Report, Centre for Entrepreneurship, Dunedin: University of Otago.

Collini, S. (2009), 'Impact on Humanities', *Times Literary Supplement*, 55 (63): 18.

Cooper, D. (2009), 'University–Civil Society (U–CS) Research Relationships: The Importance of a 'Fourth Helix' Alongside the 'Triple Helix' of University–Industry–Government (U–I–G) Relations', *South African Review of Sociology*, 40 (2): 153–80.

Douglas, S. (2012), 'Advancing the Scholarship of Engagement: An Institutional Perspective', *South African Review of Sociology*, 43 (2): 27–39.

Etzkowitz, H. (2003), 'Research Groups as "Quasi-Firms": The Invention of the Entrepreneurial University', *Research Policy*, 32 (1): 109–21.

Etzkowitz, H. (2008), *The Triple Helix: University-Industry-Government Innovation In Action*, London: Routledge.

Etzkowitz, H. and L. Leydesdorff (eds) (1997), *Universities in the Global Economy: A Triple Helix of University–Industry–Government Relations*, London: Cassell Academic.

Etzkowitz, H. and L. Leydesdorff (2000), 'The Dynamics of Innovation: From National Systems and "Mode 2" to a Triple Helix of University–Industry–Government Relations', *Research Policy*, 29: 109–23.

Etzkowitz, H. and R. Viale (2010), 'Polyvalent Knowledge and the Entrepreneurial University: A Third Academic Revolution?', *Critical Sociology*, 36: 595–609.

Evans, M. (2004), *Killing Thinking: Death of the University*, London: Bloomsbury.

Giroux, H. and K. Myrsiades (2001), *Beyond the Corporate University: Culture and Pedagogy in the New Millennium*, US: Rowman & Littlefield.

Gove, J. (2015b), 'Social Sciences and Humanities Faculties "To Close" in Japan after Ministerial Intervention', *Times Higher Education*, 14 September. Available online: https://www.timeshighereducation.com/news/social-sciences-and-humanities-facultiesclose-japan-after-ministerial-decree (accessed February 2016).

Harvey, D. 2004. 'The "New" Imperialism: Accumulation by Dispossession', *Socialist Register*, 40: 63–87.

Hotson, H. (2011), 'Short Cuts', *London Review of Books*, 33 (11): 19.

Jackson, D. (2011), *What is an Innovation Ecosystem?*, Arlington, VA: National Science Foundation, 1–11.

Jeffreys, B. (2019). 'The University Timebomb', BBC Radio 4 documentary. Available online: https://www.bbc.co.uk/sounds/play/m0004gy7

Levin, M. and D. J. Greenwood (2016), *Creating a New Public University and Reviving Democracy: Action Research in Higher Education*, Oxford: Berghahn.

Lewis, N. and C. Shore (2017), 'Managing the Third Mission: Reform or Reinvention of the Public University?' in S. Wright and C. Shore (eds), *Death of the Public University*, 41–68, Oxford: Berghahn.

Lyotard, J. (1994), *The Postmodern Condition: A Report on Knowledge*, Minneapolis, MN: University of Minnesota Press.

Marginson, S. and M. Considine (2000), *The Enterprise University: Power, Governance and Reinvention in Australia*, Cambridge: Cambridge University Press.

Martin, E. (1991), 'The Egg and the Sperm: How Science has Constructed a Romance Based on Stereotypical Male–Female Roles', *Signs*, 16 (3): 485–501.

McGettigan, A. (2013), *The University Gamble: Money, Markets and the Future of Higher Education*, London: Pluto.

Molas-Gallart, J., A. Salter, P. Patel, A. Scott and X. Duran (2002), *Measuring Third Stream Activities*, Brighton: SPRU.

Nedeva, M. (2007), 'New Tricks and Old Dogs? The "Third Mission" and the Re-production of the University', in D. Epstein (ed.) *Geographies of Knowledge, Geometries of Power: Framing of the Future of Higher Education*, World Yearbook of Education 2008, Routledge: New York.

Robertson, S. and F. Kitagawa (2011), 'University Incubators and Knowledge Mediation Strategies: Policy and Practice in Creating Competitive City Regions', Centre for Learning and Life Chances in Knowledge Economies and Societies. Available online: http://www.llakes.org.

Shore, C. (2010), 'Beyond the Multiversity: Neoliberalism and the Rise of the Schizophrenic University', *Social Anthropology*, 18 (1): 15–29.

Shore, C. (2017). '"100% Pure New Zealand": National Branding and the Paradoxes of Scale', in U. Hannerz and A. Gingrich (eds), *Small Countries: Structures and Sensibilities*, 47–66, Philadelphia, PA: University of Pennsylvania Press.

Shore, C. and L. McLauchlan (2012), '"Third Mission" Activities, Commercialization and Academic Entrepreneurs', *Social Anthropology*, 20 (3): 267–86.

Shore, C. and S. Wright (2000), 'Coercive Accountability: The Rise of Audit Culture in Higher Education', in Strathern, M. (ed.) *Audit Cultures: Anthropological Studies in Accountability, Ethics and the Academy*, 00+00, London: Routledge.

Shore, C. and Wright, S. (2017). 'Privatising the Public University: Key Trends, Counter-trends and Alternatives', in S. Wright and C. Shore (eds) *Death of the Public University? Uncertain Futures for Higher Education in the Knowledge Economy*, 1–27, Oxford: Berghahn.

Slaughter, S. and G, Rhoades (2004), *Academic Capitalism and the New Economy: Markets, State and Higher Education*, London: Johns Hopkins University Press.

Tsing, A. (2009), 'Beyond Economic and Ecological Standardization', *The Australian Journal of Anthropology*, 20 (3): 347–68.

Tsing, A. (2011), *Friction: An Ethnography of Global Connection*. Princeton, NJ: Princeton University Press.

University of Auckland (UoA) (2013), 'Spark $100K Challenge Qualifiers Revealed', Business School, The University of Auckland, Available online: https://www.business.auckland.ac.nz/en/about/news-and-media/news/mr-2013/08/23/Spark-100K-Challenge-qualifiers-revealed.html.

Vernon, J. (2010), 'The End of the Public University in England', *GlobalHigherEd*, 27 October. Available online: https://www.insidehighered.com/blogs/globalhighered/the_end_of_the_public_university_in_england (accessed November 2016).

Whitcher, G. (2013), *Building an Entrepreneurial Ecosystem in Auckland*, Auckland: University of Auckland Business School.

Whittred, G. (2014), 'Greg Whittred – Dean, The University of Auckland – Entrepreneurs' Challenge 2014'. Available online: https://www.youtube.com/watch?v=D7j4oUPQbXA (accessed December 2016).

Williams, R. (1977), *Keywords*, Glasgow: Fontana.

Wright, S. (2016). 'Universities in a Knowledge Economy or Ecology? Policy, Contestation and Abjection', *Critical Policy Studies*, 10 (1): 59–78.

Wright, S. and C. Shore (eds) (2017), *Death of the Public University? Uncertain Futures for Universities in the Knowledge Economy*, Oxford: Berghahn.

2

Leave a Light On For Us: The Future of a Collaborative Anthropology in the Neoliberal University

Fiona Murphy

Collaborations and engagements in the neoliberal university

Something smells of bullshit. It has for a long time. Caught in the spectacular entanglements of the neoliberal university, academic work is being actively 'bullshitized' (Graeber 2018). Audit cultures (Shore and Wright 2011), the intensification of administrative duties, the politics of intellectual egos and academic 'assholery' (Dunn 2018), hierarchical academic freedoms, an exploitative publishing industry and an increase in zero-hour contracts means the precariat of academia are subject to the combination of some very particular horrors. So, something does indeed smell of bullshit. It will, no doubt, linger long in the gloaming of too many precarious academic careers. These inequalities and exploitative practices are the buttresses upon which some contemporary successful academic careers are built, at the expense of others, gadflies turned horses. The key to the ivory tower has been hidden away, with only academic 'elites' and senior university management remaining inside; all others must wade knee-deep through work-practice bullshit, deprived of labour dignity, equality and solidarity.

Intimately connected to the evolution of this kind of work-practice is the manner in which ideas of collaboration and impact have acquired a neoliberal hue, spoken in a language which often undermines some of the core goals of many anthropologists. This chapter discusses the complexities of collaboration in this particular regard for precarious anthropologists. It reflects on how ideas of collaboration, engagement and impact, while fundamental to the work of anthropology, can also, in their neoliberal guise, serve to diminish and undermine what it is we set out to do and achieve in our scholarly projects. Collaboration, in its many forms, whether with our research participants or non-academic partners, is in principle an ideal. For precarious academics, collaboration and public engagement in many cases is not a choice, it is a mechanism of survival. It is of course critical that our work finds value outside of the ivory tower, and this is an important part of how we work as anthropologists, but the pathway to this kind of impact is a challenging one for many precarious academics.

As such, within the confines of the neoliberal university, collaboration is often something which is foisted upon scholars at all levels in an attempt to win large grants or to produce an image of 'impactful work'. Inherent in such neoliberal goals is the quantitative measurement by universities of collaboration and impact – a practice which ultimately undermines the work of anthropology, and indeed, the social sciences and humanities more broadly. This is particularly acute in the context of the UK's research excellence framework (REF system), where metrics have become the modus operandi of higher education. Disciplines such as anthropology are frequently called upon to justify their existence within the neoliberal university, while principles of metrics devalue our work and undermine our place in the university. All of this is doubly complicated for precarious academics, who are much more vulnerable to the vagaries of such measurements and justifications as well as neoliberal discourses of responsibilization.

Precarious academics occupy a neoliberal university in which they are second-tier academics; more often than not they are expected to offer a sizeable proportion of their labour for free, with the neoliberal university offering the false promise of future employment as 'the affective currency of unpaid work' (Coin 2017: 713). In addition to this, precarious academics often need publishing and grant outputs far in excess of senior permanent academics when they were at an equivalent career stage. The 'privilege' and 'pleasure' of doing academic work is often deemed as having more weight than decent employment contracts and working conditions; to be someone who complains about this 'labour of love' is to be someone who may possibly imperil their chances of ever acquiring security of tenure. It is clear then that an entire cycle of exploitation is made possible by the corporate and managerial university in which many permanent/tenured academics act as neoliberal agents (often willingly). Grant culture often plays into this as well in the ways it perpetuates a cycle of temporary and short-term contracts. Further, many precarious positions are occupied by women in the arts, humanities and social sciences (Courtois and O'Keefe 2015; Ivancheva 2015; McKenzie 2017, 2018; Thwaites and Pressland 2017) making the issue of precarity a highly gendered one. This culture of competition, expectation and forced mobility in a two-tiered system makes everyday life for precarious academics an ongoing struggle; the notion of collaboration in such spaces is often much more complex than is credited.

Like a number of the chapters in this book, I construct this chapter in an autobiographical vein. Herein, I document my professional trajectory in academia – a CV of a female anthropologist subject to precarity for the entirety of her career thus far. Indeed, I do so in order to highlight the challenges of 'precarious collaborations' in the neoliberal university. However, in writing publicly about precarity, one can attract criticism, and so, like other precarious scholars who publicly express their dissatisfaction, I make myself vulnerable in this very act. As such, in drawing on different kinds of engagements and collaborations from my professional life, from a PhD with Indigenous Australians (Murphy 2018; 2019) to work in a business school (Murphy and McDonagh 2016) and with policy makers on issues of displacement (Murphy and Vieten 2017), I highlight the continuities and discontinuities of collaboration in a neoliberal setting. Further, the value of being self-reflexive, of drawing on my own professional curriculum vitae, while still occupying a precarious academic position is key to thinking about how my journey into various collaborative projects and settings has not always been by choice. This is anchored in a deeply complex and affective relationship to the issue of precarity in academia. In spite of this precarity and almost universal expectations around a kind of volunteerism or free labour in the neoliberal university, I have always attempted to work as an engaged anthropologist – one who believes that collaboration and writing for the public is an appropriate personal, moral and ethical response to the kind of work I do. This is something many of us in this collection share: an ethical and moral reflexivity and a strong awareness of the privilege of doing the kind of anthropology that we do, albeit from the perspective of different career trajectories. I, however, use the word 'privilege' with caution, given how the very notion of privilege with respect to academic labour has been a trope much deployed to circumvent, even purposely obscure the issue of precarity. This connects with issues of gender and caring responsibilities, indeed, in my own personal case, of the challenges of being a mother in a precarious role. This privilege play entwined with the willful blurring of definitions of impact, collaboration and engagement by the neoliberal university agenda, anxieties about the moral imperative to act, engage or have impact, also lead to bigger questions about the nature of knowledge production (and its reception) in the social sciences and humanities.

In a context where we find ourselves under ongoing critical scrutiny in the crucible of neoliberalism, I believe that we should take anthropologist Michel Trouillet's (2004: 139) provocation that we must approach such questions with a moral optimism very seriously. We do indeed owe it to ourselves and in particular to our interlocutors to proclaim as loudly as possible that as anthropologists we have seen many alternative visions of humankind – indeed, often many more than other academic disciplines. It is within these alternative visions and an approach informed by moral optimism that anthropology and, indeed, the social sciences and humanities more broadly carry their deepest value. Such a vision should play a critical role in our decisions to collaborate, to engage and to have impact, and this sits well beyond the reach of neoliberal processes of measurement and justification. The challenge is finding a unified voice through which to accomplish this.

As an anthropologist, I have worked in a number of different settings, on projects connected to Indigenous Australia, asylum seekers and refugees on the island of Ireland, France and Turkey, and a project on sustainability in the context of austerity Ireland. I have worked with policymakers and industry, and have researched and taught in anthropology departments, schools of business, and interdisciplinary settings such as the Senator George J. Mitchell Institute for Global Peace, Security and Justice in Queen's University Belfast. These pathways and my academic trajectory have been multifaceted, due in no small part to graduating with a PhD in 2009, the point of critical global economic crisis and the beginning of severe austerity measures in the Republic of Ireland, where I currently live. This, coupled with the growth of neoliberal agendas within universities, has meant that like many of my fellow early career colleagues who graduated in and around this time, I have had to be innovative with my skill set. The standard and, in comparison, relatively easy academic pathways of my senior colleagues are not available to me or my early to mid-career colleagues. The difference in coming out into the world with a PhD before the global economic crash and the increased tightening of neoliberal agendas is quite substantial. Many of these academics are comparatively lucky (although some fervently deny this) and work in contrast to their colleagues who graduated a mere short number of years after them.

George Morgan (2016: 162) goes as far as to describe these academic trajectories as having been limited by precariousness in a number of ways; he says that 'precariousness has also limited scholarly horizons and ambitions: a gentle nudge to public policy here, an incremental contribution to some scholarly sub-specialism there'. It is indeed this culture of precariousness that has robbed many anthropologists of the chance to become embedded in singular spaces of depth. However, in losing, we also gain, in terms of our ability to be flexible and adaptable with our subject matters and to bring diversity to the departments in which we teach. But ultimately, as Morgan (2016) reminds us, the force of precarity is fast altering the university landscape, recasting it as a place where all notions of security and permanency are absented, resulting in what he calls a 'lost generation of academics'. This is the heavy burden many early to mid-career anthropologists now have to bear, its impact having a bearing on our mental and physical health, our sense of place, our financial well-being, even our ability to build a life in one place, and ultimately, our desire to remain working in universities where we are ill-treated and exploited almost on a daily basis. Indeed, the emergence of an abundance of academic 'quit lit' (Coin 2017) testifies to many of these feelings – in particular, how a strong sense of exploitation and alienation ultimately pushes people out of the neoliberal university.

Indeed, this 'lost generation of academics' is heavily 'dependent' on permanent/ tenured academics, as both Vita Peacock (2016) and Lara McKenzie (2018) have pointed out in their work on precarity. Peacock (2016: 97) characterizes academic precarity as a hierarchical social relation, in which the precariat is 'one side of a reciprocal dynamic in which one lives at the will or pleasure of another person'. Such co/dependencies impact and shape the everyday work/life experience of the precariat in numerous ways, but with respect to issues of collaboration can engender hierarchies, subversions and betrayals which push precarious academics even further into the dark margins of the neoliberal university.

Such limited scholarly horizons also ensue due to the fact that jobs in anthropology departments remain thin on the ground, so anthropology PhDs find themselves working in increasingly varied settings as anthropological purpose itself is continually redefined. While the evolution of the discipline's reach is a positive, it does, however, remain to be said that the heightened precarity of those graduating with PhDs in anthropology runs the risk of devaluing the space for anthropology in the university. Such issues beckon towards questions of responsibility within the discipline with respect to how we 'produce' and then treat our PhD candidates, and what might be the responsibility of senior anthropologists towards new generations of anthropologists. The question also remains as to whether we are in fact producing too many PhDs, setting them up – rather unethically, it must be said – for a career full of struggle, precarity and mistreatment. The controversy in 2018 regarding the anthropological journal *HAU* and its playing out on social media is indeed a synecdoche for the entrenched and unwavering dominance of such work practices and institutional culture in the discipline of anthropology and the university at large (Neveling 2018). It is an interesting controversy to reflect on, given how it brought about a larger discussion on the nature of precarity within anthropology more specifically as well as collaborations between different kinds of scholars. Many commentators have highlighted how, at its inception, *HAU* was presented as an alternative vision for anthropological publishing, part of the open access movement, with much in common with the sharing economy's attempts to disrupt and circumvent capitalist relations of production and consumption. *HAU*, however, became little more than a reflection of the neoliberal system of which it was a part, especially in its active debasing of the principles of mutuality, solidarity and equality on which it was founded.

The tense unfolding of *HAU*'s story on social media, beginning with David Graeber's apology, is a marker of the extent to which many academics inhabit a twilight of knowing and unknowing in their everyday work, particularly with respect to the complex experiences of early and mid-career academics in their midst. In terms of how collaborative practices within academia emerge and are dis/considered, this also holds strong relevance. Perhaps it is this Lethean bad faith that is most disappointing and frustrating, but which also points to the challenges of career formation, and indeed, collaboration for precarious academics.

Like many of my fellow anthropologists, I followed #hautalk closely, while my various messenger systems intoned pings of distress, disappointment, anger, curiosity and, of course, relief – finally, at least one silence was broken. One of my closest anthropologist friends reminded me that a 'nasty, brutish, and short' career was indeed all that many early career anthropologists might expect. However, what wounded most in this unfolding simulacrum of structural harm were the obvious entanglements of silence, complicity, power and disavowal, alongside the delays and absences of particular and necessary engagements. The refusal or the absence of engagement with issues of precarity from those with security of tenure is not unusual, but is particularly shocking in a discipline that prides itself on speaking truth to power in a diversity of ways. In fact, Rosalind Gill asked us as early as 2009 what it would mean to:

> make links between macro-organisation and institutional practices on the one hand, and experiences and affective states on the other, and open up an exploration of the ways in which these may be gendered, racialised and classed? How might we engage critically with the multiple moments in which individuals report being at breaking point, say 'my work is crap' or 'I'm going to be found out' – as well as those moments of gratuitous attack and cruelty, so often seen – for example – in anonymised referee processes (yet rarely challenged) – and

connect these feelings with neoliberal practices of power in the Western University? In short, how might we begin to understand the secrets and silences within our own workplaces, and the different ways in which they matter?

2009: 229

Controversial or shocking events should neither rob us of complexity of thought nor absolve us from the responsibility of speaking out, of responding, or of being in solidarity. However, in the accretion of *HAU*'s symbolism as a microcosm of the ills of academic anthropology, a full scholarly reckoning from all actors did not become apparent. Some argue that social media is not the space for such critique, that the mediatization or condensation of such issues, coupled with the endless plasticity of social media responses, only serves as spectacle – an expansive, blurry mess of finger-pointing and name-calling. However, in a world where both academic freedom and freedom of speech are unequally distributed resources, the constraints and affordances of social media have nonetheless created a space, otherwise lacking, for precarious and untenured academics to connect in solidarity. This connection with some formal, horizontal organizing of precarious groups (such as Precanthro, to name one) has opened up more spaces of possible critique of precarity. Without some ontological and economic security from one contract to another, those academics in this curious mix of feudal and neoliberal space find critique strangled. Those daring to speak out and speak back fear being shut out. While calls exist for a slowing down of scholarship of response, of not fetishizing the digital, but, of protecting the open access ideal, early and mid-career anthropologists, more than most, need this kind of engagement, away from the binds of tenured approval and thus capable of greater activism. Social media creates just this space to call out the bullshit many have been subjected to in their indentured journey to so-called professionalization. Indeed, the instance of #hautalk arrests the rush to habits of responses that follow scripts of resignation and denialism in its decrying of personal, institutional and structural abuses. It also reflects a layered, deeply affective, transnational anthropological response with all its points of conjuncture and disjuncture. This is a collaboration of another kind, one which is outside of the remit of my focus herein, however, significant to point to in terms of how a collective of precarious anthropologists can work collaboratively (very publicly) to highlight their everyday work challenges.

Such controversies, while not only visible in anthropology, also relate to the political economy of how knowledge production is constrained by a perceived utility to the market (of which the university is an increasingly willing accomplice). Knowledge is not produced, negotiated, preserved or disseminated in a vacuum and anthropologists, as much as anyone, follow a dream of new ways of knowing, but struggle to maintain themselves in neoliberal contexts, which the *HAU* controversy illuminates in part. It also marks out how in such conditions precarious anthropologists are forced to reinvent themselves, thus needing to find new collaborative spaces to work in. Given the fact that some disciplines in the university operate as almost akin to imperial or colonizing disciplines, producing what Henry Giroux (2001: 30) calls 'compliant workers' who serve consumers or clients while abstracting from disciplines in the humanities and social sciences, the notion of collaboration can thus be a strange bedfellow in neoliberal universities; its pull being both attractive and necessary but often also forced, ignited by the struggle to be an academic in what is an increasingly confined and limited environment. My views on collaboration, as such, remain mixed. I have had little choice in my career to date *but* to collaborate. These collaborations have taught me a lot about the limits of my own discipline and broadened my skill set and world view. However, some of these very many collaborations have also been a failure, thereby highlighting how truly difficult, even false, some constructions of interdisciplinarity and multidisciplinarity can be. Ultimately, I remain open-minded, but also mindful of how deeply challenging any attempt to collaborate can be, especially for precarious academics, in the context of the neoliberal university, where academic egos and competition define and shape our place of work and partly diminish the value of attempting to work together in spaces beyond our discipline.

The shaping of an engaged anthropologist

I have worked on a diverse range of projects since the award of my PhD in 2009, both individual and collaborative. My views herein are clearly ambivalent about the notion of collaboration and as such, I see it as having both positive and negative connotations. It was, however, my PhD research that played a pivotal role in how I see the positive elements of engagement and collaboration – in short, how I aim to continue to approach collaboration in spite of many negative experiences in my journey. My doctoral research focused on the removal and institutionalization of Indigenous Australians (otherwise known as Stolen Generations) with a particular interest in how modalities of trauma and suffering become politicized. The process of doing this research was instrumental in terms of seeing how collaboration with one's research participants is an important part of anthropological fieldwork. Collaboration over the course of fieldwork assumes diverse forms; in fact, many anthropologists argue that fieldwork is collaborative by its very nature (Lassiter 2005). Collaboration in fieldwork is a form of communicating, rapport building, shaping, of action, advocacy and also of engagement beyond scholarly publics. Researching in a particularly politically fraught context such as among Indigenous Australians evinced how critical a collaborative rapport between researcher and research participants is to the very *doing* of ethnographic work.

In Australia, for those who work with Indigenous Australians, issues of representation feature large, to the degree that such debates can often have a vitriolic and angry hue. I struggled as a PhD student with what my work meant for the very many members of the Stolen Generations who gave me their time and their stories. Many of my research participants saw this as helping to craft a more public narrative of their experiences, the end goal being that my work would reach publics that they themselves could not. Given the limitations of scholarly journals, it concerned me (and still does) that I would not realize their ambitions for my work. Indeed, this was revealed to me in the harshest of ways. Towards the end of my two-year fieldwork period I had a brief encounter with one of my colleagues, an elderly lady called Jane, an Aboriginal activist who had been working for a number of years in Aboriginal education within the walls of the university. When I told her that I would soon be returning to Ireland, she admonished me and told me that I had no right to return to Ireland with the stories of Indigenous Australians, where in her view they would not have any impact (see also Murphy 2019). While I was shocked at this suggestion, I understood that what Jane was pronouncing was the question of 'acting with' my research in impactful ways and the need to do this in a mode of ethical responsibility (see also Murphy 2019). A few weeks later, just days before I was about to leave, during a farewell lunch with two elderly members of the Stolen Generations, they also asked to me to think about who I was going to tell their stories to when I returned home. They advised me to move beyond the university into what they called the real world, to tell their stories in as many forums as I possibly could, so as to bring their experiences to a variety of different people and hence, different publics.

My research participants were merely echoing some of my own concerns at the nature of bearing witness and writing about the experiences of the Stolen Generations, of doing justice to their lifeworlds, but also about the value of an anthropology engaged with suffering and trauma of this kind. They were also setting out the importance of engaging different kinds of publics beyond the university context and understood as well as anyone the value of engaging what

Michael Burawoy (2005) has called 'different potential publics'. My research participants viewed their engagement with my PhD dissertation as a kind of collaboration oriented towards public engagement.

On my return home, while embroiled in the writing up experience, I did indeed heed their advice and spoke to a number of different publics about the story of the Stolen Generations and my research. Burawoy argues that through this kind of engagement we can contribute to both the creation and transformation of various publics. But how we go about this project of engagement, beyond paying lip service to a neoliberal understanding and requirement of 'impact' in the higher education system (particularly in the UK), is a bigger question, one that requires an approach which Burawoy (2004) believes should be based on an open, meaningful dialogue, which reflects a strengthening of the 'internal democracy' of the sociological community – or in the case of this book's public, the anthropological community. In recent years, there has been broad discussion on how the kind of writing anthropologists engage in can do an injustice to the life experiences of our research participants. In our quest for epistemological interpretations of our subject matter, our words and our theories can do harm in a way that, while often unintended, can undermine the very notion of collaboration inherent in the ethnographic project. These are concerns which the discipline of anthropology has taken very seriously and continues to dwell upon, particularly since the writing culture debate in the 1980s. Indeed in their 2016 text *A Passion for Society: How We Think About Human Suffering*, scholars Iain Wilkinson and Arthur Kleinman address the issue of how anthropological research with a particular focus on suffering and trauma can have direct ameliorative societal value. They argue:

> We understand research and writing on problems of social suffering to necessarily involve a commitment to understanding how the moral imperative to care for others is met, experienced, and negotiated under real-life conditions and is thereby either left frustrated or provided with a social space to nurture humanity. We are committed to the project of promoting care as a means to positively transform society and conditions of democracy. We preface would add, however, that we also see this as a fundamental requirement for the invigoration of human-social understanding.
>
> Wilkinson and Kleinman 2016: xii

Books such as this one go some way in addressing a range of different publics and collaborations that anthropologists engage with and in, particularly with respect to Wilkinson and Kleinman's call for anthropological work to positively transform society. Anthropologists such as Thomas Erikson, Michael Jackson, Paul Stoller and Alisse Waterson (this volume) have also spoken at different points in their careers about strengthening our modes of collaboration and engagement at a more unifying level within the discipline as a whole. In other ways, the recent anthology on writing, *The Anthropologist as Writer: Genres and Contexts in the Twenty-First Century* (2016), edited by Helena Wulf, also underlines the importance of seeing how collaboration should shape the contours of our different kinds of writing lives. Collaboration in ethnographic work is a process, both reciprocal and incremental, one that acquires a second life in and through writing for different kinds of publics. This is the kind of critically engaged anthropology that Alisse Waterson (this volume) argues requires continual self-reflexivity, the kind of anthropology from which there is no turning back. Like many of the contributors herein, my academic trajectory is one anchored in an interdisciplinary ethos; indeed, what many of us have in common in this collection is the ability to be flexible with our training and skill sets.

My PhD journey equipped me with a particular approach to collaboration and engagement as many of my research participants continually questioned my motives and intentions. While I have tried to meet my research participants' interpretations to some degree, I feel I have not yet fully realized their objectives. In writing of my ethnographic encounters, I have published in traditional journals, and been warned by the REF-hungry that I need to think more carefully about the kind of book I will write in developing my monograph from my PhD work. I have been urged to go quickly down the well-trodden path of using traditional academic publishers, but this sits in conflict with the desires of my research participants. While some academic publishing houses are starting to open up and become more innovative, thus embracing the need for something to be both scholarly and public in the same moment (in particular the University of California Public Anthropology series and Routledge Innovative Ethnographic series), such efforts are otherwise minimal. The challenge, therefore – in particular for the more junior precarious anthropologist who works in a fashion cognitive of the ethical importance of collaboration and engagement for one's research participants – is how to do justice to their desire for public engagement while also meeting the scholarly demands of the neoliberal university. The precarious are thus caught in this double bind of exceptionalism in terms of how we approach and engage in collaboration in our writing. As someone caught in these shrinking frames of writing engagement, I have had lots of moments of deep reflection on what it is I owe my research participants and how I should close off those debts in the writing directions that I take. This also pushed me to think of how significant to my project of collaborative anthropology the act of *decolonizing* is, in terms of who I cite, how I write and ultimately, who my writing ends up serving (see also Murphy 2019). Some might say such dilemmas and quandaries were good preparation for my years ahead as an anthropologist in a business school.

A portrait of a lone anthropologist in a business school

Concerns with instrumentality, application and use value in the social sciences and humanities are indeed age-old (if we look to the work of Adam Smith we can see this) and increasingly, highly contentious within the neoliberal university; however, they have continually impacted on my own career trajectory. On graduating with a PhD in 2009, right at the beginning of a global economic crisis and the introduction of a particularly severe form of austerity in Ireland, my career in anthropology intersected both in terms of subject matter and direction with global crises. By 2011, I found myself working in a large business school in Dublin on a project on sustainable consumption in austerity Ireland. However, as a lone anthropologist also called upon to teach business topics, it was here I was asked most about the utility of my discipline with respect to a particular set of business school objectives. I had to frequently justify why I should be allowed to include elements of my discipline in some of the consumer behaviour and marketing courses I found myself teaching. I also witnessed the rolling back of critical subjects or critical elements of certain topics, with a larger focus on application, in opposition to theory. This was during a time where the particular business school I was working in was insisting more and more that their singular public was industry. While much has been written in the press about the responsibilities of business schools, particularly post the economic crisis, to produce ethical leaders and thinkers (O'Connor 2013), many business schools do not pay heed, preferring instead to play the model citizen of the neoliberal university (Bennis and O'Toole 2005).

Anthropologists work very successfully in industry, with large corporations such as INTEL and Google employing them to work on a variety of projects (including in INTEL Ireland, which employs a team of anthropologists working in smart cities) and other anthropologists such as Gillian Tett writing very successfully within financial journalism. However, I did not feel that this should be constantly engaged as a 'justification' of why I could be useful to their students and their particular public. Midst the Irish economic crisis, however, I did feel that the role of critical thinking and reflection in our business schools was now needed more than ever before. Indeed, eminent feminist scholars such as Martha Nussbaum and Judith Butler have argued throughout their careers that critique belongs to the entire university and so the value of sharing this across and within disciplines is paramount to producing students as ethically engaged citizens. Anthropologists who are readily dispersed in different departments and schools in different universities play an important role in this intellectual project of critique. But this snapshot begs a larger question – that of the way in which social science and humanities scholars are called upon to justify the work they do to various publics. Indeed, the work of Helen Small (2013) in *The Value of the Humanities*, which is an excellent treatise of the various justifications of the humanities, highlights the need 'to make persuasive to others and the need to find a language in which we can advance claims about public values and their relation to private languages without the language becoming quickly co-opted to other ends and as quickly losing its appeal' (2013: 22). It also supports the view that collaboration in certain kinds of contexts can indeed be strained and challenging, particularly when the value of one discipline is openly pitted against another, in terms of its instrumentality and use value. In a number of universities across the globe, this has been articulated in an aggressive fashion in the form of attempting to close down particular disciplines, such as anthropology, which university management construct as economically unviable.

In the particular research which I undertook while working in a business school, that of understanding sustainability in the context of austerity, I came to understand very well the challenges of a multidisciplinary collaboration. But I also came to understand how ethnography is greatly fetishized within business schools and other disciplines. Ethnography has become somewhat of a buzzword in certain contexts, in particular marketing and industry, more broadly. While this is exciting for anthropologists who want to collaborate in industry contexts, there is also the danger of a distillation of methods and a general misconstruction of the value of doing ethnography in certain kinds of projects. I have taught ethnography to marketing and business students for a number of years, and they are always delighted with the depth and richness it affords as a method, thus there is a real need for it to be taught properly (in all its richness as an approach) within other disciplines.

However, the value of ethnography and anthropology to a topic such as sustainability stood out, particularly when working with business academics. Indeed, Charles Redman (2011) points to this by positing that anthropology and its methods can be hugely helpful in developing a more coherent sustainability science, in both an academic and applied sense. He is also quick to point out that engaging with the very current issue of sustainability will reflect back on the development and positioning of anthropology within the broader context of academia. Redman's conviction emerges out of a belief that anthropology, through its long relationship to notions of value and belief, should allow us to find a route to combine value and science. He argues:

> We all get, as anthropologists, that it takes lots of different ways to understand why people do what they do and what they're like. The past, the present, the biology, the language – we've always understood that a variety of lines of evidence can help enrich our understanding of something. This is a sustainability message too. We can't just invent a new hybrid car and not worry about who can use it and who can't. We can't just put a solar panel on a roof and think that we've saved the world. We need to look at it from all different directions and the impacts. Anthropology is a natural for that. In sustainability, what we have to get across is that there are not only multiple lines of information that we need to incorporate, but there are multiple ways of knowing the same information.
>
> Redman 2011

What Redman and other anthropologists (Trigger 2004) are debating (for both applied and academic anthropologies) is the need to move beyond the simple statement that anthropology has a lot to offer sustainability science (or indeed a number of other research contexts) and to begin to engage with what are and continue to be the barriers to communicating ethnographic discoveries and anthropological analyses to different disciplines and audiences. In a collection of papers on this very topic entitled *Sustainable Environments, Sustainable Communities: Potential Dialogues Between Anthropologists, Scientists and Managers* (2004), a number of anthropologists working in the area of sustainability and environmental management in Australian contexts argue to varying degrees that the anthropologist must find a meta-language with which to communicate anthropological insights (see Minnegal 2004). Equally, anthropologists must employ the tools of anthropology itself to learn how to communicate with and to business and science worlds. Collectively, the anthropologists in this collection argue for collaborative working contexts, stressing that anthropologists must learn to be translators, the conduit between oppositional world views. Anthropologists must act too as initiators, providing the catalyst for different kinds of exchanges between local people, communities, experts and broader publics (see Minnegal 2004). In sum, then, the anthropologist is well placed to facilitate a rapprochement between different disciplines and world views, one that through collaboration and co-creation can engender a space to further important conversations. It is within these debates that a notion of rethinking the scale and form of a collaborative anthropology crystallizes. Working in business school environments taught me a lot about how anthropology is viewed and utilized, but also how enlivening it can be to some disciplines, should we and they allow it to be so.

From the business school to policy makers: Shifting focus

At the time of writing in 2018, I work as a research fellow in an interdisciplinary setting which focuses on conflict, peace and social justice in Queen's University Belfast (QUB). I have found myself a home in the Senator George J. Mitchell Institute for Global Peace, Security and Justice, which takes the task of engaging different publics seriously. One of the more important projects that I worked on in my time in QUB was on a tender for the Northern Ireland Executive Office in Stormont, which focused on the integration of asylum seekers and refugees in Northern Ireland. Working with my colleague Ulrike Vieten, a sociologist also based at the Mitchell Institute, we interviewed forty-seven asylum seekers and refugees from ten different countries in order to ascertain their views on their everyday life experience in Northern Ireland, as well as fifty individuals working in service provision and the NGO and civil sector society over a period of six months. The results of this research will feed directly into the development of a first refugee integration strategy for Northern Ireland, thus making this project one of the more engaged and, indeed, significant projects I have worked on to date (Murphy and Vieten 2017). Conducting this research moved me into a space of collaboration with policy makers and NGOs which was entirely new to me, extraordinarily challenging for both myself and my colleague, but ultimately rewarding in a way that makes me want to continue collaborating in this vein.

Policy-oriented work is certainly not part of the remit of all areas within the social sciences and humanities (and is a very particular orientation). Indeed, like other attempts at application or public engagement, it creates particular tensions. Much of this is summed up in the excellent collection edited by one of the authors in this volume, Cris Shore (and colleagues Wright and Pero) entitled *Policy Worlds: Anthropology and the Analysis of Contemporary Power* (2011). The book evinces how critical it is for anthropologists to engage with policy worlds and to think critically, in our engagements, of how policies work more broadly as technologies of power as well as maps of action.

While it is important collaborative and impactful work to do, the speed of doing policy research (not unlike industry-engaged projects) can indeed be compromising alongside the challenges and complexities of dealing directly with policy makers. Anthropologist Thomas Erikson argues in his book *The Tyranny of the Moment* that a culture that favours fast thinkers over slow ones (2001: 117), in which superficiality and simplification flourishes to the detriment of deeper engagement (2001: 60–61), is a culture in which 'something has run out of control' (2001: 77) – one, he argues, that categorically impacts on the production of knowledge and modes of thought, being, as such, a concern for us all both within and outside the academy. While speed was indeed a defining part of the particular policy project I worked on, my broader feeling was that it did not diminish the results of the project overall. While what we conducted was certainly not ethnographic and did not offer up the same depths of an ethnographic engagement, it nonetheless provided a breadth of perspective through more structured one-to-one interviews and focus groups. In doing this kind of collaborative work, the challenge of methodological approaches often features, and many anthropologists are resistant to adapting their methods, wanting to stay true to their identity as an ethnographer. Personally, I see this as limiting. While I argued earlier in this chapter for a refusal to let ethnography become distilled, as it often does in industry contexts, what I want to stress is that in our big data-driven contemporary world, anthropologists have to be willing to more deeply engage with other methods and approaches to complement our already rich, diligent ethnographic approach.

Doing policy work in this way can allow it to be multilayered and have a multilevelled appearance in other parts of our scholarly lives. With permission from the Executive Office in Stormont, Ulrike and I continue to write out our policy work in different kinds of forms, storying it in scholarly fashion, but also writing it out on public platforms such as The Conversation UK and RTE Brainstorm. The approach we adopted in doing so, however, was only possible with the permissions of both the Executive Office and our very many research participants, who were happy to see this work evolve and assume different forms, many of which are necessary to advocate for better rights for asylum seekers and refugees in Northern Ireland and beyond. The freedom to do this kind of work in the institute in which I work has allowed me to greatly develop my skills and approach to collaboration in a way which sits much differently in my scholarly life to some of my previous collaborative engagements. What this points to, is that successful collaboration can take many different forms, but in part, it requires anthropology to be more malleable in how it defines itself with respect to its broader engagements.

Concluding thoughts: On cabinetmakers and fish fryers

In David Graeber's (2018) work on bullshit jobs, he points to the proliferation of jobs in the contemporary moment that seem to be both pointless or meaningless to both the performer of this type of work and the overall output or impact on the world. Graeber's thesis resonates loudly, particularly in the context of the intensification of pressures to collaborate as well as increased administrative duties in the neoliberal university. Graeber asks us to imagine how if someone was hired as a cabinetmaker but ended up spending large amounts of their time frying fish, they may become obsessed by the fact that some of their colleagues were getting much more time to make their cabinets, thus not engaging in the meaningless, even needless, frying of fish. For the fish fryers, as well as creating stacks of unwanted fried fish, a politics of resentment emerges. This analogy works well in contemporary academia, where some tenured cabinetmakers are often complicit actors in the bullshitization of academic work, while precarious fish fryers not only feel resentful and angry, but are continually silenced and exploited as second-tier academics, the sous-chefs in the academic kitchen. In such spaces, there is a lack of solidarity, basic humanity, and thus a growing inequality between different kinds of academics and networks. It should also remind us to ask, in the midst of silencing and structural, institutional limitations, what it is that the fish fryers are owed? What are indeed the ethical responsibilities of the cabinetmakers toward the fish fryers to help achieve 'new ways of being' (Hey and Morley 2011) if, as it seems, the neoliberal university is here to stay?

In a context where a culture of speed pervades not just policy work, but many other of our engagements, including our scholarly writing, and stems from and connects to the vagaries of work in the neoliberal university, we are asked to be everything from administrators to teachers to publicly engaged scholars. As such, the paths we follow in doing so often crumble as we rush to do it all, striving to become what the neoliberal university has imagined for us. For precarious scholars, resistance to this often means failure in terms of carving out a position or a place in the neoliberal university. Further, the challenges of cobbling together a salary often makes meeting the testing limits of being a scholar in this world almost impossible. I argue, following Rolfe (2013: 80), for a 'paraversity' embracing a collaboration and collegiality between disciplines that moves to:

> subvert . . . the mission of a disintegrated, task-centred university as a commercial enterprise and to propose in its place a parallel 'fourth mission', which aims to reunite and reintegrate the vision, structure, people, relationships and activities

of the academy as a rhizomatic network dedicated to the practice of radical scholarship.

2013: 77

It is, I believe like Rolfe, the 'paraversity' which will move towards spaces of collaboration, diversity, inclusion and equality while convincing the neoliberal university to somehow allow it to run in parallel. It is up to us both precarious and permanent/tenured academics to reinvent this space in collaboration with one another.

In the earlier part of this chapter, I depicted a brief snapshot from one of my research participants, Jane. In Jane's admonishment of my move back to Ireland to complete my PhD, she in fact urged me to think of stories as a gift; which, like all gifts, compel recognition, acknowledgement, and which also instantiate an ethics of responsibility and equitable return (see also Murphy 2019). This points to the important role of reciprocity in our work – with our fellow scholars, but in particular with the 'different potential publics' (Burawoy 2005) with which we engage. The question of what we owe one another in these diverse and sometimes unequal relationships should figure large in our thinking on how anthropology should conceptualize and collaborate with and relate to various publics. That is the only pathway for a collaborative anthropology in the neoliberal university.

References

Bennis, W. and J. O Toole (2005), 'How Business Schools Lost Their Way'. Available online: https://hbr.org/2005/05/how-business-schools-lost-their-way (accessed 12 October 2018).

Burawoy, M. (2005), 'For Public Sociology', *American Sociological Review*, 70: 4–28.

Coin, F. (2017), 'On Quitting', *Ephemera: Theory and Politics in Organisation*, 17 (3): 705–19.

Courtois, A. and T. O'Keefe (2015), 'Precarity in the Ivory Cage: Neoliberalism and Casualization of Work in the Irish Higher Education Sector', *Journal for Critical Education Policy Studies*, 13 (1): 43–66.

Dunn, E. (2018), 'The Problem with Assholes', *Public Anthropologist*. Available online: http://publicanthropologist.cmi.no/2018/06/20/the-problem-with-assholes/ (accessed 12 October 2018).

Eriksen, T. (2001), *Tyranny of the Moment: Fast and Slow Time in the Information Age*, London: Pluto Press.

Gill, R. (2009), 'Breaking the Silence: The Hidden Injuries of Neo-liberal Academia', in R. Flood and R. Gill (eds), *Secrecy and Silence in the Research Process: Feminist Reflections*, 228–44. London: Routledge.

Giroux, H. (2001), *Theory and Resistance in Education: Towards a Pedagogy for the Opposition*, London: Greenwood Publishing Group.

Graeber, D. (2018), *Bullshit Jobs: A Theory*, London: Simon and Schuster.

Guyot, J. (2011), 'Anthropology as Key to Sustainability Science: An Interview with Charles Redman', *Anthropology News*, 52: 12.

Hey, V. and L. Morley (2011), 'Imagining the University of the Future: Eyes Wide Open? Expanding the Imaginary Through Critical and Feminist Ruminations in and on the University', *Contemporary Social Science*, 6 (2): 165–74.

Ivancheva, M. P. (2015). 'The Age of Precarity and the New Challenges to the Academic Profession', *Studia Europaea*, 60 (1): 39–47.

Lassiter, L. (2005), 'Collaborative Ethnography and Public Anthropology', *Current Anthropology*, 46: 83–106.

McKenzie, L. (2017). 'A Precarious Passion: Gendered and Age-based Insecurity Among Aspiring Academics in Australia', in R. Thwaites and A. Pressland (eds), *Being an Early Career Feminist Academic: Global Perspectives, Experiences, and Challenges: Studies in Gender and Education Series*, 31–49, Basingstoke: Palgrave Macmillan.

Minnegal, M. (ed.) (2005), 'Sustainable Environments, Sustainable Communities: Potential Dialogues Between Anthropologists, Scientists and Managers', Proceedings of a Symposium hosted by the School of Anthropology, Geography and Environmental Studies, the University of Melbourne, 2 October 2004, Research Paper, School of Anthropology, Geography and Environmental Studies, University of Melbourne, Australia.

Morgan, G. (2016), 'Cannibalising the Collegium: The Plight of the Humanities and Social Sciences in the Managerial University', in J. Habjan, S. Gupta and H. Tutek (eds), *Academia and the Production of Unemployment*, 151–65, London: Palgrave Macmillan.

Murphy, F. (2018), 'When Gadflies Become Horses: On the Unlikelihood of Ethical Critique from the Academy'. Available online: https://www.focaalblog.com/2018/06/28/fiona-murphy-when-gadflies-become-horses/ (accessed 12 October 2018).

Murphy, F. and U. Vieten (2017), *Asylum Seekers' and Refugees' Experiences of Life in Northern Ireland: Report of the First Study on the Situation of Asylum Seekers and Refugees in Northern Ireland*, Northern Ireland: The Executive Office, Stormont.

Murphy, F. (2018), 'The Whisperings of Ghosts: Loss, Longing, and the Return in Stolen Generations Stories', *Australian Journal of Anthropology*, 29 (3): 332–47.

Murphy, F. (2019), '"Friend or Foe": A Reflection on the Ethico-politics of Friendship and Ethnographic Writing in Anthropological Practice', *Ethnofoor, Special Edition on Friendship*. Available online:

Neveling, P. (2018), 'HAU and the Latest stage of capitalism. Available online: https://www.focaalblog.com/2018/06/22/patrick-neveling-hau-and-the-latest-stage-of-capitalism/ (accessed 12 October 2018).

O'Connor, S. (2013), 'The Responsibility of Business Schools in Training Ethical Leaders', *Forbes*. Available online: https://www.forbes.com/sites/shawnoconnor/2013/05/15/the-responsibility-of-business-schools-in-training-ethical-leaders-2/ (accessed 12 October 2018).

Rolfe, G. (2013), *The University in Dissent*, Abingdon: SRHE and Routledge.

Shore, C. and S. Wright (2011), *Policy Worlds: Anthropology and the Analysis of Contemporary Power*, EASA Series, Oxford: Berghahn Books.

Small, H. (2013), *The Value of the Humanities*, Oxford: Oxford University Press.

Thwaites, R. and A. Pressland (2017), *Being an Early Career Feminist Academic: Global Perspectives, Experiences, and Challenges: Studies in Gender and Education Series*, Basingstoke: Palgrave Macmillan.

Trouillot, M. (2004), *Global Transformations: Anthropology and the Modern World*, 1st edn., New York: Palgrave Macmillan.

Wilkinson, I. and A. Kleinman (2016), *A Passion for Society: How We Think About Human Suffering*, Berkeley, CA: University of California Press.

Wulff, H. (2016), *The Anthropologist as Writer: Genres and Contexts in the Twenty-First Century*, Oxford: Berghahn.

3

Most Humanistic, Most Scientific: Experiencing Anthropology in the Humanities and Life Sciences[1]

Jonathan Skinner

Introduction: What and where is anthropology?

The suggestion that 'Anthropology is the most humanistic of the sciences and the most scientific of the humanities' is generally attributed to the renowned American cultural anthropologist Alfred Kroeber (Kroeber 2003: 144). By this, Kroeber – one of founding father Franz Boas's students – is considered to have safeguarded the humanistic approach to culture alongside one with natural science influences (Steward 1962: 202), a stance that ushered in a four-field approach to anthropology that influences the discipline to this day – particularly in the United States. In the UK, the newly branded Department of Anthropology and Archaeology at the University of Bristol – formerly one of Archaeology and Anthropology, and Archaeology before that – is the sole location in the social anthropology-dominated UK for this diverse and holistic approach to the study of humanity with its distinctive 'fields' of archaeology, social anthropology, evolutionary anthropology and linguistic anthropology (Bristol 2018). Kroeber would be rolling his eyes, then, at the American Anthropological Association's Executive Board, where a suggestion came from Krystal D'Costa (2010) in response to the Executive's motion to excise 'science' as the main qualifier for anthropology (cf. Lende 2010) in their long-term goal statement at the 2010 New Orleans general meeting.[2] At that conference which I attended, there was a buzz of discussion as to the nature – or is that nurture? – of anthropology and its intent that speaks of disciplinary positionings, associations and boundaries, and the distinctiveness of its research methods – the subject of this chapter and this edited collection.

Anthropology is continually under positioning: whether establishment of a discipline differentiated from others (early twentieth-century founding fathers carving out academic territories); whether young Turks pressing new theoretical movements (structural functionalism, Marxism, structuralism, postmodernism); or critical cultural turn inspired from other subjects – 'interpretive [reading] communities' for Fish (1988: 325) – challenging representational technique; or more recent ontological (re)turns (traditionally metaphysical though more recently also methodological [cf. Holbraad and Pedersen 2017]). It is '[a]n inquisitive, challenging, uncomfortable discipline' (Firth 1981: 200), 'born omniform' (Geertz 1983: 21), perhaps even an 'anti-discipline' according to Keith Hart (2004: 5), who laments the changing anthropological object post-empire: the transition from traditional subject – subjugated, to complex society – fragmented. The result has been, for Hart (2004), an ensuing loss of a distinct unitary discipline with clear intellectual mission in favour of more compartmentalized subdisciplines associated with public institutions. He cites feminist anthropology, medical anthropology, the anthropology of development (Hart 2004: 4), to which we can add dance anthropology and the anthropology of tourism, among others. His argument is a precursor to the science-free suggestion for anthropology at New Orleans, a humanitarian anthropology of advocacy and cultural preservation.

If the debate can be characterized as one between 'genes and texts' (Lende 2010), then the textualists were seen to be taking the upper hand in New Orleans. The potential shift for the anthropological endeavour was perceived to undermine the weight of science, its gravitas, in favour of a more beneficent cultural studies – from 'a scientific endeavour to a public forum', to return to D'Costa (2010). For Peter Wood (2010) it was an attempt at 'un-disciplining anthropology'. This 'gerrymandering' (Lipo 2010) by 'cultural anthropologist fluff-heads' (Dreger 2010) against the more Popperian hypothesis-testing anthropologists (Skinner 2004) – such as the more nature-leaning primatologists, and biological and evolutionary anthropologists often held up as being more empirically minded – was not successful in the online documents but provoked much debate, angst-blogging and media comment. While little comment arose from the excision also of 'ethnology' in the proposal, it did give an impetus to notable academics to qualify their own current positioning. Under the title 'Anthropologists Unite!', for example, Adam Kuper and Jonathan Marks (2011) referred to the need to return to the traditional anthropological mission to build 'a truly comparative science of human variation' (2011: 166), interdisciplinary and integrated under both nature and culture approaches.[3] The fear was that without the rigours of a scientific approach, much of anthropology is reduced to journalism and travel writing (cf. Kamrani 2010; Wood 2010; Skinner 2008). This portmanteau discipline – 'a data-driven comparative science' (Lende 2011) for some; 'an inclusive discipline ... a glorious hodgepodge' (Downey 2010) for others – continues to mean different things to different people. This mobility, I would like to suggest, is an advantage when repositioning within the more nimble university structures, such as at the University of Roehampton.

The metrics of recruitment

It's a dreich Saturday afternoon on campus. A colleague and I have been drummed into a mid-morning and lunchtime recruitment session for those on guided tours of the university. They get deposited into our room and we introduce them to our programme of studies: Zoology in one room, Sports Science in another, Nutrition and Health the large room at the end of the corridor; the Biological Sciences and Biomedical Science have their own lecture rooms, given the large interest in the programmes. My programme is Anthropology BSc. It is a three-year degree course costing £9,250 per year for UK/EU applicants and is marketed as an integrated social anthropology and biological anthropology degree course. I have been working on recruitment to the programme for the last five years, ever since I left Queen's University Belfast where I worked as a senior lecturer in social anthropology and head of undergraduate recruitment in the School of History and Anthropology. I feel that I am on comfortable ground today. I have been talking to parents and school leavers for the last twelve years; writing careers leaflets; developing promotional materials (posters, publicity stands, flyers, websites, mailshots, PowerPoint presentations); hosting school leaver days; and training student ambassadors and sending them on local and national school visits. I can break the ice and give a soft sell of the discipline, allaying parents' concerns with information about employment rates and likely jobs in different sectors with case studies from my former students. I can also switch into a hard sell mode and give KIS information, NSS scores and the latest REF results in our sector.[4] The 'take home' message is our interpretation of student satisfaction scores running year-on-year at 100 per cent satisfaction. This year we have added 100 per cent employment or higher education within six months of graduating with a degree in anthropology from our 2015–18 cohort.

We are very proud of our anthropology programme at Roehampton. It has excellent satisfaction and graduation results. Every single one of our third-year students is glad that they came to study at Roehampton. We have an integrated

*social and biological anthropology programme that gives you the best of both
worlds and means that you will gain proficiency in the sociocultural issues as
culture brokers and producers, but also have a competence in the sciences and be
able to handle data sets and statistical analysis. This opens up employment in the
arts as well as the sciences. We are research intensive in that the lecturers will be
exploring their work with you and you won't just be reading about anthropology
second-hand. Some students will be involved in ongoing research projects working
with the remains of bones unearthed in Godalming. Why did they die and how did
they live? You will be mentored in your own research dissertation and become a
world-leading expert on your topic – this will make you stand out in any interview
from other candidates!*

*In terms of teaching, we have small class sizes and are on first-name terms with
our students: there is a low staff/student ratio. Teaching at first year is often joint
teaching: two for one in the classroom, value for money with a bio and a social
anthropologist debating on a topic such as food, violence, health. The students can
see the arguments in practice and make their own decisions on where they stand.
They love these interactive sessions with this truly integrated degree. There are field
trips in the first year to London Zoo, the Wellcome Collection and the Natural
History Museum as part of your studies. In the second year I will take you all to
Northern Ireland to work with tour guides in Belfast, explore the murals in Derry/
Londonderry and examine tourism regeneration at the Giant's Causeway and new
Titanic Belfast visitor experience. This is all included in your fees – flights, travel, all
but food and drink! There is also an optional South Africa field school in the Kruger
National Park working with guides, trackers, conservationists and home stay with
the Zulu for extra module credit.*

*The first question of the morning was from a parent asking about anthropology's
TEF scores.*[5]

Anthropology at the University of Roehampton

The University of Roehampton is a post-1992 university that presently offers two
pathways towards anthropology degrees: BSc Anthropology single honours, and
BSc Social Anthropology combined honours. The single honours programme is
delivered at Whitelands College through staff in the Department of Life Sciences.
The combined honours programme is linked with Sociology on another campus
site. Students on both programmes have the possibility of paying for an optional
South Africa field course to look at conservation from social and biological

perspectives during the summer of their second year. Students on the single honours programme have training in a more integrated biological and social anthropology with parity between the two orientations until students specialize in their final graduation year with three options and a dissertation. This means that at first-year level, for example, single honours students study an 'Introduction to Social and Cultural Anthropology' and 'Fieldwork: Theory, Practice and Product' from the social side. From the biological side they have modules on 'Human Ecology and Adaptation' and an 'Introduction to Evolution', both of which are cross-listed with the Zoology BSc. Their core integrated modules are 'Being Human' and 'Special Topics in Anthropology'.

In practice, these are innovative team-taught cross-disciplinary modules that bring together the biological and the social. Being Human covers large fundamental topics such as conflict and violence, health and well-being, sex and incest, living and dying. This module is complemented by Special Topics, a platform for discussion-based learning on the material introduced in Being Human. The unique feature of the two modules is the integrated and team-taught structure. In each Being Human session there are two lecturers debating a topic. Over a fortnight, the Special Topics students meet as a group with each of the lecturers to work through some of their selected readings from Being Human. To give an example, in 'Conflict and Violence' I examine the underlying causes of The Troubles in Northern Ireland as an ethno-national conflict, a case of culture and competition for resources, which is extended into a field trip to Northern Ireland in the second-year module 'Cultural Politics on Tour'. This is compared and contrasted with primatologist Stuart Semple's presentation on the genetics of aggression in humans and other primates. The students enjoy the Socratic style of academic argument, and they learn how to evidence a point to persuade the listening or reading audience. Most importantly, experiencing academic debate at first hand, students gain confidence in testing and critiquing theoretical positions themselves.

For us – the teaching and researching staff in the Centre for Research in Evolutionary, Social and Inter-Disciplinary Anthropology (CRESIDA) in the Department of Life Sciences – the research as well as the teaching is collaborative and cross-disciplinary. This is particularly appealing to the funding bodies, where we can demonstrate real-world impact for our work. As a social anthropologist specializing in the Caribbean region, fieldwork with the Montserrat National Trust and my expertise on carnival and the contested heritage around the Africanization of St Patrick's Day on Montserrat – the day of a failed slave insurrection on the island in 1768 (Skinner 2015) – has led on to recent involvement in a major EU Biodiversity and Ecosystem Services in Territories of European Overseas (BEST) grant (2016–19) on neighbouring British Overseas Territory Anguilla (see Figure 1.0). There, I work as co-investigator with colleagues in Zoology in the Department of Life Sciences at Roehampton, assisting the Anguilla National Trust and Anguilla Department of Fisheries and Marine Resources in their sea turtle conservation programme. My role is to facilitate the development of local fishermen into tour guides, and to use the traditional performing arts to influence public perception towards turtle conservation. To date, we have achieved this through educational events about Anguilla's maritime and marine heritage (radio, newspaper, public local school engagement), an adopt-a-beach programme, involvement in the BBC2 documentary series *An Island Parish*, introducing conservation-themed carnival floats to the island-wide Festival of the Sea, and partnering the Anguilla National Trust to provide tour guide and research methods training sessions.

This interdisciplinary collaboration will provide Roehampton with unique anthropology/zoology research publications and an excellent impact case study for the forthcoming REF2021 on the importance of heritage and the performing arts in social transformation. It has been directly facilitated by the cross-disciplinary structures within the department that range from the informal (shared offices, group lunches, varied seminar culture) to the formal (cross-disciplinary teaching, departmental meetings, shared administration). CRESIDA is one of four research centres within the department, along with the Centre for Research in Ecology, Evolution and Behaviour; Health Sciences Research Centre; and Sport and Exercise Science Research Centre. Nearly sixty members of staff within these centres contribute to undergraduate pathways from zoology to biological sciences, nutrition and health to sport and exercise sciences. Prior to 2016, CRESIDA was known as the Centre for Research in Evolutionary and Environmental Anthropology (CREEA). It was rebranded to reflect several social anthropological appointments who were not working in evolutionary or environmental anthropology subfields.

The integrated BSc Anthropology degree was developed in 2010 by Professors Ann Maclarnon and Garry Marvin,[6] primarily as a response to the existing combined honours degrees in Social Anthropology and Biological Anthropology taught on different campuses. The rationale was pedagogic as well as economic and strategic. It fosters a more cohesive experience for the student with a pathway designed to build on student learning rather than rely upon natural synergies between social anthropology and sociology or criminology, for instance, or biological anthropology and biological sciences or psychology. The 2010

Programme Validation Document notes that '[t]he development of this degree is in line with both department and university strategies to foster cross-discipline collaborations' (Roehampton 2010: 4). It is seen as an opportunity to develop a niche area in Roehampton, with only four other departments offering single honours degrees covering both social and biological anthropology (University of Kent, Oxford Brookes University, Durham University, and University College London). The merger builds on the strength of Biological Anthropology's high RAE2008 results. It also took place in the context of the start of a new 'A' level qualification in Anthropology supported by the Royal Anthropological Institute. This is all recognized in the case for support put to the university for collaboration between biological anthropology and social anthropology.

Disciplining anthropology: The anthropology of tourism and dance anthropology

How the discipline of anthropology is reproduced within the higher education context is of central concern to Marilyn Strathern and other academics in her edited volume *Audit Cultures* (2000). Each discipline, school and department has to contend with new auditing cultures that entered higher education institutional management from the 1980s and which has 'massified' (cf. Gibbons et al. 1999) with the introduction in the UK HE sector of intense Research Excellence Framework audits, impact assessments, and now Teaching Excellence Frameworks. While these initiatives stress interdisciplinary practice as part of the audit process, they reward the antisocial neoliberal academic enmeshed within a system of ranking and accountability – those trapped in cycles of self-scrutiny, as contributor Ananta Giri (2000) opines. The conditions of anthropology's disciplinary reproduction are contradictory. One might position Strathern's text and our volume as example of self-disclosure of this context which Strathern (2000: 11) aptly describes as 'academic self-closure'. 'The discipline', Giri (1998) notes in a lead-in article to Strathern's volume, is a modern mode of inquiry, one of boundedness, closure and specialization. As such it is associated with modernity: disciplines produce knowledge capital and act as cultural frames, but also, Giri adds, they become locations of social identity. 'Academic disciplines not only help us classify the world but also classify ourselves' (Giri 1998: 380).

There is fluidity on the borders where disciplines' subdisciplines relate, collaborate and even emerge with new modes of engagement. Often perceived as dangerous liminal places, Giri (1998: 381) proposes that we look at them more constructively as 'alchemical meeting points'. Rigid boundaries of knowledge and inward-looking genealogies of modern academic disciplines are associated more with the advance of the nation state, colonial governance and the structuration of the modern university system, to paraphrase Giri (1998: 382). They are exciting places to be and to work in. This is where new things happen. Giri uses anthropology and sociology disciplines as examples of contrived disciplinary territories within a modern academic division of labour. Anthropology traditionally pursued the trope of 'the savage' whereas sociology traditionally did not, suggests Giri, with an invocation towards Caribbean anthropologist Michel-Rolph Trouillot. Practitioners serve as policers of the disciplines, self-identifying and objectifying themselves and their subject area using the label 'anthropologist' or 'sociologist' to describe themselves, to which one can add 'dancer' or 'non-dancer'. How these disciplines are negotiated in practice, how they are preserved, policed and breached or 'interpenetrated' and developed in collaboration are thus important questions for the academe. They are illuminated by the cross-currents, in the border zones, through the twilight. The disciplines are useful 'frames' (Giri 1998: 396), useful contrivances in the mission of knowledge production. But they are subject to profound change, movement and renegotiation. In Geertz (1983, cited by Giri 1998: 397), they are considered to be intellectual cultures with their own conventions – quite literally. Dance anthropology and the anthropology of tourism at Roehampton are, I suggest, particular examples of this dalliance with disciplinary boundaries.

'Cultural Politics on Tour' is a level two module introducing anthropology students to the tourist contact zone. It is where we look at places where people, when at leisure, spend their time. This varies in topic from touring and sightseeing to sunbathing and dancing. How do they act and, more critically, how do they interact? We look at how The Troubles of Northern Ireland are reanimated by the tour guide on the Falls Road; why sexual relationships in Jamaica between tourists and locals are so prone to fall apart; how heritage is mobilized in stately homes, and through international organizations such as UNESCO; and how tourism has influenced cultural performances such as Maasai welcome dances in the Serengeti, initiation rites among the Chambrai of Papua New Guinea, and healing tarantella dances in southern Italy. This module was billed as a level three Anthropology of Tourism specialist choice module, but we moved it to level two and made it core so long as it opened out its content to cover more general anthropological topics from cultural contact to debates about authenticity, the commoditization of culture, indigenous performance, and the fault lines and fractures in conflicted heritage and dark tourism. The material is redeveloped from modules taught at my previous institutions: Queen's University Belfast (2003–13) 'Leisure, Tourism and Culture' and the University of Abertay Dundee (1997–2003) 'The Sociology of Leisure and Tourism'. In the former institution the module had a Caribbean inflection to it and in the latter it was more about the rise of the leisured class in British society. Both modules, however, stressed the impact of tourism upon the destination and took Valene Smith's 1977 foundational volume *Hosts and Guests: The Anthropology of Tourism* as a starting point.

Smith's 1977 *Hosts and Guests*, updated in the 1989 revision, was based upon proceedings from a panel in the 1974 Mexico City meeting of the American Anthropological Association (Smith 1989: ix). It often marks the emergence of the subdiscipline of the anthropology of tourism, when a corpus of scholarship focused on knowledge production in a particular niche became apparent. Stronza (2001) echoes Graburn's title in her article in *Annual Review of Anthropology*, consolidating the academic profile of the subdiscipline despite her attention to the anthropological focus on tourism and new forms such as ecotourism. Michael Di Giovine recently referred to this period as the first wave in the emergence of the subdiscipline, one not without anthropologist critics, who see tourists as unwanted flotsam in their fieldsites. For Giovine (2017: 80) '[t]he anthropology of tourism is ultimately concerned with touristic discourses, practices, and imaginaries in everyday social life – socioculturally and biologically'. Nelson Graburn, a contributor to Smith's original volume, suggested in a special issue on the anthropology of tourism in *Annals of Tourism Research* (founded by cultural anthropologist Jafar Jafari) that 'the anthropology of tourism is a recently developed field' (1983: 9) – one unified, for him, topically around the study of tourists and the impact of tourism; conceptually through anthropological notions of ritual, play and pilgrimage; and methodologically through distinct ethnographic fieldwork. Thirty-five years later, it has perhaps come of age with the recent publication of Owsianowska and Banaszkiewicz's (2018: 1) *The Anthropology of Tourism in Central and Eastern Europe: Bridging Worlds*, an explicit attempt 'to dispose of limitations on the anthropological study of tourism', no longer the preserve of the West. As part of a world anthropologies movement, this volume – with a contribution from Graburn – rebalances the 'geopolitics of knowledge' (2018: 5) in the anthropology of tourism with scholarship both of and from Central and Eastern Europe. The attention to the particular political context in the production of anthropological knowledge decolonizes the discipline, opening it out to Hispanophone and Lusophone 'anthropologies of tourism scholarship'

(Milano 2017: 737), to even anthropologies of tourism that link to the development of the nation state such as China with the rise of national interest in ethnic tourism (cf. Zhu, Jin and Graburn 2017). This scholarship extends the anthropological canon.

Critics of the anthropology of tourism subdiscipline suggest that it is not there yet in terms of its development, that there is no clearly defined or delimited academic area. Kaaristo contends that this is a difficulty with tourism studies in general as a subject area approached from anthropology, but also a bevy of subjects including management, sociology, cultural studies, development studies, psychology and political science. This is the 'indiscipline' of studying tourism (Tribe 1997). Anthropologists working on tourism need to be making a more distinct theoretical contribution for a subdiscipline to live up to its claim: '[t]here is ... a need for more theorizing in the field, in order for it to be fully realized as a subdiscipline', Kaaristo (2018: 73) qualifies. This suggests that external recognition and a clear theoretical territorialization of knowledge are some sort of litmus tests for the subdiscipline in general. It should also have a recognized nucleus for disseminating best practice: dedicated journals, book series, conferences and associations, all of which are emerging, especially the Anthropology of Tourism Interest Group in the American Anthropological Association (ATIG in the AAA) and the Commission on the Anthropology of Tourism in the International Union of Anthropological and Ethnological Sciences (AoT in the IUAES). Graburn himself readily accepts this developmental position; publishing a half-way position with Naomi Leite (2009: 35) in the *SAGE Handbook of Tourism Studies*, they expressed their work as 'anthropological interventions in Tourism Studies' rather than an anthropology of tourism, because of the need for 'coherence' but also the advantage of not having to re-frame work for a different, non-anthropological audience. This is after presaging this anthropological turn to tourism decades earlier as an inevitable new direction when Graburn wrote in 1980 about first teaching an anthropology of tourism class. Then, tourism was a new topic for anthropology, as the core discipline shifted emphasis away from taxonomy to engage more with contact and change: 'from the study of classification and structure to that of process and interaction' (Graburn 1980: 65).[7] Leite and Graburn suggest that future research directions can be 'postdisciplinary' (2009: 54), a position shared by tourism scholars Munar, Pernecky and Feighery, who consider the compartmentalization of knowledge production an 'evolutionary cul-de-sac' (2016: 344).

What constitutes tourism anthropology, or the prefix 'the anthropology of' plus a subject area, as in 'the anthropology of tourism', is the focus of Les Roberts and Hazel Andrews' article '(Un)Doing Tourism Anthropology: Outline of a

Field of Practice' (2013). This is a particular 'model of intellectual taxonomy' (Roberts and Andrews 2013: 14) for them and the only reference I could find to tourism anthropology rather than the anthropology of tourism. The question for them is what constitutes the doing of the anthropology of tourism as a field of practice. What are its parameters and how stable are they, to which we can add the extent of collaboration? Anthropology is the discipline and tourism is the subject matter, with the two being able to be tacked together, or there can be an 'anthropology of' all sorts of subject matters, as though anthropology has the (st)ability to colonize and grow subject areas. It begs the question why it is not doing anthropology as though the two can be explicitly framed differently – anthropology from the anthropology of tourism. To use a spatial metaphor, there are 'striations' (Roberts and Andrews 2013: 32) associated with these types of confined interdisciplinary pathways. For Roberts and Andrews (2013: 13) doing – as well as undoing – a tourism anthropology is 'in part the practice of reinforcing the anthropos while at the same time looking critically askance at the category of "the tourist"'. This is bringing the anthropological gaze to the tourist gaze, if you will; using an anthropological imagination and methodology to the tourist and tourism, cognisant of a particular subdisciplinary lineage (from Smith to Graburn, including Victor Turner, Edward Bruner and more recently Noel Salazar) to the main disciplinary canon.

Similar histories of collaboration are available in the anthropology of dance or dance anthropology – a different sort of leisure mobility, a similar sort of off-piste pathway or anthropos striation. At Queen's University Belfast, my appointment within first the School of Anthropological Studies and more latterly the School of History and Anthropology – now both disciplines set within a wider School of History, Anthropology, Philosophy and Politics (HAPP) – was to span the ethnomusicology and anthropology units. Informally it was to offset ethnomusicology being absorbed within music. Besides continuing tourism anthropology teaching and research, I was given the support to turn the school's performance room into a dance studio with mirrors and laminate floor (we used a former secretarial pool room at night for its sprung floor for the more high-impact social dancing!). The school is renowned for Professor John Blacking's establishment of the discipline of ethnomusicology with former student Suzel Reily continuing his music-making traditions, teaching by ensemble, end-of-year recitals and drumming circles. This was an opportunity to teach dance anthropology, a growing area of research with several years' ethnography of modern jive in Scotland and England, and now salsa as a cross-community leisure activity in Belfast, but also Sacramento, California.

Ethnomusicology was seen as distinct but complementary to anthropology at Queen's, with two core members of staff plus additional input from myself and Fiona Magowan. The emphasis was on the social production and meaning of music. 'Dance, Health and the Body' was a cross-listed anthropology and ethnomusicology module examining the place, function and meaning of dance in society: a module structured around Wulff's (2001: 3210) division of US/UK Blacking-influenced meaning-centred approach, continental dance ethnology/ choreology, or a mix of the two. In an encyclopaedia entry on the anthropology of dance, Wulff notes that in the 1960s and 1970s pioneering dance anthropologists established the subdiscipline with debate on the origins and definition of dance, following the theoretical currents of its 'parent discipline' (Wulff 2001: 3209) anthropology. By the 1980s the interdisciplinary influences were with dance and movement studies, with gender and body critique and literary and cultural studies (cf. Wulff 2001: 3209). More contemporary dance anthropology research extends into the popular Western and non-Western dance forms, whether social dancing, hip-hop, ballroom or Bollywood. Wulff makes the point that the modest position of dance anthropology may come from its female dominance rivalled by the male dominance of ethnomusicology (2001: 3211). Further to this, she notes that there is a tendency towards a lack of accumulation of expertise in dance anthropology, as anthropologists undertake one study in the field of dance before moving on to other subject matter. Dance anthropology, for Wulff, has had a sporadic growth. This is set alongside an extensive range of subdisciplines in the encyclopaedia: political anthropology, psychological anthropology, economic anthropology, linguistic anthropology, urban anthropology and visual anthropology.

At Roehampton, the dance anthropology influence creeps into the 'Cultural Politics on Tour' module and classes on Victor Turner's classic anthropology. It is not just apparent in the anthropology cluster but is more deeply embedded in the teaching and research of the dance department cultivated by the late Andrée Grau, Professor of the Anthropology of Dance. Professor Grau was a student of Professor Blacking at Queen's before going on to develop with Professors Ann R. David and Theresa Buckland the anthropology of dance at Roehampton from 2000 to 2017 and leading an EU Master's programme – Choreomundus: International Master in Dance Knowledge, Practice and Heritage MA – training an international cohort of the best new dance (and music) scholars. Grau strove to expand dance beyond 'the parochialism' (Grau 1997: 56) of Western theatre dance by challenging notions of dance and dancers and pressing for the integration of dance forms and performers from all around the world. The anthropology of dance lends itself to disciplinary collaboration, between dance and music especially. Collaboration has been critical to the establishment and development of the discipline in an environment of austerity and academic capitalism, according to dance anthropologists Gore, Grau and Koutsouba (2016). Difficult and oppressive educational and free market environments have stimulated collaboration through an anthropological model of 'reciprocity' based around an international seminar series for new ethnochoreologists, collaboration through 'shared but limited resources' with the intention of establishing 'dance anthropology as a legitimate discipline within academia across Europe and the globe' (Gore, Grau and Koutsouba (2016: 187). This model of collaboration across disciplines (dance, anthropology, ethnomusicology, ethnochoreology) and countries (Greece, France, Norway, Hungary, UK) draws upon the passion of the dance practitioners and the social cohesion created from the intensity of the all-day and late-into-the-night nature of the events, with social networking added in. It is activated by the social communitas of solidarity with scarce resources.

Anthropology of dance pioneers Gore and Grau, joined more recently by Koutsouba, draw from traditional anthropological concepts in their development of dance anthropology – of the anthropology of dance subdiscipline that Grau occasionally refers to. They are personally invested in the establishment of this discipline. This personal connection in collaboration is more heavily articulated in the development of the discipline than the anthropology of tourism striations or pathways. In its sociality it is different to the idea – also culled from anthropological thought – of trading zones and scientific exchange languages put forward by history of science scholar Peter Galison (2010) in Michael Gorman's (2010) edited volume, *Trading Zones and Interactional Expertise: Creating New Kinds of Collaboration*. Galison describes post-Cold War disciplinary mapping as one of constant rearrangement. These spaces between disciplines are characterized as 'subversive' and where an 'interlanguage' develops (Collins, Evans and Gorman 2010: 11), a hybrid pidgin or creole between the two disciplines. For this to occur, there has to be a degree of stability and distinctiveness in and between the disciplines, and an attraction or advantage to approach and explore the border zone, those 'intersections of discursive and material practice' (Galison 2010: 32). For all this territory marking, the space is subject to change over time and culturally specific influences. As Galison (2010: 33) notes, '[w]hat is exchange work today may well become the disciplinary pillars of tomorrow: science is forever in flux, not just in its results but in the contours of its disciplines'. Galison is writing about disciplines where the boundaries break down and the partitions become permeable: biology and chemistry combining as 'biochemistry', algebra and geometry to fashion 'algebraic geometry', but he also includes the humanities such as art and history that reconstitute as 'art history'. Unsuccessful interdisciplinary mergers are also significant for their failure to gain traction, such as 'neutronics' (an association between nuclear science, engineering and health) or 'iatrogenics' (Newtonian mechanics and physiology) (Galison 2010: 43).

Significantly, the exchange relations between the partner disciplines are seldom egalitarian, but typically feature a subordinate discipline. For Galison,

> [i]n instances of unequal exchanges between scientific-technical subcultures, what precisely does make it to the interlanguage from each side? It is a question that cannot even arise if we stop our analysis with proclamations about 'interdisciplinarity', 'collaboration', or 'symbiosis'. Those terms point at the problem; all the interest, in my view, lies in unpacking what the nature of this coordination is and how it evolves over time.
>
> 2010: 39

This inequality, we might read, could be presaged in the pairing of the disciplines. Notably it is the anthropology of tourism as opposed to tourism anthropology in the former, and dance anthropology rather than the anthropology of dance in the latter. This connotes subtle emphases that need unpacking and contextualizing in the university environment as above. Interestingly, while I would not refer to myself as a tourism anthropologist, I would consider labelling myself a dance anthropologist. This is not just because dance is more personal as a calling and is more than a discipline. It is because sometimes one just 'becomes' on the dance floor and loses oneself in the music, the movements and the collaborations with other dancers. As Grau (2007: 199) explains, 'anthropologists [come to] embody cultural knowledge'. One can 'go native' as a dancer but not 'go native' as an anthropologist. Identification and personalization take place with dance but not tourism, though one can practise both extensively.

Policing these distinctions, one seeks recognition and legitimation in both (of) one's disciplines. Dance identity is more than academic, it is social and physical. One embodies a dance anthropology more so than treating it as just some form of analytical framework. These emphases inflect dance departments that I am familiar with, including Roehampton but also Surrey, Chichester and now Royal Holloway, where dance is expanding as a new BA degree within the Department of Drama and Theatre, now rebranded Drama, Theatre and Dance. This is where, as Grau (1995: 77) points out, the lecturer and supervisor's interests and expertise – aboriginal Tiwi and Western classical ballet for Grau (1983, 2005) – play a significant part in shaping the development of a university degree structure. As in the case of the anthropology of tourism, Grau and Jordan (1995: 78) also note the influence of professional associations such as the Society for Dance Research with its *Dance Research* journal as outlet. 'Dancing on the canon' is how popular dance scholar Sherril Dodds expresses the disciplinary shifts and reorientations in dance after only receiving training in vernacular dance in her MA dance anthropology module (Dodds 2011: 2). The tensions between dance, dance studies – charged with 'intellectual imperialism' by Grau (2007: 203) for its disciplinary debates divorced from the dancer – performance studies, theatre and theatre dance; their interrelations as macro- or micro-disciplines; and whether or not, for example, dance history is or should be 'a discrete discipline' as a recognizable field of studies (cf. Carter 2004: 1–2) are all neoliberal academic tensions akin to those between anthropology and sociology, anthropology versus cultural studies.

Critics of the disciplining of the academic press for more collaborative approaches, one that anthropology appears to be particularly responsive to. Performance studies scholar André Lepecki (2004) chastises scholarship on contemporary European dance for being too divisive, partitioning and academically dry, and hence unable to pick up the essence or authenticity of human movements. For Lepecki (2004: 172), '[t]he very possibility of open and endless naming suggests that the truth of the work resides in its performance rather than its accommodation to previously fixed, establishes hermetically sealed aesthetic and disciplinary boundaries'. Movement transcends semantic fields. It is transdisciplinary, he opines: dance, visual, political and performance art. This situates – if we can and if we should be considering this – dance anthropology as a transdisciplinary collaboration and, to follow this example, the anthropology of tourism, then, as an interdisciplinary collaboration. This is a different position to one of dance anthropology as a discipline in its own right, as proposed by dance historian Theresa Buckland (1999: 5) with its specific 'academic discourse' of 'empirical and conceptual inquiry' and ethnographic methodology as well as audience. These facets of the dance anthropology discipline were subsequently chronicled by Andrée Grau and Georgiana Wierre-Gorre (2005). In France, as well as through the Choreomundus programme, the two writers – 'writers à deux', as Gore recently lamented[8] – collaborated extensively to develop 'Anthropologie de la danse' as a discipline in its own right – the title of a reader they collated (*Anthropologie de la danse: Genèse et construction d'une discipline* [2005]). This is, according to Grau and Wierre-Gore (2005: 17), identifiable from an initial review of dance ethnology by Kurath in 1960. Kurath used this piece to define the parameters of this 'emerging discipline' (Kurath 1960: 234), shifting dance scholarship beyond decades of formative folk dance collecting; such comparative approaches have been castigated as idle 'butterfly collecting' by Edmund Leach (1971: 2), lacking in insight or explanation. Where Adrienne Kaeppler (1978: 31) notes that this was, for Kurath, considering dance as 'a branch of anthropology', Grau and Wierre-Gore (2005: 17) go further and propose that its publication marked a historical turning point in the emergence of this discipline, before going on to add, in the introduction to their reader, the particularities of a dance anthropological approach (an overview, questions of method and eclecticism and openness) (Grau and Wierre-Gore 2005: 26).

It would appear that dance anthropology and the anthropology of tourism fulfil criteria for interdisciplinary collaboration. They have stability and coherence in their histories, canons, readings and readers. They cross disciplines. They have their own conference and publication outlets and appeal to differing audiences. There is a developing consensus as to what they are and what they are not. They contribute and add theoretical and empirical academic knowledge and debate, enriching not just their hybrid collaborative ground but also their parent disciplines. It is in the new university environment that there is a nimbleness to respond to these new interests, subject areas and research grounds that are opening up. In Queen's, the anthropology unit was repositioned during restructuring, reflecting differing staff interests, new collaborations and REF investments from ethnomusicology to history and now to politics. At Roehampton, the shifts have been between social sciences and life sciences with the integration of anthropology, and the key development of a new discipline that is undergoing new changes and challenges. While the boundary frames of the collaborative new disciplines are taking shape and reifying, optimistically the picture within is being storied, advanced and shaded in by bold, imaginative scholars drawn to these interstitial new spaces.

Notes

1   I am grateful to my co-editors for their suggestions and constructive comments, as well as Ann R. David and Theresa Buckland.
2   Kamrani (2010) details the proposed changes to the long-term mission statement.
3   Smith, Gurven and Borgerhoff (2011) critique Kuper and Marks (2011) noting that large-scale 'integrative' research is taking place in the field of anthropology and that it is more interdisciplinary than they suggest.

4   KIS – Key Information Statistics; NSS – National Student Survey; REF – Research Excellence Framework: these are all official public metrics for comparing programmes and universities in terms of cost, employment prospect, satisfaction, research strength.

5   TEF – Teaching Excellence Framework: a new government metric to measure excellence in teaching and learning, awarded institutionally as Bronze, Silver, or Gold.

6   My thanks are to both colleagues for their accounts of the development of anthropology programmes at Roehampton.

7   See also Burns (1999) on an anthropology of tourism themed around tourism-as-pilgrimage and tourism-as-imperialism, and Nash on tourism as 'super structure' (1996) and 'extradisciplinary borrowing' (2007: 24) in early and initial contributions to the subdiscipline.

8   Georgiana Wierre-Gore speaking at a research seminar ('Honouring Andrée Grau: A Roundtable on Her Research and Scholarship in Dance') dedicated to the celebration of the work of her friend, colleague and writing partner Andrée Grau (1954–2017), 21 February 2018.

References

American Anthropological Association (2016), *AAA Long-Range Plan* (revised and approved by the AAA Executive Board November 2016). Available online: http://www.americananthro.org/ConnectWithAAA/Content.aspx?ItemNumber=1985 (accessed 25 March 2018).

Banaszkiewicz, M. and S. Owsianowska (2018), 'Introduction: Anthropological Studies on Tourism in Central and Eastern Europe', in S. Owsianowska and M. Banaszkiewicz (eds), *The Anthropology of Tourism in Central and Eastern Europe: Bridging Worlds*, 1–24, Lanham, MD: Lexington Books.

Bristol (2018), Anthropology and Archaeology Department website. Available online: http://www.bristol.ac.uk/study/undergraduate/2019/anthropology/ (accessed 24 March 2018).

Buckland, T. (1999), 'All Dances are Ethnic, but Some are More Ethnic than Others: Some Observations on Dance Studies and Anthropology', *Dance Research: The Journal of the Society for Dance Research*, 17 (1): 3–21.

Burns, P. (1999), *An Introduction to Tourism and Anthropology*, London: Routledge.

Carter, A. (2004), 'Making History: A General Introduction', in A. Carter (ed.), *Rethinking Dance History: A Reader*, 1–9, London: Routledge.

Collins, H., R. Evans and M. Gorman (2010), 'Trading Zones and Interactional Expertise', in M. Gorman (ed.), *Trading Zones and Interactional Expertise: Creating New Kinds of Collaboration*, 7–24, London: Massachusetts Institute of Technology.

D'Costa, K. (2010), 'Anthropology Just Says No to Science?' *Anthropology in Practice: Exploring the Human Experience*. Available online: http://www.anthropologyinpractice. com/2010/12/anthropology-just-says-no-to-science.html (accessed 26 March 2018).

Dodds, S. (2010), *Dancing on the Canon: Embodiments of Value in Popular Dance*, New York: Palgrave Macmillan.

Downey, G. (2010), '"Late to the Science-Anti-Science bum fight . . ." Neuroanthropology: Understanding the encultured brain and body'. Available online: http://blogs.plos.org/neuroanthropology/2010/12/20/late-to-the-science-anti-science-bun-fight. . ./ (accessed 20 December 2010).

Dreger, A. (2010), 'No Science, Please: We're Anthropologists', *Psychology Today*, 25 November 2010. Available online: https://www.psychologytoday.com/us/blog/fetishes-i-dont-get/201011/no-science-please-were-anthropologists (accessed 3 April 2018).

Firth, R. (1981), 'Engagement and Detachment: Reflections on Applying Social Anthropology to Social Affairs', *Human Organization*, 40 (3): 193–201.

Fish, S. (1988), 'Interpreting the Valorium', in D. Lodge (ed.), *Modern Criticism and Theory: A Reader*, 311–29, London: Longman.

Galison, P. (2010), 'Trading with the Enemy', in M. Gorman (ed.), *Trading Zones and Interactional Expertise: Creating New Kinds of Collaboration*, 25–52, London: Massachusetts Institute of Technology.

Geertz, C. (1983), *Local Knowledge: Further Essays in Interpretative Anthropology*, London: Fontana Press.

Gibbons, M., M Trow, P. Scott, S. Schwartzman, H. Nowotny, H. and C. Limoges (1999), *The New Production of Knowledge*, London: Sage Publications.

Giovine, M. Di (2017), 'The Anthropology of Tourism', in L. Lowry (ed.), *The SAGE International Encyclopedia of Travel and Tourism*, 77–81, Thousand Oaks, CA: Sage Publications.

Giri, A. (2000), 'Audited Accountability and the Imperative of Responsibility: Beyond the Primacy of the Political', in M. Strathern (ed.), *Audit Cultures: Anthropological Studies in Accountability, Ethics and the Academy*, 173–95, London: Routledge.

Giri, A. (1998), 'Transcending Disciplinary Boundaries: Creative experiments and the critiques of Modernity', *Critique of Anthropology*, 18 (4): 379–404.

Gore, G., A. Grau and M. Koutsouba (2016), 'Advocacy, Austerity and Internationalisation in the Anthropology of Dance (Work in Progress)', in *Cut & Paste: Dance Advocacy in the Age of Austerity, Proceedings of the 40th Annual Congress on Dance Research (CORD), Joint Conference with the Society of Dance History Scholars (SDHS)*, 180–90, Cambridge: Cambridge University Press.

Gorman, M. (ed.) (2010), *Trading Zones and Interactional Expertise: Creating New Kinds of Collaboration*, London: Massachusetts Institute of Technology.

Graburn, N. (1980), 'Teaching the Anthropology of Tourism', *International Social Science Journal*, 32 (1): 56–68.

Graburn, N. (1983), 'The Anthropology of Tourism', *Annals of Tourism Research*, 10 (1): 9–33.

Grau, A. (2007), 'Dance, Identity, and Identification Processes in the Postcolonial World', in S. Franco and M. Nordera (eds), *Dance Discourses: Keywords in Dance Research*, 189–207, Abingdon: Routledge.

Grau, A. (2005), 'When the Landscape Becomes Flesh: An Investigation into Body Boundaries with Special Reference to Tiwi Dance and Western Classical Ballet', *Body & Society*, 11 (4): 141–63.

Grau, A. (1997), 'Dance, South Asian Dance, and Higher Education', *Choreography and Dance*, 4 (2): 55–62.

Grau, A. (1995), 'Dance Research in the United Kingdom', *Dance Research Journal*, 27 (2): 77–80.

Grau, A. (1983), *Dreaming, Dancing, Kinship: The Study of Yoi, the Dance of the Tiwi of Melville and Bathurst Islands, North Australia*, PhD thesis, Queen's University Belfast.

Grau, A. and S. Jordan (1995), 'Dance Research in the United Kingdom', *Dance Research Journal*, 27 (2): 77–80.

Grau, A. and G. Wierre-Gore (2005), 'Introduction Générale', in A. Grau and G. Wierre-Gore (eds), *Anthropologie de la Danse: Genèse et Construction d'une Discipline*, 7–28, Paris: Centre National de la Danse.

Hart, K. (2004), 'What Anthropologists Really Do', *Anthropology Today*, 20 (1): 3–5.

Holbraad, M. and M. Pedersen (2017), *The Ontological Turn: An Anthropological Exposition*, Cambridge: Cambridge University Press.

Lepecki, A. (2004), 'Concept and Presence: The Contemporary European Dance Scene', in A. Carter (ed.), *Rethinking Dance History: A Reader*, 170–81, London: Routledge.

Kaeppler, A. (1978), 'Dance in Anthropological Perspective', *Annual Review of Anthropology*, 7: 31–49.

Kamrani, K. (2010), 'The AAA Does Away With Science, Seriously', Anthropology.net: Beyond Bones and Stones, 30 November 2010. Available online: https://anthropology.net/2010/11/30/the-aaa-does-away-with-science-seriously/, (accessed 21 March 2018).

Kaaristo, M. (2018), 'Engaging with the Hosts and Guests: Some Methodological Reflections on the Anthropology of Tourism', in S. Owsianowska and M. Banaszkiewicz (eds), *The Anthropology of Tourism in Central and Eastern Europe: Bridging Worlds*, 71–88, Lanham, MD: Lexington Books.

Kroeber, K. (2003), 'Curious Profession: Alfred Kroeber and Anthropological History', *Boundary 2: An International Journal of Literature and Culture*, 30 (3): 144–55.

Kuper, A. and J. Marks (2011), 'Comment: Anthropologists Unite!', *Nature*, 470, 10 February 2011: 166–8.

Leach, E. (1971), *Rethinking Anthropology*, University of London: The Athlone Press.

Leite, N. and N. Graburn (2009), 'Anthropological Interventions in Tourism Studies', in T. Jamal and M. Robinson (eds), *The SAGE Handbook of Tourism Studies*, 35–64, Thousand Oaks, CA: Sage Publications.

Lende, D. (2010), 'Anthropology, Science, and Public Understanding', *Neuroanthropology: Understanding the Encultured Brain and Body*, 1 December 2010. Available online: http://blogs.plos.org/neuroanthropology/2010/12/01/anthropology-science-and public-understanding/ (accessed 31 March 2018).

Lipo, C. (2010), 'Whither Anthropology as a Science?', *LipoLab: Evolution, Archaeological Science, and Surfing*, 26 November 2010. Available online: http://www.evobeach. com/2010/11/whither-anthropology-as-science.html (accessed 29 March 2018).

Milano, C. (2017), 'Otherness Anthropologies: Toward Ibero-American: Anthropologies of Tourism', *American Anthropologist*, 119 (4): 736–41.

Munar, A., T. Pernecky and W. Feighery (2016), 'An Introduction to Tourism Postdisciplinarity', *Tourism Analysis*, 21: 343–7.

Roberts, L. and H. Andrews (2013), '(Un)Doing Tourism Anthropology: Outline of a Field of Practice', *Journal of Tourism Challenges and Trends*, 6 (2): 13–38.

Roehampton (2010), BSc Anthropology, BSc Biological Anthropology, BA Social Anthropology: Programme Validation Document. Unpublished document.

Skinner, J. (2008), 'Glimpses into the Unmentionable: Montserrat, Tourism and Anthropological Readings of "Subordinate Exotic" and "Comic Exotic" Travel Writing', *Journeys: Studies in Travel Writing*, 12 (3): 167–91.

Skinner, J. (2004), 'Popper in the "Open": Science, Morality, Culture and the Open Society' in, N. Rapport (ed.), *Democracy, Science and the 'Open Society': A European Legacy? Anthropological Journal on European Cultures Special Edition*, 13: 133–50.

Smith, E., M. Gurven and M. Borgerhoff Mulder (2011), 'Correspondence: Anthropology: It Can Be Interdisciplinary', *Nature*, 471: 448.

Smith, V. (1977), 'Preface', in V. Smith (ed.), *Hosts and Guests: The Anthropology of Tourism*, ix–xi, Philadelphia, PA: University of Pennsylvania.

Steward, J. (1962), *Alfred Kroeber (1876–1960): A Biographical Memoir*, Washington, DC: National Academy of Sciences.

Strathern, M. (2000), 'New Accountabilities: Anthropological Studies in Audit, Ethics and the Academy', in M. Strathern (ed.), *Audit Cultures: Anthropological Studies in Accountability, Ethics and the Academy*, 1–18, London: Routledge.

Stronza, A. (2001), 'Anthropology of Tourism: Forging New Ground for Ecotourism and Other Alternatives', *Annual Review of Anthropology*, 30: 261–83.

Wood, P. (2010), 'Anthropology Association Rejecting Science?', *The Chronicle of Higher Education*, 29 November. Available online: https://www.chronicle.com/blogs/ innovations/anthropology-association-rejecting-science/27936 (accessed 1 April 2018).

Wulff, H. (2001), 'Dance, Anthropology of', in N. Smelser and P. Baltes (eds), *International Encyclopedia of the Social & Behavioral Sciences*, 3209–12, New York: Elsevier Ltd.

4

Polyphony for the Ivory Tower Blues: Critical Pedagogies in Graduate Professional Development

Tracey Heatherington

Developments over the past decade have left many of us singing the ivory tower blues. Those lucky enough to remember the fertile intellectual environment of the 1960s and 1970s typically feel some nostalgia for the way the academy used to be, while the rest of us can only imagine it with envy. In his book, *The Last Professors: The Corporate University and the Fate of the Humanities* (2008), Frank Donoghue explored the erosion of the academic tenure system in the United States. In an email exchange about the themes of his book, he told a reporter from *Inside Higher Education*:

> The tenure-track professoriate will never be restored. Two factors seal its fate. First, the hiring of adjuncts continues to outpace the hiring of tenure-track professors by a rate of three to one. It's silly to think we can reverse the trend toward casualization when, despite a great deal of attention and effort, we can't even slow it down. Second, the demographics of American higher education don't help us either. For 40 years, students have been moving away from the humanities toward vocationalism ... Tenure-track professors don't have a place in this new higher education universe. Much as it pains me to say it, I never considered putting a question mark at the end of my title, *The Last Professors*.
>
> quoted in Jaschik 2008

Although some educators predicted more optimistic trends ahead in faculty hiring (for example, Ehrenberg and Kuh 2010), there is no doubt that young scholars confront considerable uncertainties in the academic market. Public higher education faces intensive pressure from funding cuts in much of the world, and austerity discourses only intensified in the wake of the great recession of 2008. In the United States, for example, Christopher Newfield (2016) has pointed to a 'devolutionary cycle' in which the devaluing of higher education as a public good is part of a feedback loop that makes that education decreasingly accessible. That same cycle, we should note, makes faculty positions less accessible to new PhDs. The operations of elite, well-endowed, private institutions in the United States are less vulnerable to fluctuations in state budgets and political priorities in comparison to public universities, and because of their prestige, the graduates they produce may do quite well. Overall, however, there are relatively few academic jobs available for those finishing their doctorates, many of whom will remain underemployed and insecure if they do go to work in colleges and universities. The implications of this are system-wide. They necessarily influence the reproduction of anthropology and all its sister disciplines, since the failing prospects for dignity and security in academic employment directly impact the viability and orientation of graduate academic programmes.

Recognizing that research universities represent a diminishing sphere of career opportunities for those with advanced degrees, many have called for graduate programmes to produce more versatile and flexible PhDs, capable of succeeding in the 'real' world. Recent studies emphasize the necessity to make multiple career paths accessible to students who might once have aspired to take faculty positions.[1] And here is where our very imagination of the so-called 'ivory tower', including its role – or its much-lamented obsolescence – in the twenty-first century, begins to transform disciplinary trajectories writ large. Individual scholars might feel the impact of changing structural contexts in terms of their own career challenges, but in fact, every field of study is being fundamentally reshaped by the effects of neoliberalism in the academy.[2] What does this mean for the future of anthropological research, and what are the possibilities for anthropological traditions to critically inform emerging paradigms in graduate education?

Although we often reflect on interdisciplinary collaborations in research, it is easy to overlook that the reproduction of disciplines entails cooperation (and competition) with a broad range of academics and non-academics, both within and across our institutions. As an a priori fact of its structural location in the university, anthropology already exists in symbiotic relationship with higher education management. Engaging with the scholarship and practice of academic leadership is therefore important. Some of us encounter this sphere directly, as we serve in university governance and administrative roles. This might be considered a curious site for 'applied anthropology' and a most challenging venue for 'engaged anthropology'. In my four years as Associate Dean of the Graduate School on our campus 2015–18, I took part in university-level projects that reminded me of doing fieldwork in a very strange and unfamiliar place. Rooted as they are in entrepreneurial and managerial orientations, the current literatures on graduate education and academic leadership provoked some cognitive dissonance for me. Ideas about innovations, efficiencies and 'best practices' for American graduate programmes are shaped by aggregate studies produced by organizations such as the Council of Graduate Schools, the Mellon Foundation and the Carnegie Foundation. Their 'evidence-based' insights are meant to be relevant at the national and institutional levels, so they utilize different scales, methods and concepts from those of ethnography. Incentives for colleges and universities to achieve high rankings in national-level research assessments (such as the Carnegie rankings in the United States) and lists of 'top schools' are implicitly about consolidating revenue streams by attracting students, philanthropic donors and corporate partners to invest in the institution.

Today, there are a growing number of critiques that explicitly consider the unfolding impacts of market-based logics and accounting models introduced into the academy. Advocacy organizations such as the American Academy for Arts and Science and the American Association of University Professionals have contributed important statements about conditions of higher education and academic freedom. Many professional organizations have been forced to consider the future of research in their specific disciplines, while journalists and public intellectuals continue to raise relevant questions about access to education and the problem of rising student debt.[3] Spirited conversations about the future of the humanities and the arts have been ongoing. Even the future of STEM (science, technology, engineering and mathematics) research and education in the United States was drawn into question after announcements of new White House budget priorities in 2017, leading to a phenomenally broad-based 'March for Science' on Capitol Hill and across the country in April of that year. All of these debates energized my anthropological inclinations to reflect on structural conditions and cultural practices in graduate education.

This chapter considers our ivory tower blues in the context of these reflections. Neoliberal discourses interpret the challenges facing universities today as problems arising from a combination of economic 'realities' and changing times. They insist that academics simply need to become more flexible, nimble and efficient entrepreneurs, prepared to tear down the outmoded traditions of the 'ivory tower'. Ironically, few such narratives are pitched to attack the university system; instead, many aspire to advocacy and benevolent 'solutions' to the problems defined in this way. As these homophonic discourses meld, and strategic compromises forge new hegemonies in higher education, a blunt critique of the neoliberal university may find little resonance. The most revealing analyses may go no farther than our own intellectual circles, if we cannot find ways to make them relevant to a broader community. Yet by transposing these critiques into our practices of graduate education, we not only find that community, but also mobilize enormous commitment to nurture the young people who are simultaneously embedded – as are all academics – both inside and outside the social field of the university.

My undertaking explores how emerging models for the production and professionalization of PhDs tend to discipline neoliberal subjects, and how this affects the quality of participation in debates about the future of universities. For who will confront the 'devolutionary cycle' (Newman 2016) of declining public investment in higher education if an emerging generation of scholars and scientists perceives it to be natural? Building on the experience of academic leadership in the American Midwest, I argue that we need a polyphony of voices, disciplines and critical approaches to answer the urgent challenges facing us in the academy today. Adding polyphony to the ivory tower blues means breaking up the lonely melody of crisis that seems set on 'repeat' by becoming more aware of the contexts in which our disciplines are (re)produced, and learning to add different counterpoints. Polyphony addresses some of the core issues associated with interdisciplinary collaboration in the context of austerity and neoliberalism, because it requires us to imagine ourselves in kinship and common interest not only with other anthropologists, but also with other academics, professionals, administrators and staff with different backgrounds, priorities and visions of research. The musical metaphor suggests expressive possibilities for world-weary academics, with hope of weaving conscientious questions into the very tune that would silence them. It shifts our perspective as social agents, no longer sounding our instruments in isolation, but joining in together to collectively shift the chords.

Supporting the professional development of students in advanced degree programmes

My administrative portfolio as Associate Dean of the Graduate School at the University of Wisconsin Milwaukee (UWM) included the update and expansion of graduate professional development across all the disciplines. Our 2016–17 series on 'Preparing Future Faculty and Professionals' integrated emerging priorities to enhance graduate student access to non-academic career tracks.

There had been several earlier initiatives for graduate professional development on campus; each reflected the disciplinary orientations of leaders as well as the evolution of 'best practices' disseminated through pilot programmes and studies conducted by the Council of Graduate Schools (CGS).

The first of these was a graduate course called 'Introduction to Academic Life' developed by a previous Associate Dean of the Graduate School at UWM, sociologist Dale Jaffe, in the early 2000s. This followed the best practices modelled by CGS 1993–2003, under an initiative called 'Preparing Future Faculty'. The objective of this programme was to provide 'opportunities to observe and experience faculty responsibilities at a variety of academic institutions with varying missions, diverse student bodies, and different expectations for faculty'.[4] Accordingly, the course at UWM focused on the needs of PhD students aspiring to enter academic careers. The curriculum featured a number of guest speakers including faculty and administrators, exploring topics around university service, faculty governance, research ethics and compliance, and academic integrity. It was a curriculum that would help bright, committed young scholars to make the leap successfully into faculty positions, giving students a 'sneak peek' at a faculty perspective on university life.

The second initiative followed ten years later, under the interim leadership of educational psychologist Patricia Arredondo, with the assistance of a doctoral student from administrative leadership. This was a more flexible, informal series of events coordinated with staff of various centres on campus, including the library, the women's resource centre, the career centre, the office of sponsored research and the health centre. As the student coordinator continued through her own trajectory as a dissertator with family responsibilities, the series demonstrated a particular concern with mentorship ties, peer support, career planning and job search skills, work/life balance and personal wellness. This was a student-centred perspective that filled a significant need for some individuals, particularly given the number of non-traditional students on our campus.

Over time, the CGS 'Preparing Future Faculty' initiatives faded into the background. Another CGS model focused on 'Scholarly Integrity and the Responsible Conduct of Research' took shape 2004–2012, in collaboration with the Office of Research Integrity (US Department of Health and Human Services) and the National Science Foundation. On our campus, a standalone 'Responsible Conduct of Research' (RCR) series was established under the wing of the Office of Sponsored Research. This series offers certification for research funding compliance and maintains records of student completion (but does not offer course credit and does not appear on the transcript). Run by academic staff, the series is comprehensive and interdisciplinary in exposing students to the gamut of ethical, integrity and responsibility issues, from animal research and human subjects research to plagiarism and mechanical safety.

By 2016, CGS had begun new initiatives related to enhancing professional development in STEM fields, and exploring new career pathways in the humanities.[5] Both represent shifts in the aftermath of the 2008 recession, recognizing the declining job market for faculty. Today's models for graduate education favour programmes that explicitly build 'career skills' and 'interdisciplinary' components that undertake to enhance the preparation of young scholars to enter non-academic careers, particularly in the private sector. This is typically separate from the training of teaching assistants for future academic careers; for example, the Mellon Foundation's strategic plan in 2014 established programme funding in 'Higher Education and Scholarship in the Humanities' that included an emphasis on 'Reforms of doctoral education that broaden the intellectual and professional preparation of students' and 'Initiatives that involve humanities scholars in grand challenge questions that require interdisciplinary collaboration'.[6]

Our efforts to reassess and upgrade professional development at UWM owed much to the enthusiasm of Dean Marija Gajdardziska-Josifovska, a physicist with first-hand understanding of issues in the STEM fields and strong engagement with the CGS models of best practice. A graduate intern from English, Danielle DeVasto, worked with me to design and coordinate events in 2016–17.[7] Our collaboration, augmented by the dean and other staff, helped us reach across the disciplines. Our institutional resources were limited as a result of Wisconsin's notorious budget cuts in 2015. Yet in 2016, UWM was recognized as an 'R1' (very high research activity) doctoral institution by the prestigious Carnegie rankings, partly due to the research productivity associated with academic dissertations in a growing portfolio of graduate programmes. This paradox – severely reduced operational budgets coupled with the need to ensure the best possible recruitment, retention, graduation and placement of doctoral students, in part to retain our newly christened, top-tier research ranking – demanded that we learn to do more with less, as good managers must.

At the same time, however, the institutional structures supporting higher education everywhere were swiftly changing before our eyes (cf. Shore and Wright 1999, 2015; Wright and Shore 2017; Saunders 2010; Hyatt, Shear and Wright 2015; Heatherington and Zerilli 2016, 2017). This is not simply a management problem. Increasingly, it is a political problem that cuts to the very heart of public, doctoral research universities in the United States. At UWM, a variety of federal and state supports to research and education are fundamental to fulfilling mandates that include both research excellence and enabling access to education for underrepresented minorities and first-generation students, particularly in our home state. To equip all our students to thrive at the graduate level and beyond, professional development initiatives are essential. Ultimately, this is about much more than an institutional imperative. As a cultural anthropologist, I see graduate professional development as part of the bigger picture that will shape possible futures for whole academic fields, the nature of the academy, and American society itself.

Helping graduate students succeed in challenging times

The Graduate School at UWM administers and supports Master's, PhD and certificate programmes in all twelve schools and colleges across the campus, serving just over 4,600 students in 2017. In 2016–17, we launched an expanded and updated professional development programme at UWM in order to support student retention and graduation. The new initiative revitalized the vision of the older 'Preparing Future Faculty' model, in synthesis with the new initiatives targeted to enhancing preparedness of PhDs for a variety of non-academic, professional and entrepreneurial careers. The content of the series was partly determined by the institutional ecology of UWM, where the Center for Excellence in Teaching and Learning maintains primary responsibility for training teaching assistants, while the Office of Research continues to run its accreditation series in RCR. We also had to take into account the needs and interests of Master's students, creating a 'one-room schoolhouse' to provide enrichment to every stage of the graduate trajectory. The goal of the series envisioned 'cross-cutting seminars, workshops and discussion forums to help students get acquainted with the expectations associated with graduate studies, move successfully through degree milestones, acquire a variety of transferable core skills, and also understand the "big picture" of higher education and academic life'.[8]

Events included an established portfolio of topics such as library research and data management, job hunting skills and interview strategies, funding strategies and grant writing for both the sciences and humanities. These depended on collaborations with other units on campus whose non-academic staff volunteered to do presentations targeted to the interests of graduate-level students. We added topics related to the Institutional Review Board process, financial literacy and campus climate. Yet, while staff shared important information and resources with the students, other perspectives were relevant and fundamental to graduate professional development. For this reason, we began to bring PhDs from off-campus to discuss their own career trajectories after graduate school, and share valuable skills and perspectives. A popular workshop on public speaking skills involved a retired guest with a PhD in theatre and experience in small college administration, ministry, performance and nonprofit organizations. Two other panels on the prospects for non-faculty academic ('alt-ac') jobs as well as non-academic jobs for PhDs also involved guests from off-campus. Thematically divided across broad disciplinary categories, a STEM version was organized in collaboration with alumni relations and the UWM Foundation, while an AHSS (arts, social sciences and humanities) version invited 'alt-ac' staff on campus and outside guests via faculty connections. Learning to think 'out of the box' when it comes to career choices after graduate school is vital for the majority of students now. While online resources[9] for alternative career paths are growing in popularity, it is very productive for students to interact directly with role models who have applied the skills they acquired through graduate study to a spectrum of careers.

Faculty were brought back into the mix to contribute to graduate professional development at a campus-wide level. Thinking in interdisciplinary terms about academic skills and professionalization is not always intuitive. The socialization processes inherent in disciplinary acculturation impart highly particular knowledges, orientations and expectations about how to be a particular kind of scientist, artist, scholar, researcher, practitioner or manager. During an event conceived by Danielle DeVasto on 'succeeding in graduate seminars', a senior faculty member from English co-presented with a mid-career scholar from geosciences. They shared only a few expectations about how advanced seminars were run, what they expected from students, and what the key skills were to do well. Yet the general discussion of what seminars are *for* changed how students and faculty alike understood the project. Few students had previously considered class presentations as practice for conferences and job talks, or class discussions as valuable opportunities to build professional networks with other students. Similarly, some were surprised to think about seminar papers as a chance to grow mentorship relations with teachers and build research proficiencies in anticipation of the thesis or dissertation. On the other hand, not all faculty deliberately teach their classes how to break down and analyse readings and research results. Instead, they reify the talent of some students who immediately grasp the format. Answering general questions about seminars made our faculty speakers freshly aware of the basic mentorship and explicit structure necessary for all students to do well. This highlights that the point of professional development is not to break down disciplinary competences, but to add new dimensions of skill, understanding and creativity.

Although certain events on academic integrity, conferencing and finding an advisor drew on individual faculty presentations, most of our faculty-led events adopted a panel discussion or co-presenter approach that addressed multiple, diverse, disciplinary constituencies. This multidisciplinary approach was important for panels related to the academic job market and preparing job applications. Students were grateful for the access to wider insights and strategies regarding a process that looms large with their approaching graduation. But as we know, it is not enough just to get an academic job; an increasing number of them are highly precarious or short-term positions. The skills and preparation required to compete for scarce tenure-track positions and eventually achieve tenure are moving targets. A degree with a bit of symbolic capital is no longer enough; nor will focus and productivity guarantee a place among the diminishing professoriate. One must also be equipped with good judgement, determination, resilience, and simple luck. In these cruel times for aspiring young scholars, the market threatens to transform our subjectivities in ways that leave the lucky few surviving academics complacent with confidence in their own transcendent merit, while a generation of other promising creative minds are banished or marginalized. Thinking about the bigger picture therefore cannot be left until after they all find jobs. If we want the academy to embody our visions of democratic society, then we should embrace and cultivate a sense of active citizenship within our own institutions. Professional development must therefore address critical issues in higher education, including the circumstances of institutional (re)production.

Critical perspectives on graduate education

Anthropologists writing about the impacts of neoliberal policies in higher education have brought powerful qualitative and reflexive analysis to bear (see Shore and Wright 1999, 2015, 2017; Strathern 2000; Hyatt, Shear and Wright 2015; Heatherington and Zerilli 2016, 2017). Ultimately, our very sense of well-being is vulnerable to the changes wrought by the logics of austerity and accountability. Jon Mitchell has noted how academic subjectivities are transformed by new ways of assessing our research and teaching:

Evidence is starting to emerge about the levels of stress and anxiety being generated by this entrepreneurialisation of university life (Berg and Seeber 2016: 2). We might identify three inter-related sources of stress. First, the need to perform, to maximize, to generate outputs, income, impact and high levels of satisfaction. Second, the stress inherent in compromising principles that this generates. We are drawn towards tailoring our research interests towards those of the funders or of policy; and tailoring our teaching towards that which is satisfying. Maintaining principles in such a context can lead to contradiction and compromise. Third, there is the stress inherent in competition. Although academics have always competed – intellectually, and over jobs and resources – it is its collegiality and sense of collective endeavour that has attracted and sustained many careers – including my own – through difficult and stressful times. The neoliberal regime of audit, accountability, entrepreneurialism and competition cuts across this collegiality, producing an entrepreneurial subjectivity that is by definition competitive, rather than collegial. As a result, the very thing that holds us together is eroded.

2016: 89

The ongoing intrusion of audit cultures into the academy produces a climate that can seem unwelcoming even to faculty who already have established positions in the university system. Graduate professional development is not only about the graduate students themselves, but also about the larger academic community and its role in society. It is about the future of the university, access to education and participation in knowledge production and cultural innovation. It is about the possibilities for critical research perspectives to thrive no matter what the contemporary political climate. Our subjective anxieties and critical concerns are therefore important to share with each other, and with our students.

In an essay on graduate education and training at the University of Georgia, anthropologist Meredith Welch-Devine reflected:

I spend much of my time assisting faculty as they write proposals for new programs. This involves encouraging them to think about whom their new program will attract, how their new program will serve the workforce of the state and the nation, and what their economic impact will be. At the same time, I encourage them to be entrepreneurial: new programs are all but obliged to apply for training grants, to apply to foundations, or to otherwise secure the means to fund their graduate students … the need to continually rejustify my existence forces me to carefully document the ways in which I contribute to the university, particularly in how I help increase our offerings, our training grants, and the quantity and quality of graduate students. This necessarily takes time and energy away from my ability to serve those students and to think creatively about training programs that advance knowledge and create passionate and curious people ... I feel acutely the tension between my roles as handmaiden of neoliberalism and critical scholar committed to the democratization of knowledge production, management and transfer.

2016: 83–5

This gives some ethnographic perspective on how graduate programmes are being shaped by policy models that invest less and less in public education. Welch-Devine's account tells us how it feels to be caught up in a system that focuses more on revenue and enrolment management than building programmes that fulfil the highest visions of science and scholarship. There is a risk that 'Graduate students become the cogs in the machine, teaching courses and labouring in labs, with their work conditioned primarily as service to undergraduates and to PIs rather than as opportunities and contexts for their own growth and development as scholars' (2016: 84). Young scholars are unlikely to find this environment rewarding. In fact, few of us do.

Shore and Wright have described the evolving naturalization of the performance indicators and accounting structures in institutional systems as a potential 'glass cage of coercive transparency' that recalls Weber's critique of early twentieth-century bureaucracies (2015: 422). They ask:

How can we reclaim the professional autonomy and trust that audit practices appear to strip out of the workplace? Is it possible to sustain critical practice when what counts in modern rankings no longer reflects the central role and purpose of a professional and public institution?

2015: 422

Welch-Devine's discussion offers an ambivalent perspective on changes in the academy, and critically addresses her own position within it. She herself occupies an 'alt-ac' administrative role without the benefit of tenure, so she enjoys limited capacity to resist the forms of bureaucracy she must negotiate.[10] Nevertheless, her ability to recognize pressures to compromise fundamental academic values, while assessing opportunities to foster collaborative skills and the spirit of interdisciplinarity, opens space for creative agency. This reflexive and critical capacity itself demonstrates the agency of anthropological subjectivity and practice within an institutional context. Accordingly she sees possibilities for some positive effects to come out of the neoliberal turn:

Many authors decry the 'vocationalization' of training (e.g. Giroux 2010), and while I do believe that our graduate programs should focus more on creativity and inquiry, I also think it is perfectly reasonable and responsible to train students with other skills as well. Turning out graduates who can communicate and work in teams certainly serves the interests of capital, but that does not mean it does not also serve the interests of the students and society more broadly ... And perhaps the arranged marriage of arts and humanities programs with the sciences will not simply produce bland humanities in the service of STEM but rather confer benefits in expanding the horizons of both partners.

Welch-Devine 2016: 85

I agree with Welch-Devine that we cannot afford to focus only on the negative aspects of neoliberalism, not only because it is impractical, but also because we might miss out on positive opportunities. We cannot simply repeat the 'worried notes' of academic nostalgia, the ivory tower blues, over and over. Our students must be equipped with skills that give them the best chance to take up vocations both within and beyond the academy, skills that could help change the world. Many faculty and staff volunteers have gone above and beyond the call of duty to contribute to this project.

Yet even as we worked to support improved graduate professional development on our campus, I was aware that discourses about the professionalization of PhDs also authorized the very models that produce good neoliberal subjects. The kinds of studies that emphasize making advanced degrees more adaptable and versatile are typically generated through collection and analysis of big data in higher education. They are primarily concerned with institutional outcomes, such as student retention rates, rates of degree completion and rates of placement. They usually have little or nothing to do with the fine-grained approaches that anthropologists value, so they rarely address big contrasts across various public and private universities, let alone the funding and culture of different kinds of PhD programmes. They do poorly at the towering qualitative task of integrating student perspectives, and poorly at attending to differences between them. They generally refrain from challenging political analyses, and they do not seek to cultivate such critical awareness among the students. Instead, they focus on preparing students to be competitive, flexible labourers in a field of precarious employment. While students facing a ruthless job market may be strongly motivated to acquire masteries that might give them any competitive advantage, we also want them to become thoughtful representatives of their respective fields, and of public education writ large. Above all, this entails bringing our students along into lively conversations about the academy and its contributions to society.

Freire and Gramsci in the grad school

My role in university administration gave me occasion to examine a significant portion of writings on graduate studies that fall into the 'self-help' category. These are chiefly marketed to graduate students hoping to pull themselves up by the bootstraps, as it were. There are blogs, essays and books that promise secrets to success in graduate school, dissertation writing and the job market afterwards, as well as those that claim to reveal the mysteries of academic life and the tenure process. There are even books that assure to help faculty advisors become optimal mentors so that their graduate students will be able to get jobs. Sometimes written by experienced faculty, sometimes by other PhDs who were either dissatisfied with the academy or unable to enter it, these narratives about self-professionalization can be ridden with guilt, blame, or alienation. Much of this literature now talks about the internal flaws and failures of the 'ivory tower' and risks promoting anti-intellectualism, even though it is meant to support the success of graduate students and academics. Whether confessional, patronizing, jocular, inspirational or passive aggressive, these voices usually personalize individual agency. As a result, they tend to obscure structural conditions and ignore the role of community as factors in individual outcomes. Our updated graduate student professional development series in 2016–17 attempted to frame graduate education in a different way.

We adopted an approach that subtly infused the critical pedagogical traditions of Antonio Gramsci and Paolo Freire into discussions about academic and alternative careers for those with advanced degrees.[11] Critical pedagogies insist upon the role of students as critical subjects and protagonists in a socio-economic and political field characterized by implicit structural inequalities. These pedagogical strategies are rooted in an understanding of knowledge as an ongoing process, rather than a reified object that must be acquired. As Tim Ingold (2018) contends, education is at heart a process of exposing oneself to the world, learning to attend to others, and opening up to new understandings and possibilities, even if they are uncomfortable. This perspective is vital to transform perceptions of advanced study as a prestige mechanism or commodity into a meaningful, productive and emancipatory practice. Critical pedagogies rely upon mutual mentorship between students and teachers and a willingness to open-ended debate. From an ethnographic perspective, they are fundamentally self-reflexive and collaborative in orientation, seeking to generate co-produced insight into the larger context in which all the actors find themselves variously situated. Panels focused on various topics around professionalization were not intended to disseminate expert knowledge 'from the top down', but rather, asked both panellists and audience members to reflect upon the nature of their experiences, and engage one another as interlocutors and allies.

Our approach was also deliberately polyphonic. We tried to bring many different kinds of voices into the dialogue about the vision, purpose and subjective meaning of graduate degrees. We gave graduate students access to mentors and role models beyond their own disciplines, and beyond the university itself. It would be a mistake to assume that all of these mentors and role models agreed on what the university is for, and what it should be about. This is especially true as we bring more alumni, donors and community members into the mix. Neither do all graduate students have the same goals, visions and priorities in mind when they are working on their degrees. Such differences are not only about disciplinary orientations, but also about their identity as individuals, as well as the expectations of their family members. At UWM, we have many non-traditional students at different life stages. Many of the participants in our professional development series were international students and faculty, as well as under-represented minorities. Everyone was grappling with the significance of the structural transformations at the state and institutional level, as we became a test case for one model of austerity. It was the very diversity and marginality of both students and faculty in this university that enabled important perspectives to take shape. Building community across the disciplines – a community that seeks to bridge divides between town and gown, and validate the role of advanced education as a valuable public resource – became more vital than ever.

Starting conversations about 'the big picture' of higher education was high on my list of priorities for our updated series on graduate professional development. The first of our 'big picture' events was dedicated to concerns about academic freedom.[12] In the wake of policy changes to University of Wisconsin system statutes that affected conditions of tenure and promotion for academics in 2016, it became apparent that principles of academic freedom were poorly understood by the general public. This is also true for much of the student body, who tend to perceive the tenure system as an undeserved guarantee of job security that they themselves will probably not enjoy. For our professional development series, we brought together a panel including a climate change scientist, a freshwater ecologist, a civil rights historian and an immigration rights historian. Their commentaries illuminated the fundamental need for academic freedom to guarantee independent research opportunities not only for faculty, but also for graduate students. An unexpected benefit of the conversation was that faculty in the humanities were not previously aware of issues facing their colleagues in the sciences, and vice versa. The discussion generated a sense of alliance across the disciplines and shared individual faculty experiences with students and colleagues. It also enabled a means of reflecting on current events in a context framed by academic concerns rather than polarized partisan politics.

Another event considered the experience of women academics, engaging a panel of faculty from information studies, health sciences, education and the humanities. In a country where women with advanced degrees are typically paid only 74 per cent of what their male counterparts earn and are significantly less likely than men to reach the highest-paying leadership and executive positions (AAUW 2017), it is important for women graduate students to recognize ongoing sources of institutional bias and discrimination that implicitly shape their experiences within and beyond the university. According to an analysis of data collected by the American Association of University Professors (Newman 2014), women academics in the United States generally earn about 90 per cent of what their male counterparts are paid in the same field, but are disproportionately represented at lower (and more precarious) ranks, in less prestigious institutions and in lower-paying fields. They are much more likely to fall out of the 'leaky pipeline' of tenure and promotion as a result of reproductive choices and family responsibilities, and they are apt to get less recognition for the intellectual contributions and institution building they achieve. Very few are recruited into the ranks of full professor or upper administrative leadership. The statistics are more exaggerated for women of colour, who often bear disproportionate burdens of university service precisely because they are expected to mentor and encourage others. These career trajectories begin in graduate school, although the continuing gender gap is typically obscured and disavowed by the 'merit culture' of academics. Sharing personal stories across fields and generations had a transformative impact for everyone who attended, including the men in the room.

In general, we tried to balance offering events that focused on building skills for success in graduate school and beyond with 'big picture' events that deliberately considered critical concerns and debates about the future of the academy. Fittingly, we also video-streamed and recorded events to further discuss and disseminate in the future, so that the panels themselves were just the beginning of ongoing conversations that could continue to recalibrate our collective vision of the academy.

Polyphony and resonance

As a result of growing austerity in the public sector, academic leadership models for graduate education are pushed in particular directions. The intensive focus on budgets and 'bottom lines' now favours programmes that leverage various forms of prestige and sponsorship from organizations outside the academy. While this might support wonderful community-based research activities, it very often affirms research orientations that benefit profit-seeking partners, or attempt to satisfy the priorities of private donors. This can jeopardize academic freedom by narrowing the range of research options that are incentivized, or even feasible to undertake. The growing reliance on alumni campaigns and philanthropic development also emphasizes research that seems to promise direct social, economic or cultural impacts for the local community. In resource-challenged institutions, this can have unintended effects on international research, so that the world becomes smaller. The importance of some research may be inscrutable to the public, while high-profile research comes under acute scrutiny. And as the political winds shift, more provocative and controversial research creates new risks in an environment where tenure lines are increasingly limited, and unreliable protection from harassment. Thus, as the budgets of key national research funding agencies come under attack, the work songs of the university assume a monotonous, repetitive, worried progression – what I call the ivory tower blues.

For graduate programmes to survive and recruit students under these conditions, many are forced to highlight their applicability to 'real world' or 'professional' careers. In anthropology, this includes a range of possibilities from marketing research and business, development, government agencies, elementary and high school teaching, public service and administration, to project management for international and non-governmental organizations. Certain options, such as the recent Human Terrain Project, suggest ethical concerns (see CEAUSSIC 2009). Even if we attempt to assert and maintain the highest ethical standards in applications of research, there is a danger that the discipline as a whole will be driven away from fundamental research that maintains a critical perspective not undermined by particular private or political interests. Nevertheless, there are good reasons for sending many of our young scholars into non-academic vocations. We hope that they will better the world by translating their expertise into new contexts, and that their work will ultimately reinvigorate the discipline by bringing new insights and ideas into focus. Both applied anthropology and public anthropology have broadened the intellectual capacity of our field. This is also true in other disciplines, even where training has usually focused on academic orientations. The declining job market for academics has simply highlighted that there should be many alternatives available to us.

Polyphony is the art of blending distinct lines of melody into a harmonic musical texture. A polyphonic approach to the professional development of our graduate students is a broad-based approach that brings an ensemble of instruments (methodologies) and voices (intellectual traditions and positionalities) into a meaningful pattern. This approach accepts the need to enable students at a pragmatic level, by nurturing diverse competences and transportable skills that cross-cut a range of potential professional and academic roles. It also produces counterpoints to this neoliberal tune, however, by integrating dialogues that foster critical thinking and active participation in debates about the future of higher education. This harmonizes a shared commitment to the academy as a vital public resource, and a means to democracy and social justice, rather than a mere mechanism of the 'knowledge economy'. Our graduate students have much at stake in what our universities may become, whether or not they remain in academia. In Tim Ingold's words,

> In today's world, we need universities more than ever. We need them to bring people of all ages and from all nations together, across their multiple differences, and we need them as places where these differences can be voiced and debated in an ecumenical spirit of tolerance, justice and fellowship. No purpose is more important, and no institution, apart from the university, currently exists with the capacity to undertake it.
>
> Ingold 2018: 78

Critical perspectives on the neoliberal university come from many different experiences. To achieve polyphonic resonance, we need community across the disciplines. Adventuring in the unfamiliar terrain of academic leadership, the eclectic disciplinary articulations common in anthropology equipped me to think about a wider field of interdisciplinary engagements. In turn, the odyssey into administration informed my growing awareness of academic community in the broadest sense, defined not only by anthropology, but by all of us who believe that our institutions matter. We need each other. Graduate students from across campus have broadened my own horizons, as have the faculty, staff and others who generously contributed their time and energy to engage with our fledgling scholars. Their affective labours in transdisciplinary graduate mentorship renew bonds of collegiality, notwithstanding the splintering effects of the audit culture.

Notes

1 See for example CGS 2015, 2017; Denecke et al. 2017.

2 Cris Shore and Susan Wright use the term 'neoliberalism' to highlight aspects of policy reform agendas impacting universities that 'include an emphasis on creating an institutional framework that promotes competition, entrepreneurship, commercialisation, profit making and "private good" research and the prevalence of a metanarrative about the importance of markets for promoting the virtues of freedom, choice and prosperity' (2016: 47).

3 See for example Newfield 2008, 2016.

4 http://cgsnet.org/preparing-future-faculty.

5 These were based on the results of two special nationally funded research grants from the National Science Foundation and the Andrew W. Mellon Foundation.

6 https://mellon.org/resources/news/articles/continuity-and-change-andrew-w-mellon-foundation-strategic-plan-programs-executive-summary/.

7 We also benefitted from input from our counterparts at Marquette University, who had launched a non-credit course for graduate student professionalization and teacher training on their campus: http://www.marquette.edu/pffp/.

8 http://uwm.edu/graduateschool/professional-development/.

9 See for example 'The Versatile PhD', https://versatilephd.com.

10 The term 'alt-ac' is used to define a growing number of quasi-academic roles in colleges and universities, where PhDs accept administrative or staff roles and continue to be engaged in their fields, without tenure-track faculty status.

11 For discussion see for example Freire 2000; Fischman and McLaren 2005; Giroux 2013; Mayo 2015.

12 See DeVasto and Heatherington (n.d.).

References

AAUW (American Association of University Women) (2017), *The Simple Truth About the Gender Pay Gap*, Spring 2017 edition. Available online: http://www.aauw.org/resource/the-simple-truth-about-the-gender-pay-gap/ (accessed 2 May 2017).

Andrew W. Mellon Foundation (2014), *Continuity and Change: The Andrew W. Mellon Foundation Strategic Plan for Programs*. Available online: https://mellon.org/resources/news/articles/continuity-and-change-andrew-w-mellon-foundation-strategic-plan-programs-executive-summary/ (accessed 30 April 2017).

Berg, M. and B. Seeber (2016), *The Slow Professor: Challenging the Culture of Speed in the Academy*, Toronto: University of Toronto Press.

CEAUSSIC (Commission on the Engagement of Anthropology with the US Security and Intelligence Communities) (2009), *Final Report on the Army's Human Terrain*

System Proof of Concept Program. American Anthropological Association. Available online: http://s3.amazonaws.com/rdcms-aaa/files/production/public/FileDownloads/pdfs/cmtes/commissions/CEAUSSIC/upload/CEAUSSIC_HTS_Final_Report.pdf (accessed 19 April 2017).

Council of Graduate Schools (2015), *Understanding PhD Career Pathways for Program Improvement,* Report, Washington, DC: Council of Graduate Schools.

Council of Graduate Schools (2017), *Promising Practices in Humanities PhD Professional Development: Lessons Learned from the 2016-2017 Next Generation Humanities PhD Consortium,* Washington, DC: Council of Graduate Schools.

Denecke, D., K. Feaster and K. Stone (2017), *Professional Development: Shaping Effective Programs for STEM Graduate Students,* Washington, DC: Council of Graduate Schools.

DeVasto, D. and T. Heatherington (n.d.), 'Getting the Big Picture into Graduate Professional Development', Unpublished essay.

Donoghue, F. (2008), *The Last Professors: The Corporate University and the Fate of the Humanities,* New York: Fordham University Press.

Ehrenberg, R. and C. Kuh (2010), *Doctoral Education and the Faculty of the Future,* Ithaca, NY: Cornell University Press.

Fischman, G. and P. McLaren (2005), 'Rethinking Critical Pedagogy and the Gramscian and Freirean Legacies: From Organic to Committed Intellectuals on Critical Pedagogy, Commitment and Praxis', *Cultural Studies – Critical Methodologies,* 5 (4): 425–47.

Freire, P. (2000), *The Pedagogy of the Oppressed.* 30th Anniversary Edition. London: Bloomsbury Academic.

Giroux, H. (2010), 'Bare Pedagogy and the Scourge of Neoliberalism: Rethinking Higher Education as a democratic public sphere', *The Educational Forum,* 74 (3): 184–96.

Giroux, H. (2011), *On Critical Pedagogy,* London: Continuum/Bloomsbury.

Jaschik, S. (2008), 'The Last Professors'. Email interview with author Frank Donoghue. *Inside Higher Education.* Available online: https://www.insidehighered.com/news/2008/06/11/lastprofs (accessed April 30, 2017).

Heatherington, T. and F. Zerilli (eds) (2016), *Special Issue: Anthropologists in/of the Neoliberal Academy,* Forum, *Anuac,* 5 (1): 41–90.

Heatherington, T. and F. Zerilli (eds) (2017), *Special Issue: Anthropologists Witnessing and Reshaping the Neoliberal Academy,* Forum, *Anuac,* 6 (1): 23–98.

Hyatt, S., B. Shear and S. Wright (2015), *Learning Under Neoliberalism: Ethnographies of Governance in Higher Education,* Oxford: Berghahn.

Ingold, T. (2018) *Anthropology and/as Education.* London: Routledge.

Mayo, P. (2015), 'Antonio Gramsci's Impact on Critical Pedagogy', *Critical Sociology,* 41 (7–8): 1121–36.

Mitchell, J. (2016), 'Let our Profs be Profs', in T. Heatherington and F. Zerilli (eds), *Special Issue: Anthropologists in/of the Neoliberal Academy,* Forum, *Anuac,* 5 (1): 87–90.

Newfield, C. (2008), *Unmaking the Public University: The Forty-Year Assault on the Middle Class.* Cambridge, MA: Harvard University Press.

Newfield, C. (2016), *The Great Mistake: How We Wrecked Universities and How We Can Fix Them*. Baltimore, MD: Johns Hopkins University Press.

Newman, J. (2014), 'There is a Gender Pay Gap in Academe but it May Not Be the Gap That Matters', *Chronicle of Higher Education*, 11 April. Available online: https://www.chronicle.com/blogs/data/2014/04/11/there-is-a-gender-pay-gap-in-academe-but-it-may-not-be-the-gap-that-matters/ (accessed 17 March 2017).

Saunders, D. (2010), 'Neoliberal Ideology and Public Higher Education in the United States', *Journal for Critical Education Policy Studies*, 8 (1): 41–77.

Shore, C. and S. Wright (1999), 'Audit Culture and Anthropology: Neo-liberalism in British Higher Education', *JRAI*, 5 (4): 557–75.

Shore, C. and S. Wright (2015), 'Audit Culture Revisited: Rankings, Ratings and the Reassembling of Society', *Current Anthropology*, 56 (3): 421–44.

Shore, C. and S. Wright (2016), 'Neoliberalisation and the Death of the Public University', in T. Heatherington and F. Zerilli (eds), *Special Issue: Anthropologists in/of the Neoliberal Academy*, Forum, *Anuac*, 5 (1): 46–50.

Strathern, M. (ed.) (2000), *Audit Cultures: Anthropological Studies in Anthropology, Ethics and the Academy*, London: Routledge.

Welch-Devine, M. (2016), 'Graduate Education and Training in the Neoliberal University', in T. Heatherington and F. Zerilli (eds), *Special Issue: Anthropologists in/of the Neoliberal Academy*, Forum, *Anuac*, 5 (1): 83–6.

Wright, S. and C. Shore (eds) (2017), *Death of the Public University? Uncertain Futures for Higher Education in the Knowledge Economy*, Oxford: Berghahn.

5

Symbiosis or Entrepreneurialism? Ambivalent Anthropologies in the Age of the (Neo)Liberal Arts

Carolyn Hough and Adam Kaul

We offer this autoethnographic account of anthropology at a liberal arts college from a specific place, the western edge of the Midwestern state of Illinois in the United States, and from a particular institutional and political moment of ambivalence, improvisation, risk, unpredictability and liminality. As Dána-Ain Davis argues in her own analysis of neoliberal impacts on higher education, autoethnography 'can provide valuable insights into the tensions between the neoliberal environment and being an academic in such a setting' (2015: 153). Some aspects of our crisis are only now unfolding, so we offer a perspective from the disaster before the dust has settled; in fact, we write from within the confusion of the storm. As a result, we offer more questions than answers, and more problems than solutions. However, some time ago now, Renato Rosaldo pointed out that such 'indeterminacy allows the emergence of a culturally valued quality of human relations where one can follow impulses, change directions, and coordinate with other people' (1989: 112). It seems to us that responding to contingencies and constantly changing directions in order to coordinate with others is necessary for establishing anthropological symbioses in the midst of the neoliberal era of higher education. Here, we counter the seemingly univalent certainty of neoliberalism by employing an 'anthropology of ambivalence' in our attempts to speak from the crisis. Neil Smelser (1998: 5) wrote that ambivalence is

> the simultaneous existence of attraction and repulsion, of love and hate. Ambivalence is inclusive in that it can focus on people, objects, and symbols ... The nature of ambivalence is to hold *opposing affective orientations* toward the same person, object or symbol ... [It] tends to be unstable, expressing itself in different and sometimes contradictory ways as actors tend to cope with it.

Using this frame of reference, this chapter documents our attempts to cope with the uncertainty of our particular and perhaps peculiar place and time in higher education.

Our ambivalence about anthropological symbioses is the result of contradictory goals for reaching out beyond anthropological boundaries. On the one hand, neoliberalism forces a particular kind of creative connectivity, which, in the late-capitalist regime, is branded 'entrepreneurialism'. On the other, we write from a small, selective liberal arts institution where the goal is deep interdisciplinarity, epistemological syntheses, and a broad consilience of knowledge across programmes, departments and divisions.[1] In that sense, symbiosis is not forced upon us so much as it is the point of what we do. To be clear, we value these concepts differently. In the episteme of the liberal arts tradition, the highest-order knowledge is developed above and beyond disciplinary boundaries or silos, where each discipline's methods and data accumulate and combine to create new ideas that are greater than the sum of their parts. This is epistemological symbiosis, and anthropology has a pivotal role to play in the process of its creation. The difference between this and 'entrepreneurialism', it seems to us, is the intention, motivation and rationale for these creative connections. Neoliberal entrepreneurialism occurs as a result of extrinsic market forces, and adaptation to these is often fuelled by the (occasionally desperate) desire to prove one's relevance or even simply survive the external pressures. Indeed, '"[s]urvival", individual, institutional or national, becomes one of the key drivers in the neo-liberal discourse' (Davies and Petersen 2005: 88). So one goal of this chapter is to ask rather than answer the question: when is the discipline of anthropology being forced into entrepreneurialism and when is it being allowed to create symbioses?

Another contribution we make is setting the discussion in the context of a rather different kind of institution of higher learning, the small liberal arts college. At Augustana, we limit enrolment to around 2,500 students in order to maintain a very low student–faculty ratio of twelve to one. Along with the philosophy of interdisciplinary interconnection discussed more below, this intensive faculty–student interaction sets liberal arts colleges apart from most other institutions. By contrast, most analyses of the impacts of neoliberalism on post-secondary schools focus on public universities (cf. Washburn 2005; Hyatt, Shear and Wright 2015; the other contributions to this volume). However, although they exist (cf. Pfnister 1984; Lang 1999; Melomo 2013; Deresiewicz 2015), analyses about neoliberalism's unique impacts at a small private college are few and far between. It is within this context of the (neo)liberal arts that we explore our ambivalence about students' subject positions as professionalizing consumers of higher education and our own as faculty entrepreneurs.

Anthropology in a (neo)liberal arts context

As anthropologists, we are trained to pay close attention to the language that people use to talk about the problems of the day. At Augustana College, we talk a lot lately at faculty meetings, over lunch and coffee, and on 'the quad', about how the pressures of the *marketplace* are changing the state of higher education. It is understandable that parents and students want a higher *return on investment*. As costs spike and tuition increases, students and parents rightly demand to be reassured about job security after graduation and how quickly graduates will be gainfully employed. They *shop around* more intensively each year for a college or university that will give them the *best product, comparing prices*, and attempting to get the most *value for money*. Meanwhile, as the demographics of our region of the country shift, *competition* increases between our institution and our peer schools for fewer and fewer *customers*. Simultaneously, Augustana is pouring more resources into expanding our *yield* of students outside of the Midwest and into national and international *markets*. To make our case that Augustana College is a better investment, we gather more and more data and try to *market our brand* effectively, leveraging our *worth claim* and our *value proposition*.

Of course, this language is all borrowed from the corporate world. And while the monetary cost of higher education causes real concern and leads students and parents into a consumer narrative, this also creates a good deal of anxiety for faculty who wish to resist reframing the value of an education in terms of capitalist exchange-values. It seems that year after year, consumerism and college-as-primarily-professional-development creep further and further onto the campus. Meanwhile, soaring student debt in the United States has become a key talking point for politicians on both the right and the left. Part of what makes our discussion of the capitalist privatization of higher education in volumes like this one unique is that, like most small selective liberal arts colleges, Augustana was founded as, and remains, a *private* (non-profit) institution with a board of trustees and a tuition-driven annual budget. In many ways, we highly value our ability to be (semi-)independent from many strictures of the state, but that partial (in)dependence is also one of the central sources of our ambivalence.

Liberal arts colleges follow a distinct history that reaches back to the European Middle Ages, and can arguably be traced even further back to the Hellenic Age of

Ancient Greece. 'In a strict sense', writes Wagner (1983: 1), 'the term designates those arts as they were codified by the Latin encyclopedists of the 5th and 6th centuries', which include seven categories: grammar, logic, rhetoric, mathematics, music, geometry and astronomy. In the United States, the liberal arts were established in the colonial era at some of the first universities in America in the 1700s – Harvard, Yale, Dartmouth, William and Mary – with the express purpose of 'extend[ing] the values and culture of European society' (Bonvillian and Murphy 1996: 19). Following the Revolutionary War, a second goal became clear: creating 'a new breed of leaders to guide the development of a burgeoning nation' (ibid.: 20). The curriculum evolved after Independence and as the new nation expanded westward. Liberal arts colleges often began to combine their focus on subjects that fall under the umbrella of the humanities with newly circumscribed sciences and more applied training (ibid.: 20–1). By the mid- to late 1800s when the biggest proliferation of small liberal arts colleges occurred, including the founding of Augustana College, this European/American duality was firmly established.[2] Augustana fits this model insofar as it was founded as a Swedish-American school with curriculum originally taught in Swedish, but its mission in its first few decades also included an emphasis on 'learning English and becoming American' (Blanck 2006: 59). American patriotism was strongly emphasized by the end of the nineteenth century, when the college president proclaimed that there was a 'true American civic spirit' at Augustana (ibid.: 83).

Ambivalence marks the history of the model of the liberal arts college in the American context in a few key ways. One is a transatlantic duality that suggests continuity with European traditions but also a break from them. Another duality is the very purpose of the education that a liberal arts college provides, sitting sometimes uncomfortably between a more lofty or romantic goal of educating the whole person ('in mind, spirit, and body' as it is worded in our college's mission statement) and, as our college president has said numerous times in addresses to students and faculty, the more pragmatic goal of providing the right skills and adaptability for young people not just for their first job but for their last job, as well.

These ambivalences show up not only in the curriculum (discussed below), but also in symbolic representations of the adapting identities of liberal arts colleges in a late-capitalist climate. Symbolic ambivalences are not unique to our campus. William Deresiewicz's (2015) polemical essay entitled *The Neoliberal Arts: How College Sold Its Soul to the Market* points to the banners hung up around a small liberal arts college at which he was spending a semester writing and teaching. One of the banners simply displayed four words: 'leadership, service, integrity, creativity' (2015: 25). It is not unusual to encounter banners like this on any campus across the United States these days. Presumably, these four words were conceptualized as touchstones for some of the core values of the university or college community he was visiting, or perhaps ones that they hope to one day instil in their students. Seen in that light, they might be considered rather benign, if uninspiring, slogans, perhaps meant to encourage some sort of vague character development. Deresiewicz is far less forgiving, however. 'The text is not the statement of an individual,' he writes, 'it is the emanation of a bureaucracy' (2015: 26). What interests him even more is what is left off the list: thinking and learning. And this is where he begins his scathing critique of the state of higher education more generally. The banners are a kind of synecdoche of the capitalist (re)orientation of the contemporary college and university.

It was a bit of a shock to read this critique, partly because our campus has eerily similar banners mounted on light posts throughout our wooded 115-acre campus. In fact, Deresiewicz's description resonated so well that we wondered initially if he was talking about Augustana College, until we realized that the words themselves were wrong. Here, the words displayed on the banners (and on posters in the student centre) are Purpose, Openness and Respect, Accountability, Responsibility, and Care. Banners like these ostensibly present us with answers, but leave us wondering what the questions are. In case there was any mystery at Augustana, though, the banners also say in much smaller print: Community Principles. Like Deresiewicz, however, we are left wondering how these principles adhere to the primary goals of a liberal arts college. Like condensed ritual symbols, they are a touchstone for layers of meaning and a call for community action. 'A single symbol, in fact, represents many things at the same time: it is multivocal, not univocal. Its referents are not all of the same logical order but are drawn from many domains of social experience and ethical evaluation', writes Victor Turner (1969: 52). Moreover, in synch with Smelser's concept of ambivalence, Turner argues that symbols cluster around opposing semantic meanings from the physiological to the social and moral, thus 'unit[ing] the organic with the sociomoral order' (ibid.). And it is in this latter function of symbols where we perhaps see the unification of community principles on the one hand and teaching and learning on the other, because many of the accompanying photographs depict students and professors actively engaging with one another in and out of the classroom, reaching to the sky, writing on whiteboards, shovelling dirt. It is telling that two of the words that are apparently symbolic of our community principles, Accountability and Responsibility, are central to the neoliberal project. And for a campus community for which the

Figure 5.1 Accountability. Photo: Adam Kaul.

need to rapidly diversify the student body and the faculty has become a central concern, who exactly is being held accountable on the Accountability banner that depicts a faculty member and his student, both African-American? How are their bodies proclaiming a sense of moral responsibility and accountability, and to whom does this responsibility fall?

All of this is amplified in a particularly dire economic climate, beginning with the financial collapse of the US economy in 2008 and its subsequent slow recovery. Due to some careful financial stewardship from our administration, Augustana College weathered that storm comparatively well. But another crisis much closer to home, described below, began to slowly erupt in the state of

Illinois, leading to a far more acute moment of contingency. It is worth noting first, however, that the panic about marketplace pressures on higher education, and on the liberal arts in particular, are not particularly new. Reaching back to 1999, Eugene Lang, who was at the time chairperson emeritus of the Board of Trustees for one of the country's premiere liberal arts institutions, Swarthmore College, wrote that the 'liberal arts experience is battling pressures of escalating costs, rising tuitions, and increasing demands for career training as a primary component of undergraduate study' (1999: 133). His essay on the nature of the liberal arts college, which appeared in a special issue of *Daedalus*, rather rosily calls for collaboration in the classroom, across campus, in the community, and with other higher education institutions (ibid.: 146–7). A decade-and-a-half before that, Allan O. Pfnister had a somewhat gloomier view. He proclaimed that '[t]he free-standing liberal arts colleges and the university-based liberal arts colleges have been placed increasingly on the defensive over the past decade as study in professional and more applied fields has become more attractive' (1984: 145). Later in the same essay, he added that '[one] cannot help but wonder if, in the last quarter of the twentieth century, we are witnessing the passing of what has long been viewed as a peculiarly American form of higher education' (ibid.: 146). Lang and Pfnister were not alone, either, in making dire predictions about the future of the liberal arts. In 1989, Elizabeth T. Kennan warned that the liberal arts were 'under attack' (1989: 25); Barbara Ann Scott edited a volume with the ominous title *The Liberal Arts in a Time of Crisis* in 1991; a few years later, Bonvillian and Murphy claimed that the 'crisis in higher education' in the United States extended back to the early 1970s (1996: 28); similarly, Paul Neely wrote in 1999 that 'the primary threat to liberal arts colleges is found in the marketplace' (1999: 29); and more recently, Victor E. Ferrall, Jr. published his assessment entitled *Liberal Arts at the Brink* (2011).

Concerns about the survival of institutions like ours may not be new; however, the disastrous politico-economic moment we write from has only just begun. The election of Donald J. Trump and his appointment of Betsy DeVos as Secretary of Education leaves a lot of unanswered questions about higher education policies. DeVos's confirmation hearings in the US Congress focused heavily on so-called 'school choice' issues, which is code for privatization of K-12 (kindergarten through to the end of High School). It is unclear how this will impact US colleges and universities. Augustana College also sits on the banks of the Mississippi River at the extreme western edge of the state of Illinois, a state that has a famously corrupt political tradition. The list of governors and others convicted and often imprisoned for various crimes such as racketeering, embezzlement and fraud is long and extends back decades. The most recent and perhaps most spectacular incident involved the now-former Governor Rod Blagojevich, who in 2009 was convicted of corruption for trying to sell the president-elect Barack Obama's newly vacated senate seat. Coincidentally, Blagojevich would later appear on Donald Trump's reality television show *The Celebrity Apprentice* where Trump claimed he had 'tremendous courage and guts' ('Donald Trump Predicts . . .'). In addition, state pensions were so badly mishandled for years by both of the major political parties that Illinois was eventually liable for, but unable to pay out, $100 billion (Confessore 2015: A1). This made Illinois ripe for a political and economic experiment that began taking shape in 2013 at a gathering of the Economic Club of Chicago. There, a plea was made by one of its billionaire members, Kenneth C. Griffin, to create a political and economic power shift. Shortly afterwards, an unprecedented amount of money (from within Illinois but also New York, Texas, Florida and elsewhere) poured into an effort to elect a businessman and friend of Griffin's, Bruce Rauner, as Governor (ibid.). The oligarchs won. Rauner took office in 2015 with the express purpose of implementing typical neoliberal reforms like breaking up unions, slashing spending for social services, and radically shrinking the size of government to run the state like a corporation. In the process, the newly elected governor introduced an excessively austere budget. This led to a standoff in the state capital as the Democrat-controlled House and Senate rejected it. The standoff continued until August 2017, and Rauner was finally ousted at the ballot box in 2018. During nearly all of Rauner's governorship the state of Illinois simply went without a budget. In some quarters, the state's publicly funded university system nearly collapsed under the financial pressure (Bosman 2016: A12). As a tuition-driven private liberal arts college, Augustana does not depend nearly as much as many institutions on state funds, but some of our students do rely on suspended state-funded grants (particularly, the state's Monetary Award Program) to pay for tuition, and eventually those funds feed into the college's annual budget. This means that an institution like ours was owed several million dollars by the state.

The economic and political crises such as these at the state level dramatically amplify and exacerbate the local institutional pressures on our college, and the pressures placed on faculty, staff and administration to concentrate our efforts on recruiting new students, retaining current students, aggressively ramping up job and skills training, and marketing the return on investment of an Augustana education. These efforts were always present, as the next section describes, but the recent (necessary or opportunistic?) responses to a financial crisis caused by a CEO-cum-governor potentially reframes faculty and students as neoliberal subjects.

Accounting for the future: CORE, scorecards and the professionalization of students

Over the past decade we have seen this neoliberal reframing shape campus initiatives. In our first years at the college, students could seek guidance about what to do after graduation at a Career Center with a staff of two that included a Director of Internships. The Career Center occupied office space in the building that houses other administrative offices such as the Registrar, Dean of Students, and Academic Affairs. When giving walking directions to the Career Center from most academic departments on campus, you would tell students to go 'up the hill'. This is the same walk that we would make as assistant professors, delivering heavy crates of pre-tenure review materials to the dean's office, trudging up concrete stairways built into the bluffs of the Mississippi River and arriving somewhat breathless and flustered. Faculty joke that this geographical arrangement has to be intentional in order to literally knock the wind out of us before our tenure hearings. At that time, the Center for Vocational Reflection (CVR) had its offices in a newly remodelled academic building 'down the hill'. Apropos of the college's Lutheran affiliation and mission to 'educate students in mind, body and spirit', the CVR was a place for students to investigate the kinds of work to which they would direct their knowledge, skills and passion, in their college years and beyond. The 2009–2010 campus directory lists a staff of three for the CVR, including two directors and a coordinator.

The aims of the Career Center (find an internship or job) and the CVR (find your calling) were complementary, but the centrality of the CVR's offices, its greater human resources and the involvement of an associate dean, an erstwhile professor of religion, as one of the directors attested to its importance to the college's work. For several years, the CVR was an office where academic advisors could refer students who were not sure what their major should be. In these years several students declared anthropology as their major course of study after they visited the CVR to complete inventories and talk through the results with CVR advisors. When they expressed an interest in global diversity and solving human problems, they were often directed to us. In this way, the CVR had a clear role to play as students determined their undergraduate plans of study; it was not solely or even primarily focused on students' postgraduate careers.

Then in 2010, the Career Center and CVR coalesced under the umbrella of the Community Engagement Center (CEC) along with International and Off Campus Programs, and Entrepreneurial Development. The CEC occupied a suite of offices in a peripheral building that also houses diverse campus services such as Benefits, Accounting, and Campus Security. The community focus of the CEC emphasized students' engagements beyond the campus, both during and after their undergrad years. Students, faculty and administrators alike talk about the 'bubble' that is perceived to encapsulate the campus and often serves as a barrier to the urban communities that surround the college. Community engagement, then, can be understood as a remedy to limited or problematic 'town and gown' dynamics, as well as an opportunity for students to gain experiences like internships that are practical additions to their resumes and may provide postgraduate networking opportunities. Interestingly, when the CVR left its offices in the renovated academic building to join the CEC, our academic department moved into its space as the CEC morphed, expanded and colonized more central areas of the college.

The CEC was a relatively short-lived endeavour, however. With the development of a new strategic plan for the college, called *Augustana 2020*, came a renewed focus on student success before and after graduation. In this context we can understand success in neoliberal terms, as individual competitive advantage and financial gain (Bylsma 2015; Davies and Bansel 2007). The first strategy built into this plan, Enhanced Preparation, calls for the college to 'Explicitly focus the Augustana experience to better assist students in taking the next step in their vocational journeys through high graduate school admission rates and timely placement in rewarding and meaningful jobs and careers' (Augustana 2020: 2). The strategic plan was approved by the college's Board of Trustees at their January 2014 retreat, and the creation of CORE (Careers, Opportunities, Research, Exploration) began shortly thereafter. Over the summer of 2014, the CEC and Advising offices and the renamed and expanded Office of Career and Professional Development were relocated 'to the heart of campus' (Augustana 2020: 2) and integrated as CORE, taking over half of the ground floor of a central academic building plus additional offices on the third floor. At the time of writing CORE was headed up by an Executive Director of Career and Professional Development, an Assistant Director of Employer Relations, an Assistant Director of Internships, and an Assistant Director of Vocational Exploration. It is not an exaggeration to say that the resources dedicated to career planning and professional development have grown exponentially over the past several years on our campus. We have gone from a handful of administrators and staff members overseeing the Career Center and the Center for Vocational Reflection to CORE's greatly expanded and centralized presence and administrative structure.

One initiative of CORE is the 'Viking Score', a voluntary programme named for the college's athletic teams and mascot, designed to track students' degree of preparedness for professional life after college. Students earn points toward their score by doing things such as meeting with career development staff, creating a LinkedIn profile or a personal brand website, or attending a job/grad school fair or career workshop. The scorecard suggests minimum scores for each year as students move through their undergraduate education. An alumna, Valerie Lambert Kroll, is quoted on the scorecard: 'The Viking Score takes the ambiguity out of the steps students must take to acquire a full-time position following graduation' (Viking Score). As anthropologists in a liberal arts setting who encourage our students to embrace ambiguity and nuance when approaching questions and problems, our mission feels at odds with the neoliberal telos of risk management through individual self-mastery and decision making that generates outcomes commensurate with market values (Murphy 2000).

Certainly, the college has always wanted its students to achieve success after graduation, but our commitment to Enhanced Preparation for life beyond undergrad via CORE's services more explicitly articulates the terms of that success (full-time employment or grad school admissions), a quantified roadmap toward it (Viking Score) and a timeline for it (within a year of graduation). In this way, engaging with CORE shapes students' definitions of and expectations for success, and the meaning of their education, in very concrete and measurable ways. The centrality of CORE's services and the Viking Score's quantified reassurance that students are doing the right things and enough of them to achieve these goals signal a heightened concern for the professional preparation of undergraduate students and their ability to attain or maintain a middle-class or higher-class position (Lyon-Callo 2015: 80–1). The reification of the multifaceted process of preparing for life after college into a scorecard evokes critiques of the quantification built into neoliberal reforms that have permeated universities in other OECD nations (Shore and Wright 2000; Shore 2008). Cris Shore argues that we have good reason to be wary of new methods of assessment that confuse 'accountability with accountancy' and flatten complex outcomes into a singular variable (Shore 2008: 281). In this instance, consumerist values of maximized income and return on investment form the subtext of the score's quantification.

Although there are modest prizes and incentives for meeting yearly Viking Score point targets, students who participate in this programme are, in the language of neoliberalism's critics, self-regulating their time and experiences in service of postgraduate goals. In a challenging economic climate, Vincent Lyon-Callo queries,

'What alternatives are available to [students] except to struggle along with an individualized strategy of credentialising themselves while hoping and praying that they will be among the lucky ones' (2015: 96)? We see further evidence of professional subject-making in the mini-résumés that populate students' email signature files, which list their major and minor programmes of study, their employment and leadership roles, and the student organizations to which they belong. Students are the responsibilized subjects who monitor and quantify their progress on scorecards and document their participation in myriad co-curricular opportunities (Shear and Hyatt 2015: 6). From a Foucauldian perspective, we argue that through techniques of the self like the Viking Scorecard, students' subjectivities are moulded to institutional ideals of professional preparation (Foucault 1998). In systems of neoliberal governance, Anna Gradin Franzen proposes that 'individuals are not forced into conformity; rather, they are expected to willingly work on their own selves, to internalize societal norms and behave accordingly' (2015: 252).

The college also benefits when students achieve the goals of full-time employment and graduate school placement because these successes can be advertised to prospective students and their families for recruiting purposes. Further, metrics such as these expose a neoliberal model of college consumption in which 'universities sell their products to students and students choose which products – degrees and accreditations – will most benefit them in their aim to produce future revenue' (Shear and Zontine 2015: 112). Indeed, during the early drafting of this chapter, we received an email notification that our college was investigating the purchase of a Customer Relations Management system to better coordinate the recruitment and enrolment of new students.

The Viking Scorecard resonates with the rating system or scorecard for institutions of higher learning that was proposed by President Obama in 2013. Obama's rating system would assess colleges' and universities' average student debt and repayment track record, their on-time graduation rate and their graduates' workforce performance with the goal of helping students and their families weigh the value of an education at a particular institution (Obama 2013; Shear and Hyatt 2015: 1). Although a more comprehensive clearing house of data on the nation's colleges and universities replaced the narrower and more quantitative initial vision for this tool, Shear and Hyatt draw attention to the 'ideological context' of the original proposed system, in which 'education reform is necessary for individual economic success because of a broader discursive framework shaping education and economic policy today, where "greater and global competition in a knowledge-based economy" is understood as a key fact of our current lives' (2015: 2). Although US colleges and universities have long been ranked by *US News and World Report*, *The Princeton Review*, *Forbes* and others, the proposed national scorecard and the launch of the website that replaced it can be understood as an effort to gather the United States' myriad institutions of higher learning under an umbrella of assessment that resembles the academic 'audit cultures' of other OECD nations (Strathern 2000; Shear and Hyatt 2015: 1). Under a Trump presidency, chaotic as it has been from the start, it is difficult to know where any of this will end up.

Through professionalizing techniques of the self – creating LinkedIn profiles, completing internships, job shadowing, attending professional development workshops – students are acquiring experiences and skills that we anticipate will benefit them as graduates in the world of work or graduate school, but is this the learning that higher education is meant to facilitate? The Center for Vocational Reflection, with its language of calling rather than (or in addition to) career, no longer exists. At the time of writing, as one of the eight dimensions of CORE's work that were identified on its homepage, Vocational Reflection was the only one to which links and student photos and narratives were not attached. Clicking on Vocational Reflection, literally, got you anywhere. CORE crafts its own narrative about what college is for: career preparation and financial success. In this day and age of unprecedented college costs, student loan debt and economic uncertainty, it is understandable that this is a dominant narrative, and one to which colleges must respond. Students and their families want reassurances that the tens of thousands of dollars they are spending on college will generate returns, and sooner rather than later. We have to prove to them that their investment will be worth it, and that case needs to be made in financial terms.

This narrative does not necessarily direct or affect what professors do in their classrooms, although CORE does offer to lead workshops in faculty members' classes when they are travelling for academic conferences. A few years ago, the faculty adopted nine college-wide Student Learning Outcomes that include Disciplinary Knowledge, Quantitative Literacy, Collaborative Leadership, Intercultural Competency and Intellectual Curiosity. Academic departments have mapped their curricula onto these outcomes, which comprise the toolkit graduates will bring into the world. However, it is easy to see these as proximate outcomes that feed the ultimate outcome of employment, postgraduate studies and financial success. Shore suggests that we have experienced 'a wider paradigm shift from the idea of tertiary education as a "public good" geared to producing an educated citizenry to a conception of higher education as an individual economic investment' (Shore 2010: 15). What happens when students and their families are primarily focused on that ultimate outcome? We argue that it can make it more difficult for faculty members to impart the value of knowledge, skills and dispositions that do not as readily translate into financial gain for individual students. We need students who are ethically engaged and concerned with social justice. We need students who care about environmental sustainability. We need students who understand how to navigate social and cultural difference. These may ultimately be marketable interests and skills, but that is not why we are teaching them. We are teaching them because we see needs in the world for these skills and dispositions.

Symbiosis/entrepreneurialism: Liberal arts faculty as neoliberal subjects

One powerful nexus of ambivalence on our campus, mentioned in passing above, lies at the intersection of a so-called 'pure' liberal arts curriculum versus 'pre-professional' programmes (and they are often pitted against one another using the language of one *versus* another). Some liberal arts colleges do not offer any programmes with career-specific tracks. Instead of a degree in business, one would pursue economics; instead of pre-medicine, a student would study biology; and there would certainly be no programmes in pre-optometry or accounting, either. One of the common myths among the faculty, at least among those critical of the fact that Augustana mixes more traditional liberal arts programmes with pre-professional training, is that the latter have grown over the years and now dominate the college. But this is simply untrue. The college was founded in 1860 with a stated mission to train (Swedish) Lutheran ministers and teachers (Blanck 2006: 50). Very early on, Augustana added programmes in stenography, bookkeeping and secretarial skills. By the 1880s, a 'commercial department' for professional training in business was established alongside a conservatory of music and other programmes that are associated with the more traditional liberal arts such as political economy, philosophy, history and mathematics (ibid.: 51–2). By 1910, 668 graduates came out of the commercial department as opposed to 468 from the general college (ibid.: 50). Simultaneously, the religious mission of the college and its focus on Swedish language and culture diminished as it trained fewer and fewer ministers (ibid.: 57) and offered tracks in English as well as Swedish. Today, only a small handful of graduates enter the seminary each year, although the college is still (but far more loosely) affiliated with the Evangelical Lutheran Church in America, and a small programme in Swedish still exists. Despite this rather significant change in the institution's identity, one thing has remained constant over the course of a century and a half: Augustana College has always balanced a more traditional liberal arts curriculum with pre-professional training. These dual roles of the college extend back to its very origins and have led to an institutional version of what Smelser describes as the 'opposing affective orientations' (1998: 5) caused by ambivalence. The programmes that have graduated the greatest number of students over the past several years – biology/pre-medicine, business administration, psychology, education, communication studies/multimedia journalism/mass communication – indicate a strong pre-professional orientation within today's student body (Measures of Institutional Effectiveness and Mission Fulfillment 2016: 7). Like other more traditional liberal arts programmes, anthropology must compete for its students.

Most students we encounter as first-year advisors and as instructors in introductory-level courses have come to college with either a vague sense of what anthropology is, or a specific but very narrow conception of the discipline through one of its subfields, often archaeology or forensic anthropology. At best, we recruit a handful of prospective students each year who are interested in anthropology from the start. We more typically have to win them to the discipline through the courses we teach, and compete with programmes that have better name recognition and are more concretely anchored to professions. Students do not immediately connect anthropology to career prospects and there is, admittedly, an ease with which a young person can say, 'I'm majoring in accounting because I want a career in accounting', that does not often apply in the same way to our field. Although we often attract students who are fascinated by human diversity and the study of cultures for their own sake, decisions about majoring in a given discipline or programme are often grounded in practical concerns about postgraduate job prospects. As discussed above, these decisions must be understood within the current US financial climate, coupled with the market-oriented concerns that draw students to particular institutions of higher learning and academic programmes.

It is not surprising or unexpected that there would be more pre-medicine or business majors at our college than anthropology majors, and many faculty members frame the relationship between traditional liberal arts disciplines and pre-professional programmes as one that is beneficial because it broadens the scope of pre-professional students' college educations. All students are required to take courses across the curriculum to fulfil General Education requirements that constitute approximately one-third of their overall credits toward graduation. Of course, this puts programmes in a very specific relationship, with one subset serving another. This relationship shapes a pattern than can be seen in programmes in the arts, humanities and social sciences that offer many sections of introductory classes in a given academic year. Because these offerings are linked to the General Education curriculum, there is demand for them and they are almost always fully enrolled. They can also be challenging to teach because the students are extrinsically motivated to take them, a sentiment that is reflected in the unfortunate way that students often talk about 'getting General Education courses out of the way'. These classes might be said to provide the finishing touches on a practical and professionally oriented plan of study rather than structuring its foundation. At the same time, upper division courses for majors in these same departments often struggle to meet enrolment minimums.

This sometimes fraught structural relationship can unfortunately lead to resentments across this divide because each 'side' feels less valued by the other. In part this is because two notions of value are at play simultaneously. For students and faculty in the social sciences and humanities, it seems that the pre-professional programmes stake a claim to most or all of the economic capital investment of a college education. Insults about the humanities or the social sciences (which are usually referred to condescendingly as the 'soft' sciences in these instances) as 'interesting-but-useless' majors are sometimes bandied about. On the other hand, students and faculty in the pre-professional programmes feel condescended to as well because the social sciences and humanities lay claim to far more intellectual capital. Pre-professional majors are insultingly equated in this narrative with anti-intellectualism. This is all exacerbated by the language we use at Augustana and elsewhere, as if only some disciplines lead to professions, while the pre-professional fields, it seems, do not provide much more than career training and are antithetical to the liberal arts.

We would argue that anthropology is both intellectual and provides skills of central concern in an increasingly chaotic world. 'Today just about everyone – administrators, students, parents, employers, policy makers, and most professors – has accepted the notion that broad, transferrable skills are the desired product of college', contends *Chronicle of Higher Education* author Dan Berrett (2016). Skills, such as practical technologies of the self, are the twenty-first-century canon. But which skills matter? Anthropology offers students a culturally relativistic disposition that helps render the strange familiar and the familiar strange in a diverse and globalized world. Ethnographic methods are a toolkit they can utilize to better understand behaviours and beliefs across the broad spectrum of humanity. In 2008, only months before the financial meltdown, we designed and implemented a curriculum that expanded Augustana's anthropology programme from a concentration within sociology into its own major course of study in order to develop these capacities in our students, but it is difficult to 'sell' these so-called 'soft skills'. The lion's share of our students remain drawn to programmes that are more explicitly pre-professional.

From the inception of anthropology as an independent major at Augustana, we have distributed a document to prospective students that emphasizes the broad range of careers that may follow from an anthropology major. Vincent Melomo articulates the conflicts he experienced in drafting a programme review document to 'sell' to his department:

> I felt compelled to market anthropology to our administration, to turn it into an attractive product they should want to buy, to make it seem like a good investment with strong returns. I was positioning students and parents as the consumers, the college as the business, and our program as the vehicle that would bring them together. I was doing neoliberalism, and I thought I was doing it well … I want to highlight that although my serving this neoliberal logic was obviously necessary, in the end it is also by some measure problematic that I did so.
>
> 2013: 367

Melomo's experience and our own speaks to academics' neoliberal bind. For small liberal arts colleges like Augustana, aggressively marketing our value to prospective students and intensively monitoring current students' progress (via a software package called Starfish Retention Solutions) and encouraging their persistence seems the only way to endure as an institution. Promoting the practical value of an anthropological education is a taken-for-granted necessity. These are sites of ambivalence we navigate as faculty members and neoliberal subjects.

This ambivalence highlights and generates questions about interdisciplinary projects that can be read, on one hand, as a symbiotic hallmark of a liberal arts approach and, on the other, as an entrepreneurial survival strategy. Bronwyn Davies and Eve Bendix Petersen explore 'the difficulty individuals have, within neoliberal institutions, of keeping separate the performances that have become the practical, strategic base of action and funding, and the professional values that may be in tension with those practical and strategic performances' (2005: 82). They ask whether it is possible to perform as a strategic and flexible neoliberal subject without internalizing neoliberal values (ibid.). How, they ask, can we resist naturalizing the discursive frames of neoliberalism with its focus on the measurable and marketable successes of the individual academic? Without a critical perspective, these technologies of the self simply become 'the furniture in [our] mind[s] – just there, invisible, and invisibly shaping the way [we] think', and our expectations of ourselves and our colleagues (ibid.: 85). When, at a recent full faculty meeting, our college president suggested that we might add an interdisciplinary minor or certificate programme in social justice, what motivated us to mobilize and suggest that this endeavour might best be housed in our academic department? Was it an understanding that the work that we do in our department is fundamentally aligned with explorations of sociocultural diversity and inequality as well as local and global struggles for social justice? Yes. Was it an understanding that this programme might add human and material resources, as well as draw additional students, to our department? Yes. This may be an opportunity for fruitful collaboration across disciplines and meaningful work for students, but it is also necessarily tinged with 'the pleasures of mastery within the game of neo-liberalism, or with [our] own narcissistic competitive survival, combined with the economic survival of the collective' (Davies and Petersen 2005: 95). These accumulative processes of creating new courses of study, credentials, and means for tracking student success allow us to see that the academy, even in our small and relatively private corner of it, is subject to the same neoliberal demands as other enterprises. For our colleagues at publicly funded research universities, financial gain and market value are more intimately connected to the products of their research. As faculty members at a private and tuition-driven college, our flexibility and entrepreneurialism are directed at recruiting and retaining a robust student body and declaring our (inter)disciplinary value to those students as consumers of higher education. Emily Martin's research on the flexible accumulation that is characteristic of late capitalism captures both the satisfaction of successful adaptation and the exhausting realization that adaptation is a never-ending process (Martin 1994, 1997).[3]

Conclusion

Neoliberal obsessions with measurement, big data, assessment, process, responsibility, accountability and rationalization are attempts to claim authority of the *truth-of-the-matter*, no matter what subject is at hand. And yet, instead of answers, the everyday consequence of neoliberalism is often ambiguity and uncertainty. In this sense, we follow Shear and Zontine in opposing the 'strong theory' of the neoliberal capitalist enclosure around higher education, and instead offer what they label a 'weak theory' that allows for 'contingency and possibility' (2015: 120). Those who adhere to the 'strong theory' assume that neoliberal discourse is 'a totalizing, global container … [and] thus becomes "extradiscursive": it is given the status of being real, irrespective of discourse, and therefore there is nothing outside of it' (ibid.: 119). We believe, with Shear and Zontine, that 'there is not one legitimate course, that of building a coordinated oppositional politics that might lead to revolution: we can also (or instead) work on cultivating and fostering non-capitalist relations and new subjective orientations right now, where we already are' (ibid.: 120).

Anthropology is valuable and we love to be able to teach it to students, but we do so within a context in which they feel they must be practical and career-driven (understandable given the climate, but this has also become conventional wisdom – it is important to take a step back from that and cast a critical eye on it) and we feel we must be entrepreneurial (Bourdieu 1977). This might generate wonderful and rich learning opportunities for students, but the market value of these moves looms large and it is increasingly difficult to focus on one over the other. Vision gets very blurred in the midst of the storm. It is in our best interests as members of this academic community and employees of the college for it to succeed as an institution and allow us to continue teaching anthropology to students, both those who are intrinsically motivated to more deeply understand human cultural diversity and those who are not. As Melomo argues, 'The potential role that anthropology in particular can have in transforming people, society, and culture is lessened if anthropology is done only in service to the economy or, taken to the extreme, if anthropology does not exist in such institutions at all' (2013: 369). At the same time, as Shore has argued, following Bourdieu, it is critical for us to interrogate the taken-for-granted and unquestioned principles that shape our experiences as members of academic communities (Shore 2008: 279; Bourdieu 1977). In this chapter we have explored our experiences as faculty at a US liberal arts college to add a different context to the ongoing discussion of how neoliberal doxa is shaping higher education. This chapter is an attempt, in the midst of the crisis, to find a symbiotic space, ambivalent, contingent and nuanced, between neoliberal corporatism and a romantic ideal of the liberal arts.

.

Notes

1 We wish to rescue this word from E. O. Wilson's book of the same title. Although Wilson's sociobiological argument is wrong in our view, the concept of consilience itself, which goes beyond mere synthesis or multidisciplinarity, is valuable. As Wendy Doniger wrote of Lévi-Strauss, another great reductionist in his own right, "[t]he trick is to jettison [him] right before the moment he deconstructs himself" (1995).

2   Bonvillain and Murphy claim that '[b]etween 1850–1899, a total of 212 small liberal arts colleges were founded' in the United States (1996: 22).

3   Martin uses the term late capitalism, which others have suggested is interchangeable with neoliberalism (see Ortner 2011).

References

'Augustana 2020' (2014), Available online: http://www.augustana.edu/Documents/president/Augustana_2020_Strategic_Plan_Feb3_2014.pdf (accessed 25 May 2016).

Berrett, D. (2016), 'If Skills are the New Canon, Are Schools Teaching Them?', *The Chronicle of Higher Education*, 8 April. Available online: http://chronicle.com/article/If-Skills-Are-the-New-Canon/235948 (accessed 31 May 2016).

Blanck, D. (2006), *The Creation of an Ethnic Identity: Being Swedish American in the Augustana Synod, 1860–1917*, Carbondale, IL: Southern Illinois Press.

Bonvillian, G. and R. Murphy (1996), *The Liberal Arts College Adapting to Change: The Survival of Small Schools*, New York: Garland Publishing.

Bosman, J. (2016), 'Chicago State, A Lifeline for Poor Blacks, is Under Threat Itself', *New York Times*, 10 April: A12.

Bourdieu, P. (1977), *Outline of a Theory of Practice*, Cambridge: Cambridge University Press.

Bylsma, P. E. (2015), 'The Teleological Effect of Neoliberalism on American Higher Education', *College Student Affairs Leadership*, 2 (2), article 3. Available online: https://scholarworks.gvsu.edu/csal/vol2/iss2/3.

Confessore, N. (2015), 'A Wealthy Governor and His Friends are Remaking Illinois', *New York Times*, 29 November: A1.

Davies, B. and P. Bansel (2007), 'Neoliberalism and Education', *International Journal of Qualitative Studies in Education*, 20 (3): 247–59.

Davies, B. and E. Petersen (2005), 'Neo-liberal Discourse in the Academy: The Forestalling of (Collective) Resistance', *LATISS – Learning and Teaching in the Social Sciences*, 2 (2): 77–97.

Davis, D. (2015), 'Constructing Fear in Academia: Neoliberal Practices at a Public College', in S. B. Hyatt, B. W. Shear and S. Wright (eds), *Learning Under Neoliberalism: Ethnographies of Governance in Higher Education*, 151–77, New York: Berghahn.

Deresiewicz, W. (2015), 'The Neoliberal Arts: How College Sold its Soul to the Market', *Harper's Magazine*, 33 (2015): 25–32.

Doniger, W. (1995), 'Foreword' in C. Lévi-Strauss, *Myth and Meaning: Cracking the Code of Culture*, vii–xv, New York: Schocken.

Ferrall, V., Jr. (2011), *Liberal Arts at the Brink*, Cambridge, MA: Harvard University Press.

Foucault, M. (1998), 'Technologies of the Self', in P. Rabinow (ed.), *Michel Foucault: The Essential Works 1: Ethics, Subjectivity and Truth*, 223–52, New York: The New Press.

Franzén, A. G. (2015), 'Responsibilization and Discipline: Subject Positioning at a Youth Detention Home', *Journal of Contemporary Ethnography*, 44 (3): 251–79.

Kennan, E. (1989), 'Liberal Education in a Post-Modern World', in H. Costner (ed.), *New Perspectives on Liberal Education*, 25–39, Seattle, WA: University of Washington Press.

Lang, E. (1999), 'Distinctively American: The Liberal Arts College', *Daedalus*, 128 (1): 133–49.

Lyon-Callo, V. (2015), 'To Market, To Market To Buy A . . . Middle-Class Life? Insecurity, Anxiety and Neoliberal Education in Michigan', in S. B. Hyatt, B. W. Shear and S. Wright (eds), *Learning Under Neoliberalism: Ethnographies of Governance in Higher Education*, 79–102, New York: Berghahn.

Martin, E. (1994), *Flexible Bodies: The Role of Immunity in American Culture from the Days of Polio to the Age of AIDS*, Boston, MA: Beacon.

Martin, E. (1997), 'Designing Flexibility: Science and Work in an Age of Flexible Accumulation', *Science as Culture*, 6 (3): 327–62.

Melomo, V. (2013), 'The Art of Anthropology at a College in Crisis', in B. D. Lundy (ed.), *The Art of Anthropology/The Anthropology of Art*, 355–78, Knoxville, TN: Newfound Press.

Murphy, E. (2000), 'Risk, Responsibility and Rhetoric in Infant Feeding', *Journal of Contemporary Ethnography*, 39 (3): 291–325.

Obama, B. (2013), 'Remarks by the President on College Affordability – Buffalo, NY', Washington, DC: The White House, Office of the Press Secretary, 22 August. Available online: http://www.whitehouse.gov/the-press-office/2013/08/22/remarks-president-college-affordability-buffalo-ny (accessed 24 May 2016).

Ortner, S. (2011), 'On Neoliberalism', *Anthropology of This Century*. Available online: http://aotcpress.com/articles/neoliberalism/ (accessed 26 May 2016).

Pfnister, A. (1984), 'The Role of the Liberal Arts College: A Historical Overview of the Debates', *The Journal of Higher Education*, 55 (2): 145–70.

Rosaldo, R. (1989), *Culture and Truth: The Remaking of Social Analysis*, Boston, MA: Beacon Press.

Scott, B. A. (1984), *The Liberal Arts in a Time of Crisis*, New York and London: Praeger.

Shear, B. and S. Hyatt (2015), 'Introduction: Higher Education, Engaged Anthropology and Hegemonic Struggle', in S. B. Hyatt, B. W. Shear and S. Wright (eds), *Learning Under Neoliberalism: Ethnographies of Governance in Higher Education*, 1–29, New York: Berghahn.

Shear, B. and A. Zontine (2015), 'Reading Neoliberalism at the University', in S. B. Hyatt, B. W. Shear and S. Wright (eds), *Learning Under Neoliberalism: Ethnographies of Governance in Higher Education*, 102–28, New York: Berghahn.

Shore, C. (2008), 'Audit Culture and Illiberal Governance: Universities and the Politics of Accountability', *Anthropological Theory*, 8 (3): 278–98.

Shore, C. and S. Wright (2000), 'Coercive Accountability: The Rise of Audit Culture in Higher Education' in M. Strathern (ed.), *Audit Cultures: Anthropological Studies in Accountability, Ethics and the Academy*, 57–89, New York: Routledge.

Smelser, N. (1998), 'The Rational and the Ambivalent in the Social Sciences: 1997 Presidential Address', *American Sociological Review*, 63 (1): 1–16.

Strathern, M. (ed.) (2000), *Audit Cultures: Anthropological Studies in Accountability, Ethics and the Academy*, New York: Routledge.

Turner, V. (1969), *The Ritual Process: Structure and Anti-Structure*, New Brunswick and London: Aldine Press.

'Viking Score' (2016), Available online: http://www.augustana.edu/academics/core/careerdevelopment/viking-score (accessed 27 May 2016).

Wagner, D. L. (1983), 'The Seven Liberal Arts and Classical Scholarship' in D. L. Wagner (ed.), *The Seven Liberal Arts in the Middle Ages*, 1–31, Bloomington, IN: Indiana University Press.

Washburn, J. (2005), *University, Inc.: The Corporate Corruption of American Higher Education*, New York: Basic Books.

Wilson, E. O. (1999), *Consilience: The Unity of Knowledge*, New York: Vintage Books.

6

Matters of Anthropology and Social Justice: Reflections on Collaborations

Alisse Waterston

Backdrop to collaboration: Matters of morality and engagement

This chapter takes as its starting point Didier Fassin's call for a moral anthropology explored in a series of scholarly debates that appear in several articles and books (Fassin 2008, 2011, 2012, 2014; Fassin and Stoczkowski 2008; Stoczkowski 2008). Fassin's plea for the development of a moral anthropology reflects an intensification of the dilemmas anthropologists confront in the face of the world as it exists, marked by expanding globalization, militarization, inequalities, human suffering and ecological disasters (Fassin 2008: 333; see also Scheper-Hughes 1995; Escobar and Ribeiro 2006; Low and Merry 2010). Fassin's is not a new call but a reminder that the question of the anthropologist's own values, assumptions, prejudices and judgements needs to be made explicit at least in the mind of the anthropologist, considering that 'telling right from wrong and the necessity of acting in favour of the good and against the evil' (Fassin 2008: 334) shapes the who, what, where, how and why of any anthropological endeavour. The discussions between Fassin and his interlocutors go beyond this aspect, for it includes 'morals' as the object of ethnographic inquiry without prejudice (Fassin and Stoczkowski 2008: 331). Still, values, judgements and politics are partners in the dance of the dialectic between 'moral positionalism' and 'cultural relativism' (Caduff 2011: 466). The critical perspective is necessary but likely insufficient in resolving the dilemmas and contradictions of the anthropologist who hovers 'on the threshold of Plato's cave ... from where it is possible to go inside and outside' (Fassin 2011: 485; see also Stoczkowski 2008: 350), shifting between standpoints depending on the details.

In a discussion of the meanings of the word 'moral', Fassin acknowledges that 'moral anthropology' can imply 'a do-gooder's anthropology ... a moral engagement in the world with the ultimate intention to make it better' (2012: 3), as much true for the individual anthropologist as for anthropology as a discipline. Stoczkowski references the latter in his observation that 'The moral longings of anthropology, from its first founding projects right up until its most recent developments, relied on the conviction that our discipline would be able to use its knowledge about society in order to reform society' (Stoczkowski 2008: 350). Eric Wolf said as much in 1980, where he noted that anthropologists have long sought to identify 'what anthropology could offer the world [and] to address a wide range of public issues' (1980: E9). Wolf mostly talked about Margaret Mead. Today, we talk about dozens of anthropologists and could cite hundreds more (Haugerud 2016).[1]

There is no turning back from an explicitly engaged anthropology. We are left with its 'perils and promises', to use Kay Warren's words (2006: 213), which Fassin, Stoczkowski and others recognize may expand or limit knowledge, may facilitate analysis or inhibit it, may occlude or uncover information, and may advance or hinder understanding. Amid the moral longing in anthropology to do good, there is also no way to avoid critical reflexivity – no turning away from reflecting on the limitations, possibilities and contradictions of the engaged observer standing at the threshold of Plato's cave (Sanford and Angel-Ajani 2006). Feminist anthropologists and those looking to decolonize the discipline have long issued the call for critical reflexivity, recognizing that anthropologists are always 'at risk of participating in ideologies blind to [their] own', a caution Fran Mascia-Lees, Patricia Sharpe and Colleen Cohen (1989: 16) offered the discipline over three decades ago. This is not accusation but reminder that all modes of thought have social origins, the specifics of which must be brought out of the shadows of history. It implores anthropologists to be consistently mindful of their own judgements, centrisms and privileges (Jones 1991: 192; Mannheim 1966 (1935); see also Allen and Jobson 2016).

Likewise, Fassin posits that 'The more we are conscious and critical of our own moral presuppositions or certainties – instead of keeping them in the black box of self contentment – the more we are capable of respecting the epistemological grounds and of preserving the political engagements of our scientific work' (2008: 338). This brings me to the point of this chapter: in the epistemological dimensions of my critical reflection, I acknowledge the moral commitments and ethical positions that shape my world view as an anthropologist and that shape the direction of my engagement in the world. Politics, history and political economy are never far from those commitments and positions. Through the lens of critical reflexivity, in this autoethnographic narrative I explore and translate my raw experiences in three domains of my anthropological engagement – the classroom, writing and publishing, and in a professional society of anthropologists – to consider the creative dimensions of collaboration. In each of these domains, I have 'delivered anthropology differently' (Skinner, this volume): as part of an interdisciplinary undergraduate internship programme focused on social justice and social change; in relation to the production of an edited volume featuring the work of non-anthropologist local scholars and activists; and as president of the American Anthropological Association in a time of crisis. In context of the contemporary neoliberal world and considering the location of anthropology within it, I examine my experiences for what they suggest about the possibilities and impossibilities of collaboration for a 'good, right, just or altruistic' critical anthropology (Fassin 2012: 5), for meaningful engagement and for the sustainability of the discipline.

Portrait of an anthropologist engaged with the world

I was drawn to anthropology because I believed it might help me understand how disproportionate poverty could exist amid great wealth in the most powerful nation in the world. It was the 1970s, and I was a schoolteacher in a working poor neighbourhood in Brooklyn, New York. I was right: the discipline taught me to examine the multiple connections between people and the history that shapes their lives, a way to understand the lived experiences of social class and its consequences in stigmatization, racialized poverty and homelessness. My training at the City University of New York gave me the benefit of being taught by Leith Mullings, Eric Wolf, Delmos Jones and Ida Susser, who collectively raised my consciousness about capitalist political economy, the causes and consequences of racialization, feminist intellectual thought, and the application of Marxist anthropology to understand the kinds of urban poverty issues I was exploring in graduate school and beyond. That education – in which 'going public and being engaged have been cherished values' (Ribeiro 2016: 3) – and my own sensibilities made it impossible for me to imagine approaching my life's work from a neutral standpoint. From the start, I subscribed to historian Howard Zinn's position that 'You can't be neutral on a moving train ... The world is already moving in certain directions ... to be neutral, to be passive in a situation like that is to collaborate with whatever is going on' (Zinn 2005).

This orientation led me to work in areas that have been traditionally undervalued in the academy as a woman looking to craft a professional, political and personal life in context of ever-fewer secure opportunities in higher education and ever-present vulnerabilities. In keeping with the principles of anthropology, I embraced a holistic orientation, refusing a narrow, linear course. That orientation led me away from androcentric models of scholarship to align myself with global, critical race feminism, political economic theory, and those scholars looking to 'decolonize anthropology' (Harrison 1991) and to participate in engaged, public anthropology (Low and Merry 2010). It led me to centre my anthropological projects in an urban US setting, which was looked upon unfavourably by the discipline at the time. It led me to embrace and participate in professionalizing North Americanist anthropology when that area was still considered anthropology's stepchild ... It led me to alternative ways of writing anthropology, and to developing intimate ethnography (Waterston and Rylko-Bauer 2006; Waterston 2014, 2019) as a form of critical feminist anthropology that forces confrontation with motivations, beliefs and commitments, requires the surfacing of epistemological assumptions, and necessitates recognizing situatedness in a hierarchical world and thus, the importance of acknowledging positionality in ethnographic work. In all of my work, I have been driven by these principles and commitments: that engaged scholarship has value, and that knowledge moves forward by challenging convention.

I have also been guided in my life and work by Carolyn Nordstrom's wise words: 'We all, as humans, have a responsibility to creatively offer something to the world. Not more than one person can. Just our bit' (2009: 370). Even as anthropology has helped me work through concerns about inequity and its roots in complex political economy, past and present, and to understand the powerful and sometimes imperceptible apparatuses of dehumanization and displacement, I have a persistent sense of impotence in the face of powerful local and global forces and human suffering.

Collaboration I: The Vera Fellows Program

In 2008, the John Jay College of Criminal Justice of the City University of New York (CUNY) where I teach launched an innovative student-centred collaborative programme with the Vera Institute of Justice, a non-profit organization in New York City that has been dedicated to criminal justice reform for nearly sixty years (Roberts 2009). The Vera Fellows Program would be the first of its kind at John

Jay, one of the twelve senior public colleges of the CUNY system, the largest urban university in the United States. The Vera Fellows Program was the brainchild of Jeremy Travis, John Jay's president (2004–17), who would administrate the college in the context of an austerity budget and pressures to conform to the demands of the neoliberal university. As a college whose mission is 'public service', John Jay consistently faces financial shortfalls for several reasons, including that it is a public, not a private university, its graduates tend to work in the public, not the private sector and thus its alumni donations cannot match those of Columbia University up the street or New York University down the street from this midtown educational jewel that serves primarily working-class/working-poor students of colour and new immigrants (Markowitz 2004). Given the facts of John Jay's financial state, the pressure on college presidents today to focus almost exclusively on fundraising, and the college's reputation as a 'cop school', Travis might have focused on (literally) capitalizing the opportunities of the expanding national security state in the post-9/11 period. Instead, Travis envisioned the college as a major teaching and research hub for the study of 'justice' in all its manifestations. At a time when other universities were shrinking offerings in the liberal arts, between 2008 and 2014, John Jay expanded them, developing strong humanities and social science programmes to complement its preeminence in the fields of criminal justice, forensic science and forensic psychology. 'Educating for justice' became the college tagline, easily visible on a wall of bold words that grace the 59th Street entrance: EDUCATING FOR CRIMINAL – INTERNATIONAL – MORAL – RACIAL – ACADEMIC – REAL – GENDER – RELIGIOUS – POLITICAL – ECONOMIC – LEGAL – PHILOSOPHICAL – CULTURAL – ENVIRONMENTAL – SOCIAL AND POETIC JUSTICE.

The Vera Fellows Program emerged out of this context. Even as it served as a vehicle for fundraising, it offered an extraordinary and rare opportunity for John Jay's mostly working-class/working-poor students, and the possibility of bringing critical anthropology into conversation with students who would not likely become anthropologists and colleagues who are not anthropologists. The year-long programme couples an applied-oriented, paid internship with a challenging intellectual seminar for ten students taught by a rotation of three faculty – at this time, a literature professor, a professor of social welfare and myself, the anthropologist. Students intern at one among the many Vera-originated, independent non-profit agencies operating in New York City that emerged since the 1960s to address gaps and injustices in the criminal justice system.[2]

The programme is hosted by the Interdisciplinary Studies Department, a fitting home for a project that explores social justice theory and practice from multiple perspectives. The syllabus is eclectic and seminar time is devoted in part to considering the ways in which internship experiences fit or conflict with poverty theory and stated public policy goals. With the criminal justice system as their focus, the Vera Institute and its spinoff agencies offer a lens through which students explore theories on or themes from law, literature, culture, criminal justice, and structural, political and interpersonal violence in relation to their participant observation experiences on the ground, in real-life service provider settings.

In this context, I am responsible for bringing anthropology into the discussion. Since it is one among several disciplines represented by the Vera faculty and the literature we assign, anthropology does not take a front and centre place as it does in dedicated anthropology courses. In such a collaboration – involving students, faculty, mentors at social service agencies and non-profit organizations – can meaningful engagement with critical anthropology be possible? Can the discipline retain its identity as a minor participant in discussions centred on justice and injustice? Does that even matter?

The dilemma at the centre of these questions is brought home in Jason Antrosio's post-Trump election reflection on Sidney Mintz and 'Anthropology's Unfinished Revolution'. Antrosio argues the importance of teaching 'Introduction to Anthropology' to undergraduates and providing what others do not: 'a dose of global history, and especially of the interconnected history of colonialism, capitalism and slavery' (Antrosio 2016). The diluted version of anthropology that I bring to the Vera seminar cannot attend that goal.

But it can bring us closer to information, deep questioning and analyses that matter, the substance of critical thinking that also relates to relevance. 'So what?' asks Gregory Bateson in an imaginary dialogue with an imaginary daughter who interrogates the father in an epistemological exercise revealing patterns in mind and nature (1979: 225, 242).[3] Put another way, Howard Zinn observes that every teacher must ask herself: 'Why am I doing this?' (2009: 15). Antrosio connects the issue of relevance to critical anthropology and history. Quoting Michel-Rolph Trouillot (2003), Antrosio writes: 'the ultimate context of [anthropology's] relevance is the world outside, usually starting with the country within which we publish rather than with those that we write about' (Antrosio 2016; Trouillot 2003: 114; see also Peacock 1979).

In the Vera programme, we start with the country within. The critical political, economic and social issues in the United States are at its core. Some anthropology is tucked amid the assigned short stories, political commentary and essays, and scholarly articles, including works on structural violence as theoretical framework for grasping the dialectical relationship between the individual (readily seen) and larger structural forces (more difficult to observe) (Galtung 1969; Farmer 2004; Farmer et al. 2004), and culture of poverty ideological frameworks from the past that all too often seep into contemporary public policy and social service approaches (Moynihan 1965; Greenbaum 2015; DelReal 2017).

The burden on anthropology to be sustainable in the shrinking academy and to retain its identity amid interdisciplinary collaboration of this kind is not my students' problem. In the Vera programme, students engage critical anthropology, but only as one among the rich perspectives on the human condition and on the social issues with which we contend in seminar. As most of my students prepare to enter the real world of the neoliberal national security state as workers in the criminal justice system or in criminal justice reform, what matters is that I provide them with as many language and analytic tools as possible so they may think carefully and thoughtfully about the work they will be asked to do. Although anthropology provided me with those very tools when I went searching for explanation of how the world works, the discipline does not have the corner on good data, information, theory and analysis. Even as I incline towards critical anthropology for the deep understanding it offers, I also know it is not exceptional among the disciplines.[4]

Collaboration II: Gender in Georgia

The backstory of my involvement in *Gender in Georgia*, an edited volume featuring the work of non-anthropologists, local scholars and activists from the post-Soviet Republic of Georgia, began in earnest the day I received word my application was accepted by the International Scholars Program of the Open Society Foundations (Barkaia and Waterston 2017). Touted as a means of contributing to higher education reform in post-Soviet states of south-eastern Europe and Eurasia, the Academic Capacity Development Program offered financial support to 'promising local scholars' (called 'Returning Scholars') and scholarly expertise (called 'International Scholars') to social science and humanities departments in 'progressive universities' (Academic Fellowship Program 2011: 3). As an International Scholar, I was formally assigned to Returning Scholar students and faculty working to establish and grow the undergraduate and graduate Gender Studies Programme at Tbilisi State (TSU), the country's oldest university. By means of a collaboration structured by the

Open Society Foundation, over the course of three years (2013–15) I came to know and appreciate the women, the constraints under which they operate, their projects, the contradictions of their efforts and of my participation in them. The book project emerged from this collaboration and our collective labour.

For the most part, my work involved consulting with individual students, scholars and gender studies department faculty on research, writing and publishing, curriculum development and institution building. Those involved in building gender studies at TSU constituted a small cohort of women, none of whom held a full-time position at the university. For the most part, the women who envisioned and developed the undergraduate, Master's and doctoral programme in gender studies supported themselves and their families with full-time or part-time work in one among the thousands of International NGOs from the West that became integral to the Georgian political economic landscape after 1991 (Ritvo et al. 2013: 14; Dunn 2012, 2014). The women recognized the value of publishing in English language venues to advance their individual scholarly careers and to institutionalize gender studies just as hegemonic, Western-centric models of scholarship became more fully entrenched, in part due to the orientation of the Higher Education Support Program of the Open Society Institute. As my tenure as International Scholar was coming to a close and as the Open Society Foundations shifted its geopolitical focus to supporting 'Academic Capacity Development' elsewhere, well-founded uncertainty grew among the women about TSU's support for and future investment in gender studies. I heard firsthand the lack of support during a private meeting I had with a principal TSU administrator, who remarked: 'I still don't see the point of gender studies.'

At the TSU department level, I had been called upon in my capacity as International Scholar to teach seminars on writing and publishing in the academy and to work with individual women on their written papers, helping prepare them for publication. The vision for the edited volume emerged from these seminars and one-on-one discussions, and in context of the programme's precarious position within the university. We would deliver to any sceptical administrator an important volume on gender in Georgia, disseminating critical knowledge and information for an international scholarly audience by a highly reputable English-language international publisher. I served as co-editor with Maia Barkaia, a young Georgian scholar who received her PhD in gender studies from TSU in 2014.

At its core, the volume provides the first-ever, woman-centred collection of research and analysis on Georgia by mostly Georgian scholars and activists.

It offers a feminist critique of power in its many manifestations, is itself an assessment of women's political agency in Georgia, and reclaims a history that is in process of being written – themes captured in the book's full title: *Gender in Georgia: Feminist Perspectives on Culture, Nation, and History in the South Caucasus* (2017). Georgia is at a critical juncture, reinventing itself as a nation state in the post-Soviet period. The post-Soviet transition is gendered; 'gender', broadly speaking, is the lightning-rod issue around which controversy swirls and contradictions are revealed. Georgian women are manoeuvring to cope with and accommodate the new (neoliberal) economic, social and political order, activists are demanding policies to transform discourses and women's lives, and feminist scholars are struggling to institutionalize and professionalize gender studies at the country's oldest university even as they investigate, document and theorize gender in Georgia.

From my perspective, the collaborative book project is itself an instance of decolonizing post-Soviet gender research and an alternative to androcentric knowledge production. As co-editor of the volume, I have put myself to use by facilitating access to resources enabled by my sociopolitical location and professional position as a tenured professor in the United States with knowledge and experience in scholarly publishing. I have multiple motivations for collaborating on this project. For one, it is a response to the call by anthropology to recognize one's own location in multiple fields of power and to act accordingly in a responsible and ethical way. At least since the mid-1980s with the publication of the widely referenced *Writing Culture*, anthropologists have reflected deeply on the politics and poetics of representation, questioning the right, ability and reasons for speaking on behalf of others (Clifford and Marcus 1986). Many anthropologists have come to understand, as Gupta and Ferguson put it, that all participants in any project are situated within a field of power relations and are products of shared historical processes that operate in a world of culturally, socially and economically interconnected and interdependent spaces (1992: 14, 16, 17; see also Harrison 1991). With this understanding, and appreciating that I at once represent, reproduce and seek to resist Western global hegemony, in this project I adopt the Paul Farmer/Partners In Health credo to shift resources from where there are too many to where there are too few, and to use my privilege where I have it to support others seeking *their own flourishing*.

However, the contradictions of my position and my collaboration are near, starting with my status as International Scholar of the Open Society Foundations that has had a presence in Georgia since 1994 'to help the country pursue the development of a democratic and open society after Georgia gained independence from the Soviet Union in 1991 [using] donor funding, partnerships, and training to help Georgia's transition process move forward and to meet the economic, political, and social challenges it has faced' (Open Society Georgia Foundation). The organization is a vested stakeholder and operator in the unfolding of Georgia's neoliberal political economy, evidenced by its active role in 'assist[ing] the opposition' leading up to and after the Rose Revolution of 2003 (Wheatley 2005: 189; Esadze 2007: 112; Machavariani 2007: 45). The organization's interests are not necessarily aligned with the interests and motivations of actors on the ground who receive support from the Open Society Foundation. Nevertheless, it is a significant force in fashioning the contours of a field of action that make some things possible and other things impossible for local actors operating on that constructed and structured field. In the Georgian case, the contemporary field of action is shaped in large part by that Western project of modernization with newly made liberal subjects and neoliberal capitalist political economy.

This discussion offers context to understanding the collaboration and to reading the volume. *Gender in Georgia* is created almost entirely by Georgian women – scholars and activists who live, work, think, act and write within the field of action delineated by the forces and factors outlined above. Nearly all contributors have been supported by these International NGOs, including the Open Society Foundation and UN Women, which provide career opportunity and stable employment in a place with a decidedly unstable labour market (World Bank 2015; Frederiksen 2013; Sulaberidze 1999). Their situation (and mine) also reflects the historical fact of Georgia's embeddedness in 'East–West', 'metropole–periphery' and 'Soviet–post-Soviet' tensions. In context of its strategic geopolitical location at the intersection of Europe and Asia, the situation of this American (Western) 'International Scholar' collaborating with Georgian (local) scholars has broad implications for understanding larger global processes and power dynamics. Despite the contradictions that my role in this collaboration represents, I have chosen to actively participate in it and help produce the volume in solidarity with the express wishes of my Georgian interlocutors.

Collaboration III: Leadership in the American Anthropological Association

My involvement and participation in various service and leadership activities in the American Anthropological Association (AAA) began in the mid-1990s when Maria D. Vesperi, a co-founder of the Society for the Anthropology of

North America, invited me to write a piece for that section's column in *Anthropology News*, an association publication. By that time I had been an association member for over ten years yet hadn't dared enter what I imagined were its hallowed halls. AAA seemed inaccessible: large, complicated, and run by what I imagined was a cabal of upper-crust anthropologists – the most unapproachable people in the world.

I welcomed Maria's invitation, which gave me the entrée to participate as a volunteer in the organization. Having completed my own graduate training in the early 1990s when, as today, full-time, tenure-track academic positions were few and far between, I worked as a 'practising' anthropologist in a for-profit research company, and carved out a place for myself in anthropology by means of the American Anthropological Association. AAA gave me the opening I needed to enter the field as an equal, as a colleague.

Over the years, one leadership role led to another. I learned how AAA worked and whom it served, why it existed and what it did. I learned that relative to other professional associations, AAA is a small organization with large ambition to advance anthropology in all its aspects, to support the interests of anthropologists, to disseminate anthropological knowledge and to help solve human problems. This mission drives all its activities, of which there is an extraordinary number. It is only when you stand up close and centre that you can see how exceptional it is. I soon learned that my initial impression was terribly naïve and distorted.

I also learned about the significant role of the association in fostering collaborative relations with individuals and groups inside and outside the field. That role is enormously challenging: AAA sometimes sees eye to eye with sister associations and sometimes not when it comes to scholarly and political issues and approaches to policies in areas ranging from higher education and publishing to advocacy positions and cultural heritage; and AAA members don't always see eye to eye on scholarly and political issues or the association's policies and practices. Standing up close and centre as a volunteer over many years, I came to understand AAA as a collective that embraces inclusiveness and seeks to address a hugely diverse set of needs and interests in context of the real-world condition of limited resources, a condition shaped by the larger neoliberal political economy. It is difficult to resolve the tensions when operating under such conditions.

I was elected to the top association leadership positions (Vice President/ President-elect and President, 2013–17) when anthropologists, anthropology and the association were standing at a historic moment with the most difficult of issues and the most difficult of conversations before them. The notion of the collective would serve as a guiding principle during the course of my administration; I believe leadership works best when it operates as a team, collaborates with others, stays in constant communication, remains as open and transparent as possible, keeps aligned with the discipline's principles of professional responsibility, and works hard to achieve the organization's stated objectives that include connecting knowledge and information to principled actions designed to ameliorate human problems.

As I anticipated taking on the AAA presidency in late 2015, I fully expected to focus my energies on ensuring productive discussion on difficult anthropological subjects, and to helping bring anthropology more fully into the public conversation about critical local and global social issues and policy debates. Top on my agenda was *World on the Move*, AAA's new public education initiative on migration – a timely, enduring and difficult to discuss topic that matters to anthropologists and to the larger public. Migration ties to many anthropological concerns, past and present, and across the subfields; processes and dynamics of contemporary migration intersect with the global political economy, involving law, labour, ideology, policy, war and more. From so many angles, perspectives and locations, with this collaborative public education initiative involving museum exhibits, public forums and collective storytelling, anthropologists could teach each other and the world about migration.

As it turned out, the toughest topic up for discussion in the first year of my presidency was Israel/Palestine, and the courses of action the association would take in addressing the very real and painful human problems, including those concerning academic freedom, brought on by the Israeli occupation of the West Bank and Gaza. The story of that year has yet to be told in full; my preliminary reflections are offered in a June 2016 letter to the membership.[5] For now, suffice it to say that with this hot issue, the discipline seemed at great risk of permanently fragmenting along political lines. AAA's activities and actions with regard to Israel/Palestine identified sharp lines of disagreement on what engaged anthropology looks like and what it means to engage in public anthropology. Despite the disagreements – perhaps because of them – the discipline and the association survived and continue to thrive. Nevertheless, the experience revealed that collaboration may be an honorable ideal, but difficult to achieve when faced with the clash of cherished values, which in this case were the principles of academic freedom and of standing in solidarity with a non-violent, global resistance effort against structural violence and oppression.

In the second and last year of my presidency, the toughest issues related to the then newly elected Donald Trump's various statements and 'promises', not least those that attack the value of critical thinking and scientific knowledge and information, and those that constitute threats to human rights, human dignity and academic freedom. During the 2015 AAA annual meeting, a charged atmosphere was centred on the tension between advocates for and opponents of an academic boycott of Israeli institutions. During the 2016 annual meeting, the charged atmosphere was centred on a collective sense of dismay, sadness and shock at the results of the US national election, announced just one week before the anthropologists convened. Under these conditions, collaborative projects were easier to achieve.[6]

In making decisions on behalf of the association, I know firsthand the challenges facing the leadership to: act in keeping with the responsibilities of the office they have promised to uphold; be responsive to the varied points of view among its members; follow democratic process as delineated in the organization's bylaws and the laws that govern its non-profit status; align decisions with the organization's core values and mission; worry about the association's sustainability and in turn the sustainability of the discipline in context of real-world, neoliberal economic conditions; and keep a moral compass with respect to the human and political issues at hand. It is difficult to balance these multiple mandates, which sometimes operate in contradiction: taking action that addresses one goal may threaten the integrity of another. For me, the most difficult initial challenge was to separate myself as an individual anthropologist (and how I might act or how I might vote) from my duties as an officer of the association, a challenge I addressed by returning repeatedly to the organization's bylaws and keeping true to its democratic processes. As I anticipated the second year, my great challenge was retaining optimism in the face of likely intensification of harmful and draconian state policies and practices, violations of human rights, academic freedom and indigenous rights, and the systemic and structural violence of racialization and racism. In a time of intense global and local injustice and civil unrest, the question of whether our efforts are or are not worthwhile weighed on me. This is not about any one issue. It is about nearly everything important the association tries to do, the decisions it makes, and the actions it takes amid competing shouts and murmurs, sometimes without guarantee of return on the effort.

Possibilities and impossibilities: The devil in the details

The reflection I offer in this chapter enables confrontation with the real as opposed to the theoretical in a moral anthropology touted as activity with the ultimate intention to make the world a better place. My narrative constructs and maintains a historicist perspective in which the 'reading' of the collaborative engagements I depict is situated in larger conditions and social relations within which the actions and activities unfold (Jameson 2013: 11). Fassin's anthropologist may hover on the threshold of Plato's cave shifting between standpoints, but that goes only so far in identifying positionality. The dilemmas and contradictions of any standpoint depend on the specifics: the devil is truly in the details because they reveal paradox, potentialities and limitations in vision, action, collaboration and sustainability.

Critical anthropology unleashes revolutionary potential when it offers analysis of historically constituted social relations of contemporary capitalist political economy and the conditions that result. Thus, critical anthropology explains how the world works, what is wrong with it and why. However, anthropologists tend to operate in the world as it exists, not as they may like it to be. I confess I am that kind of anthropologist. In all my engagements, some of which I depict in this chapter, I take the reformist's path. I may be a Marxist in theory but in practice, I am a liberal subject working within the logics of neoliberal capitalism. In my collaboration with colleagues and non-profits, I bring critical anthropology to my Vera students not for its revolutionary implications but to offer a nudge towards consciousness as they enter the world of work as it currently exists. Likewise, my collaborations with my Georgian colleagues facilitate their entry into the Western 'modernization' project that is part and parcel of the world order of neoliberal capitalism. Having accepted the fiduciary and other responsibilities as president of the largest association of anthropologists in the world, I have agreed to accommodate the needs and interests of multiple stakeholders, collaborating with them to maintain the organization and the discipline in their current forms, which is not at all revolutionary. This analysis points to the impossibilities – or at least the limitations – of collaboration for a 'good, right, just or altruistic' critical anthropology even as our actions and experiences may contribute to sustaining the discipline.

Still, there is significance to engaging in these collaborative activities: underserved, aspiring minority students get opportunities they did not have before; access to global platforms is opened to historically silenced women looking to speak their own minds as scholars and activists; and an organization's norms, practices and policies are improved by the leader's principles, commitments and decisions. Such activities – Fassin's 'do-gooder anthropology' – comprise a creative offering to the world, one's bit in the struggle, an ongoing if imperfect process, to effect positive social change amid the most hardened and harsh of structural constraints. Satisfying the discipline's moral longings is an imperfect process, but the struggle to achieve it must be pursued. It is a responsibility that comes with having such knowledge as anthropologists do about humankind and society (Waterston 2018). In the end, meaningful engagement may be all about the struggle – concerted, collaborative efforts to work through the possibilities and seeming impossibilities with consciousness and conscience.

Notes

1   For example, Angelique Haugerud identifies the 'stakes and breadth' of engaged anthropology on such issues as the European refugee and migrant crisis, Black Lives Matter, the Occupy movement, the Ebola crisis, Israel/Palestine, climate change, same-sex marriage and the attack on the Paris office of the satirical magazine *Charlie Hebdo* (Haugerud 2016: 585–601).

2   The Vera Institute of Justice supports projects and has spawned a range of independent agencies that began with the Manhattan Bail Project and today includes alternative to incarceration programmes such as Common Justice (https://www.vera. org/centers/common-justice), a pre-trial services programme called New York Criminal Justice Agency that enables defendants to be released on their own recognizance (http://www.nycja.org/about-cja/), victim services agencies such as Safe Horizon (https://www.safehorizon.org/) and dozens of applied policy research projects in criminal justice reform (https://www.vera.org/projects).

3   For Bateson, the process of knowing requires contradictory mental processes, which humans must hold together at once for knowledge to advance: 'we know a little more by dint of rigor and imagination, the two great contraries of mental process, either of which by itself is lethal. Rigor alone is paralytic death, but imagination alone is insanity' (1979: 242). Should anthropologists heed Bateson, the so-called divide between 'scientific' and 'humanistic' anthropology might melt away.

4   In a recent *Chronicle of Higher Education* essay, Carl Cederström and Michael Marinetto remind scholars: '[Y]ou aren't the only person who can talk and write about sociological matters. [C. Wright] Mills was early to point out that journalists, filmmakers, authors, and artists are doing social science, too. And their work is by no means inferior' (2016).

5   The letter provides reflection and background on the lead-up to the eight actions taken by AAA on Israel/Palestine. The letter, the list of AAA actions and a full set of AAA resources on Israel/Palestine are available online: 1) http://www.americananthro.org/ ParticipateAndAdvocate/AdvocacyDetail.aspx?ItemNumber=20835; 2) http://www. americananthro.org/StayInformed/NewsDetail.aspx?ItemNumber=13454; and 3) http://www.americananthro.org/ParticipateAndAdvocate/CommitteeDetail. aspx?ItemNumber=2247.

6   In the immediate aftermath of the US national election and inspired by the
    2016 annual meeting and three advisory motions from the floor of business
    meeting, between 30 November 2016 and 9 January 2017, AAA: 1) issued and
    posted 'A Resolution on Behalf of the American Anthropological Association
    in the Wake of the 2016 National Elections' (http://www.americananthro.org/
    ParticipateAndAdvocate/AdvocacyDetail.aspx?ItemNumber=20963) that
    was 2) unanimously endorsed by all living past-AAA presidents (http://
    www.americananthro.org/ParticipateAndAdvocate/AdvocacyDetail.
    aspx?ItemNumber=20962); 3) reaffirmed its commitments to academic freedom
    and human rights (http://www.americananthro.org/StayInformed/NewsDetail.
    aspx?ItemNumber=20966); 4) offered #AnthroForward: Post-Election Resources:
    https://blog.americananthro.org/2016/12/15/anthroforward-post-election-
    resources/; and 5) issued a release (http://www.americananthro.org/StayInformed/
    NewsDetail.aspx?ItemNumber=21027) announcing a series of further actions
    designed to strengthen the Association's commitment to protecting academic
    freedom, as follows: a) a statement that reaffirms the Association's endorsement
    of the AAUP Statement of Principles on Academic Freedom and Tenure (http://
    www.americananthro.org/ParticipateAndAdvocate/AdvocacyDetail.
    aspx?ItemNumber=21024); b) the establishment of the Rapid Response Network on
    Academic Freedom, charged with advising association leadership and members on
    threats to academic freedom as these may emerge in the United States and
    worldwide; c) affirming active membership in the American Association for the
    Advancement of Science's Coalition for Science and Human Rights (https://www.
    aaas.org/program/science-human-rights-coalition); and d) announcing affiliation
    with Scholars At Risk, an international non-profit organization dedicated to
    protecting threatened scholars and promoting academic freedom around the world
    (https://www.scholarsatrisk.org/). By means of these actions, AAA intends to keep
    watch on and oppose threats to the academic freedom of anthropologists. As with
    any policy and practice, the tensions and contradictions inherent in them will likely
    be revealed as events unfold.

References

Academic Fellowship Program (2011), '*Academic Fellowship Program Higher Education
    Support Program*', Open Society Institute Budapest Foundation.
Allen, J. and R. Jobson (2016), 'The Decolonizing Generation: (Race and) Theory in
    Anthropology since the Eighties', *Current Anthropology,* 57 (2): 129–48.
Antrosio, J. (2016), 'The Discovery of Sidney Mintz: Anthropology's Unfinished
    Revolution', *Living Anthropologically.* Available online: http://www.

livinganthropologically.com/2016/12/26/mintz-anthropology/?utm_
content=buffere9b08&utm_medium=social&utm_source=twitter.com&utm_
campaign=buffer (accessed 30 December 2016).

Barkaia, M. and A. Waterston (eds) (2017), *Gender in Georgia: Feminist Perspectives on
Culture, Nation, and History in the South Caucasus*, New York and London: Berghahn.

Bateson, G. (1979), *Mind and Nature: A Necessary Unity*, New York: Dutton.

Caduff, C. (2011), 'Anthropology's Ethics: Moral Positionalism, Cultural Relativism, and
Critical Analysis', *Anthropological Theory*, 11 (4): 465–80.

Cederström, C. and M. Marinetto (2016), 'How to Live Less Anxiously in Academe',
Chronicle of Higher Education. Available online: http://www.chronicle.com/article/
How-to-Live-Less-Anxiously-in/237920?cid=cp79&utm_content=buffer627f8&utm_
medium=social&utm_source=facebook.com&utm_campaign=buffer (accessed 5
January 2017).

Clifford, J. and G. E. Marcus (1986), *Writing Culture: The Poetics and Politics of
Ethnography: A School of American Research Advanced Seminar*, Berkeley, CA:
University of California Press.

DelReal, J. A. (2017), 'Ben Carson Calls Poverty "A State of Mind" During Interview',
Washington Post. Available online: https://www.washingtonpost.com/news/
post-politics/wp/2017/05/24/ben-carson-calls-poverty-a-state-of-mind-during-
interview/?utm_term=.8aca8890edaf (accessed 9 June 2017).

Dunn, E. C. (2012), 'The Chaos of Humanitarian Aid: Adhocracy in the Republic of
Georgia', *Humanity: An International Journal of Human Rights, Humanitarianism,
and Development*, 3 (1): 1–23.

Dunn, E. C. (2014), 'Humanitarianism, Displacement, and the Politics of Nothing in
Postwar Georgia', *Slavic Review*, 73: 287–306.

Esadze, L. (2007), 'Georgia's Rose Revolution: People's Anti-Corruption Revolution?' in
L. Shelley, E. R. Scott and A. Latta (eds), *Organized Crime and Corruption in Georgia*,
111–20, London and New York: Routledge.

Escobar, A. and G. L. Ribeiro (eds) (2006), *World Anthropologies: Disciplinary
Transformations Within Systems of Power*, New York: Berg.

Farmer, P. (2004), *Pathologies of Power: Health, Human Rights, and the New War on the
Poor*, Berkeley, CA: University of California Press.

Farmer, P., P. Bourgois, N. Scheper-Hughes, D. Fassin, L. Green, H. K. Heggenhougen,
L. Kirmayer and L. Wacquant (2004), 'An Anthropology of Structural Violence',
Current Anthropology, 45 (3): 305–25.

Fassin, D. (2008), 'Beyond Good and Evil? Questioning the Anthropological Discomfort
with Morals', *Anthropological Theory* 8, (4): 333–44.

Fassin, D. (2011), 'A Contribution to the Critique of Moral Reason', *Anthropological
Theory*, 11 (4): 481–91.

Fassin, D. (2014), 'The Ethical Turn in Anthropology: Promises and Uncertainties', *HAU:
Journal of Ethnographic Theory*, 4 (1): 429–35.

Fassin, D. (ed.) (2012), *A Companion to Moral Anthropology*, Malden: John Wiley & Sons.

Fassin, D. and W. Stoczkowski (2008), 'Should Anthropology Be Moral? A Debate', *Anthropological Theory*, 8 (4): 331–2.

Frederiksen, M. D. (2013), *Young Men, Time, and Boredom in the Republic of Georgia*, Philadelphia, PA: Temple University Press.

Galtung, J. (1969), 'Violence, Peace, and Peace Research', *Journal of Peace Research*, 6 (3): 167–91.

Greenbaum, S. D. (2015), *Blaming the Poor: The Long Shadow of the Moynihan Report on Cruel Images About Poverty*, New Brunswick, NJ: Rutgers University Press.

Gupta, A. and J. Ferguson (1992), 'Beyond "Culture": Space, Identity, and the Politics of Difference', *Cultural Anthropology*, 7 (1): 6–23.

Harrison, F. V. (ed.) (1991), *Decolonizing Anthropology: Moving Further Toward an Anthropology for Liberation*, 1st edn, Arlington, VA: American Anthropological Association.

Haugerud, A. (2016), 'Public Anthropology in 2015: Charlie Hebdo, Black Lives Matter, Migrants, and More', *American Anthropologist*, 118 (3): 585–601.

Jameson, F. (2013), *The Political Unconscious: Narrative as a Socially Symbolic Act*, London: Routledge.

Jones, D. J. (1991), 'Epilogue', in F. V. Harrison (ed.), *Decolonizing Anthropology*, 15–23, Arlington, VA: American Anthropological Association.

Low, S. M. and S. E. Merry (2010), 'Engaged Anthropology: Diversity and Dilemmas', *Current Anthropology*, 51 (S2): S203–S226.

Machavariani, S. (2007), 'Overcoming Economic Crime in Georgia Through Public Service Reform', in L. Shelley, E. Scott and A. Latta (eds), *Organized Crime and Corruption in Georgia*, 37–49, London: Routledge.

Mannheim, K., E. Shils and L. Wirth (1966), *Ideology and Utopia; An Introduction to the Sociology of Knowledge*, with a preface by Louis Wirth, London: Routledge.

Markowitz, G. (2004), *Educating for Justice: A History of John Jay College of Criminal Justice*, New York: The John Jay Press.

Mascia-Lees, F. E., P. Sharpe and C. Ballerino Cohen (1989), 'The Postmodernist Turn in Anthropology: Cautions from a Feminist Perspective', *Signs*, 15 (1): 7–33.

Moynihan, D. P. (1965), 'The Negro Family: The Case for National Action', Office of Policy Planning and Research, Washington, DC: US Department of Labor.

Nordstrom, C. (2009), 'The Bard', in A. Waterston and M. D. Vesperi (eds), *Anthropology Off the Shelf: Anthropologists on Writing*, 35–45, Oxford: Wiley-Blackwell.

Open Society Georgia Foundation, (n.d.), Open Society Foundations. Available online: https://www.opensocietyfoundations.org/about/offices-foundations/open-society-georgia-foundation (accessed 8 July 2016).

Peacock, J. (1997), 'The Future of Anthropology', *American Anthropologist*, 99 (1): 9–17.

Ribeiro, G. (2016), 'Committed Anthropology', unpublished paper, Minneapolis, MN: American Anthropological Association.

Ritvo, R. A., G. Berdzenishvili, N. Khazalia, M. Khidesheli, A. Liqokeli and S. Samkharadze (2013), 'Public Attitudes Toward Non-governmental Organizations (NGOs) in the Republic of Georgia', *International NGO Journal*, 8 (1): 13–19.

Roberts, S. (2009), *A Kind of Genius: Herb Sturz and Society's Toughest Problems*, New York: Public Affairs.

Sanford, V. and A. Angel-Ajani (eds) (2006), *Engaged Observer: Anthropology, Advocacy, and Activism*, New Brunswick, NJ: Rutgers University Press.

Scheper-Hughes, N. (1995), 'The Primacy of the Ethical: Propositions for a Militant Anthropology', *Current Anthropology*, 36 (3): 409–40.

Stoczkowski, W. (2008), 'The "Fourth Aim" of Anthropology: Between Knowledge and Ethics', *Anthropological Theory*, 8 (4): 345–56.

Sulaberidze, A. (1999), 'Toward Poverty Eradication in Georgia', in A. Yogesh (ed.), *Poverty in Transition and Transition in Poverty: Recent Developments in Hungary, Bulgaria, Romania, Georgia, Russia, Mongolia*, 130–75, New York and London: Berghahn.

Trouillot, M. R. (2003), *Global Transformations: Anthropology and the Modern World*, New York: Palgrave Macmillan.

Warren, K. B. (2006), 'Perils and Promises of Engaged Anthropology: Historical Transitions and Ethnographic Dilemmas', in V. Sanford and A. Angel-Ajani (eds), *Engaged Observer: Anthropology, Advocacy and Activism*, 213–27, New Brunswick, NJ: Rutgers University Press.

Waterston, A. and B. Rylko-Bauer (2006), 'Out of the Shadows of History and Memory: Personal Family Narratives in Ethnographies of Rediscovery', *American Ethnologist*, 33 (3): 397–412.

Waterston, A. (2013), *My Father's Wars: Migration, Memory, and the Violence of a Century*, New York and London: Routledge.

Waterston, A. (2016), Letter to the Membership on Israel-Palestine Actions, American Anthropological Association. Available online: http://www.americananthro.org/ParticipateAndAdvocate/AdvocacyDetail.aspx?ItemNumber=20835 (accessed 10 January 2017).

Waterston, A. (2018), 'Four Stories, a Lament, and an Affirmation', *American Anthropologist*, 120 (2): 258–65.

Waterston, A. (2019), 'Intimate Ethnography and the Anthropological Imagination: Dialectical Aspects of the Personal and Political in *My Father's Wars*', *American Ethnologist*, 46 (1): 7–19.

Wheatley, J. (2005), *Georgia from National Awakening to Rose Revolution*. Burlington and Aldershot: Ashgate.

Wolf, E. (1980), 'They Divide and Subdivide, and Call it Anthropology', *New York Times*, 30: E9.

World Bank (2015), The Jobs Challenge in the South Caucasus – Georgia. Available online: http://www.worldbank.org/en/news/feature/2015/01/12/the-jobs-challenge-in-the-south-caucasus---georgia (accessed 8 July 2016).

Zinn, H. (2005), You Can't be Neutral on a Moving Train: A Personal History of our
    Time, [radio programme] *Democracy Now*, 27.
Zinn, H. (2009), 'Speaking Truth to Power with Books', in A. Waterston and
    M. D. Vesperi (eds), *Anthropology off the Shelf: Anthropologists on Writing*, 15–20,
    Oxford: Wiley-Blackwell.

Part Two

Anthropology in/of Practice

7

Anthropology, Art and Design as Collaborative Agents of Change for a Sustainable Future: The *Give a Shit* Project as Case Study

Laura Korčulanin

Social drama as inspiration for *Give a Shit*

The Chinese use two brush strokes to write the word 'crisis'. One brush stroke stands for danger; the other for opportunity. In a crisis, be aware of the danger – but recognize the opportunity.

John F. Kennedy 1959

I have been studying toilets for seven years. In the first several years, I conducted ethnographic research, observing a full range of issues related to toilets in public and private space: who uses them, when, where, how, and the degree to which people think about the various attributes of toilets and how they work. The more data I gathered, the more I realized that what I was learning was critically important and needed to be moved out of the locked-up space of the academy and brought to a broader audience. To make that move, I turned to applied and engaged collaborative practice, which became the guiding principle of my work and base for *Give a Shit*, an environmental research study and activist, performative action platform.[1]

This chapter discusses the Give a Shit project as a case study of innovative collaboration, a model of engaged action that researchers can offer society with planned and clearly articulated outcomes and benefits (Korčulanin and Ferreira 2016; Schneider and Wright 2005). The discussion presented here points to the important role of collaborative approaches for a sustainable future, such as those between anthropologists and designers in the emerging field of design anthropology (Rabinow et al. 2008; Gunn, Otto and Smith 2013; Pink, Ardèvol and Lanzeni 2016). Furthermore, I discuss my personal engagement and experiences from a collaborative interdisciplinary approach in the field of design anthropology inside and outside of academia. My project takes as inspiration Victor Turner's notion of 'social drama' (Turner 1987) to frame the environmental crisis represented by 'toilets' and how we might intervene in it. Following Turner, I recognize the need to move through a series of phases (breach, crisis, redressive action and reintegration (1987: 4); see also Kuhn 1996 on paradigm shift) in order to arrive at positive social change. The story of Give a Shit is how danger and crisis can lead to extraordinary opportunities for agents of change to positively impact society, today and into the future.

We live in a time when fast food, fast fashion, consumerism and overconsumption are ubiquitous, and where corporate interests have shaped people's expectations of hyperreal needs, which drastically and unscrupulously prevail over satisfying basic human needs. The negative impact on individuals exposed to this overwhelmingly media-monopolized world is painfully real, leading those who cannot fulfil unrealistic expectations to be seen as socially pathological. Beyond the personal crises, these expectations have also led to social and global crises (cf. Harvey 2011; Mau 2004; Ferreira 2008b). The coexistence of overlapping social, political, economic, environmental and ecological crises may seem coincidental (Bharma and Lofthouse 2007; Fry 2009). However, as Eriksen (2016) and others have documented, these crises have emerged as consequence of imprudent human behaviour (Eriksen 2016). People have become oblivious to these crises, which have become normalized by the routine of daily life: the way we think and speak; what, when and how we eat and consume; and the ways in which we relate to other people, nature and the world. The concept of the 'Anthropocene', whereby 'the Earth has moved into a novel geological epoch characterized by human domination of the planetary system' (Malhi 2017: 77), captures these dynamic relationships and their negative consequences (Olsson 2017; Tokinwise 2015; Eriksen 2016). The social drama of the Anthropocene also leads us to enter new 'game-changer' times when 'humans will become a positive force on Earth' (Olsson 2017: 5). Given that crises can lead to disaster or its opposite, an opportunity for positive change, I argue that we are at a crucial moment when more people are open to questioning the status quo, and many in the scholarly and applied sectors are eager to design novel approaches to fix the problems facing the world we live in.

I see anthropologists and other social scientists as among the main 'game-changers' for the issues we face today. Given the current crisis, more than ever we need radically innovative ways of thinking and approaching problems, building on the strengths of academic disciplines and applying what we know to addressing social needs (after Korčulanin and Ferreira 2016: 145; see Tischner and Stebbing 2015).

With the *Give a Shit* project, which I envisioned and created in 2013, I present an example of good practice where anthropological research serves as an inspiration for all levels of the project: research, education, consultancy, and artivism, through which we use art and activism as a mediating tool to pass critical messages to society through creative performative and artistic actions. The Give a Shit project is a multidimensional, interdisciplinary, awareness-raising action platform, focusing on sustainable urban water management and sanitation in cities, the goal of which is simultaneous technological innovation and social change. As will be discussed in the remainder of this chapter, the unexpected interactions among project collaborators (primarily anthropologists, artists and designers), different stakeholders and citizens have led to the creation of new narratives and new ways of moving forward out of the social drama that reflects the contemporary worldwide crises facing humankind.

Changing the rules of the game with collaboration and agents of change

You never change things by fighting the existing reality. To change something, build a new model that makes the existing model obsolete.

R. Buckminster Fuller 1982

As discussed above, we live in a very particular time, surrounded by very complex issues where paradigms used so far in our lives, policy, economy and after all in academia do not cope any more with the demands and needs of the present (Mau et al. 2004). Climate change, natural catastrophes, hunger, poverty, the refugee crisis, fake news are where the particular engagement of social studies and humanities is most needed.

Scientific research is a key to finding potential solutions for a more just and sustainable future. As such, the question I ask here is: 'how do we bridge the gap between scientific research and necessary solutions?' Therefore, this part of the discussion takes Thomas Kuhn's publication on scientific paradigm change *The Structure of Scientific Revolutions* (1970 (1962)) as a stimulus for rethinking anthropological discipline. Although Kuhn's 'scientific revolution' is based on notions coming from natural sciences, it preserves interesting aspects to reflect on them within social sciences and humanities. His futuristic vision of science in the time being is an exceptional contribution to the importance of the resiliency of science to its external factors and existing demands.

Kuhn's notion of 'scientific revolution' is based on a cyclical model: normal science, model drift, model crisis, model revolution and a paradigm change (1970 (1962)). This same model replicated to the state of anthropology makes me believe that we are in the moment of 'model revolution'. As such, it comes as no surprise that more discussions than ever are focused on the importance of interdisciplinary collaboration, transdisciplinary approaches and engaged and applied anthropology searching for new methods and technics to be applied (Dias and Gontijo 2006; Rabinow, Marcus, Faubion and Rees 2008; Fry 2009; Jordan 2013; Denny and Sunderland 2014; Podjed and Gorup 2014; Conti 2015; Manzini, 2011, 2015; Podjed, Gorup and Mlakar 2016). Subscribing to Kuhn, 'normal science' becomes confronted with crisis when:

> the awareness of anomaly had lasted so long and penetrated so deep that one can appropriately describe the fields affected by it as in a state of growing crisis. Because it demands large-scale paradigm destruction and major shifts in the problems and techniques of normal science, the emergence of new theories is generally preceded by a period of pronounced professional insecurity . . . Failure of existing rules is the prelude to a search for new ones.
>
> Kuhn 1970 (1962): 67–8

Likewise, anthropologists are being asked to rethink existing paradigms and to question the potential role we as academics play in promoting sustainable change. Demands and expectations in anthropology are already changing. The focus is on what comes after the research, how the experiences of fieldwork are gathered and narrated, and how they are made available apart from ethnographic description (Rabinow and Stavrianakis 2013). Although there is not only one model or one way to hand out solutions, there may be one truth which can serve manifold solutions. Solutions can happen only with a flexible and innovative paradigm adapted to the existing needs of society, and as Kuhn discusses, 'to do that, however, would have been to change the paradigm, to define a new puzzle, and not to solve the old one . . . Only a change in the rules of the game could have provided an alternative' (Kuhn 1970 (1962): 39–40). As such, to be able to create a change, we need actors who make this change happen – agents of change.

Throughout my professional career as a researcher, lecturer, consultant and artist, I have learned and experienced a wide range of possible applications of anthropological work in society. Nine years of experience in leading interdisciplinary teams on several independent authorship (AKULTUR–Academic.Culture.Nature 2008) and co-authorship (Žabnjek-Spatial Textbook

2009; Chambrette 2012) projects and current leadership and management of the action group Give a Shit (ongoing from 2013) has taught me the importance of resilience to the needs of the team, the project and its manifold requirements (sociocultural, economic, technological, political). As well, this same manifold professional experience has allowed me to understand that my role as educator and academic goes beyond teaching and informing people. It is to empower students, colleagues, clients and informants to become 'agents of change': contemporary visionaries and actors towards positive change (Korčulanin and Ferreira 2016; Dias and Gontijo 2006; Dexter and Prince 2007; Swing 2009; Battilana and Casciaro 2012; Manzini 2011, 2015). By empower, I mean to create an environment, situation or project with the right composition of methods, skills and techniques where individuals can feel supported, inspired and needed, and as such become engaged and active participants towards positive change. I also learned that collaboration, co-creation and social innovation should be considered as mandatory approaches towards a sustainable future and should become integrated as part of the curriculum in schools and academia. By using innovative didactic, engaging and co-creating techniques and by exposing possible ways to solutions in our educational systems, research laboratories and innovative curricula models, we are capable of constructing frameworks that would empower individuals and potentially inform agents of change. As anthropologists we should focus our objectives on combined strategies where holistic observation and problem definition is combined with solution-oriented practices.

Even so, there is still a lacuna to understand and research, especially considering the eventual application of our research in the most effective and impactful long-lasting way. As an anthropologist whose PhD research at IADE-UE (Lisbon) specializes in design, I am constantly learning new ways of applying ethnographic knowledge to living realities. Also, I am learning new methods from design (brainstorming, mind-mapping, cultural probes, empathy maps, costumer journey maps, affinity diagrams, etc.) that I am using within my projects for applied results.

To be able to bring together satisfactory systemic and innovative proposals for sustainable solutions, we need to learn new methods and techniques (from e.g. arts, performance, design, architecture) which consider innovative creative narratives for easier applications of our work closer to society. This would help us to present our written results in a simpler, more understandable way to those who might need it, especially in new policies, business models and services (Yuqiong et al. 2008; Boeijen et al. 2013).

Designing the future with collaborative design anthropology approach

> For years, I have dreamed of a liberated anthropology. By 'liberated' I mean free from certain prejudices that have become distinctive features of the literary genre known as anthropological works, whether these are field monographs, comparative studies, or textbooks.
>
> Victor Turner 1987: 1

I have learned through years of managing interdisciplinary teams, and collaborating in such teams, that individualistic approach in anthropology and some other disciplines requires various ways to accumulate experience, know-how and research into shared, cross-disciplinary framework of exchange in order to provide adequate solutions for the situations in need. In 2016, I was invited to become Lisbon's local project manager for the upcoming sixth annual event Why the World Needs Anthropologists[2] (WWNA) entitled *Designing the Future* and promoted by the European Association of Social Anthropology (EASA) within the Applied Anthropology Network (AAN). In 2018, I was proposed to become co-convenor of EASA Applied Anthropology Network WWNA, whose main objective is to become the main European network for scientists and practitioners who believe that anthropological theories, approaches, methods and skills can also be used beyond academic boundaries – to solve problems in practice. Through the experience learned from the organization and participation at Lisbon's event WWNA: Designing the Future, and all the interdisciplinary collaborations where I work mainly with designers, I have learned how significant collaboration between the two disciplines is for both fields and for our equitable and sustainable future.

For several decades, anthropology and design already meet at the crossroads of potentially beneficial collaborations (Smith 2011; Marcus 2010; Rabinow, Marcus, Faubion and Rees 2008; Korčulanin 2013). Anthropological ethnographic research and the field of design show shared interests in research subjects. In both disciplines, the main interest and focus of the research is gathered around individuals, society and behavioural attitudes. In anthropology we focus mostly on the first part: understanding and observing these concepts and defining their current state and issues surrounding them. In design we focus on the second part: production and creation of different products, services and systems that are later on used by people. From my personal experience, I would affirm that in anthropology we are mostly focused on holistic perspective and analysis of the situation/problem and its cause, while in design we mostly focus on solution-oriented methods and practices. So, it is not a coincidence that this experience and know-how from both fields starts to collide also on an academic level (Smith 2011). In the field of design anthropology practice, the place of anthropology research is to provide better insight into users' needs and their behavioural culturally differentiating habits, as well as having the potential to spark the initial creativity (Conti 2015) and encourage quality in design products, services, spaces and systems and any other kinds of project. On the other hand, design can serve anthropology by opening up new opportunities and innovative ways for applied results mediated closer to society with engaging creative design methodologies. Seeing anthropology as a *problem formulation-oriented discipline* and design as a *solution-oriented practice*, I believe that collaboration between the two represents a unique feature for systemic and sustainable solutions in the future.

Although lately human-centred design (HCD) and participatory design are becoming buzzwords in publicity models, we should not overlook the importance of quality data research within the emerging field of design anthropology, which is already showing beneficial outcomes for business, industry, communities and future cities. Overviewing some of the successful companies that base their work on quality data and ethnographic research (Anthropologerne from Denmark, VisualSigno and Stripe Partners from the UK, Horowitz Research from the United States, Beta-I from Portugal, global innovation, strategic and consulting firms Red Associates, Studio D Radiodurans, Insitum, Piece of Pie, Designit) and companies that apply and use anthropology in their services (Frog Lab, Fjord, Philips, Google, Microsoft, Volvo, Nissan) makes me believe that we have just started a cutting-edge discipline: design anthropology.

Additionally, the following research networks and networking platforms – Anthrodesign, Ethnography Matters, Ethnographic Praxis in Industry Community (EPIC), Research Network for Design Anthropology (KADK), Global Design Research Network (REACH), Ethnoborel – are affirming the importance of ethnography practice, design anthropology and applied anthropology through exchange of knowledge between academia and different sectors within their differentiating interest groups. These networks also support anthropologists to find employment outside academia.

On the other hand, within the design discipline, design labs and design projects are starting to give more attention to social design and social innovation and, as such, use ethnography and participatory design as their default method. The same design anthropology operative programmes are also apparent for educational and didactic purposes, where interdisciplinary curricula prepare students for upcoming adventures in real-life scenarios, bringing knowledge closer to society and empowering individuals to bring about necessary change.

I trust that usable results from a collaborative approach between anthropology and design will open bright new horizons in future years for both disciplines. As such, it is our responsibility as anthropologists to inform the world about the importance of ethical and critical approaches within ethnography research. Open-ended collaborative frameworks derived from interdisciplinary engagement provide valuable results for local communities, society, environment, business and industry, and are the basis of our sustainable future (Conti 2015; Bhamra and Lofthouse 2007; Denny and Sunderland 2014; Dias and Gontijo 2006; Jordan 2013; Manzini 2011, 2015; Schneider and Wright 2006, 2010; Fry 2009; Rabinow et al. 2008). In my experience, one essential purpose of the collaborative paradigm is to enrich our research, education and applied results (Bernarda, Ferreira and Neimeyer 2016). I feel that interdisciplinary collaboration creates a space for sharing experiences and knowledge. Furthermore, it encourages sharing of skills. This is why I believe a collaborative interdisciplinary approach may provide better outcomes and quality results (discussions, services, systems, spaces and products) leading out of 'social drama' towards reintegration of innovative solutions and models for well-being in our future. This kind of approach creates an environment of objective and holistic dialogue and offers possibilities to design adequate solutions. What is more, a collaborative approach with a varied palette of expertise, know-how and knowledge generated in the discipline improves quality and provides the capacity to engage with the real needs of culture, society and the world we live in. As such, it represents a potential model of agency for change and a unique feature to be integrated in anthropological work as a core value.

Give a Shit as an example of anticipated change

We need two hundred thousand dollars at once for a nation-wide campaign to let people know that a new type of thinking is essential if mankind is to survive and move toward higher levels. This appeal is sent to you only after long consideration of the immense crisis we face ... We ask your help at this fateful moment as a sign that we scientists do not stand alone.

Albert Einstein 1946

In the first place, I envisioned Give a Shit as an awareness-raising project reflecting on observed issues/crises related to water, toileting and sanitation. Due to the need to promote answers and solutions about necessary change within urban water management and sanitation, I transformed the project into an action platform, which unites individuals from different backgrounds (anthropology, arts, design, architecture, engineering, sociology and marketing) to work together in an interdisciplinary team towards a sustainable future. Give a Shit is based on an innovative model of collaboration between different disciplinary experts, bringing anthropology research closer to societal and environmental needs. Ethnography serves as a starting point in articulating creative ideas. Further developed through design thinking, system thinking methodologies and 'living lab' methodology (Ståhlbröst and Holst 2012), we include society and various stakeholders in the process of the research as essential interlocutors for the co-creation of final results/ final solution proposals. In this case, anthropology informs design and plays a crucial role in informing future stakeholders, engaging them in practice and encouraging them in more efficient implementation of sustainable sanitation systems. We use innovative creative narratives – educational, informing, shocking, engaging – and interventional artistic actions, always based on previous research, as the main mediating and communicating tools.[3] With help of new techniques, I am able to create a bigger impact within society and translate academic language into curious, interrogating and stimulating language whereby citizens, passers-by and online visitors are willing to take part in the upcoming change. I believe that this and other kinds of innovative integrative methodologies could overcome the ambiguity between theory and practice of academia and serve as models for change in the time of convergent crises we are facing today.

So far, the project has already engaged individuals from eighteen countries towards mobilizing actions around toilet, sanitation and water issues and has procreated possible solutions with the help of different creative narratives. Collaboration was established with different stakeholders: academia (research group UNIDCOM/IADE-Universidade Europeia, faculty IADE-UE, University John Jay Cummings); bathroom and water companies (Ablut, Roca, Roca Lisbon Gallery, OLI, Baur Technology); municipalities (City Hall of Lisbon, City Hall of Murska Sobota); decision-making bodies (UN-Habitat, ANQUIP, ADENE); non-governmental organizations (Sustainable Energy Youth Network, Science4 Sustainability); and artistic platform and co-work spaces (Lx Factory, Lost in Lisbon, Flecta, NOW).

Why #WeDoGiveaShit[4]

The concept of 'social drama' introduced at the beginning of this chapter, defined by Victor Turner, may be translated as disharmonic social process arising in conflict situations in society which should pass through the four main phases of public action for the change (1987, 1974). In the case of the Give a Shit project, I translate disharmony and the first two phases of Turner's social drama, 'breach' and 'crisis', related to unsustainable water use in our society, to innovative solutions through different solution-oriented steps which can be compared to Turner's 'redressive action' and 'reintegration' (1987: 4) for positive change.

Looking into contradiction and disharmony within water use, I am further presenting reasons for the concern, on the one hand, and inspiration for positive change on the other. Fresh, clean and accessible water is a common good (Ostrom 1990) and a human right declared by the United Nations, and as such should be valued and secured for future generations to come. The increasing demand worldwide for fresh water is one of the main challenges of this century. Climate change, extreme weather conditions, population growth and unsustainable water infrastructures are expected to alter the water cycle and, as such, represent the number one global risk to society (WEF 2015; WHO and UNICEF 2012). Uneven distribution of fresh water resources, bad management and increased demand from consumers and industry, urbanization and changes to global hydrology systems place our fresh water supply in peril. At the same time 'water scarcity already affects every continent' (UN-Water 2007), where 'one-fifth of the world's population live in areas of physical scarcity' (ibid.), and the prospects for the future are even more concerning. It is estimated that by 2025, half of the world's population will be living in water-stressed areas (WHO and UNICEF 2012). So far almost 80 per cent of wastewater globally is returned to the system untreated and is most probably never going to be reused (UN 2017).

Looking at the micro-scale domestic use of water – which was the starting point of the conception of the Give a Shit project – the Western system of flushing toilets means that with every flush we waste more drinkable water (between 3 and 7 litres, or with old flushing systems between 7 and 13 litres) than people in developing countries have for their daily usage (cooking, cleaning, drinking and hygiene) (UN-Water 2010). The Western flushing toilet design is one of the main users of drinkable water in our households, accounting for between 20 and 30 per cent of household drinkable water consumption (Korčulanin, Ferreira and Barbosa 2015a). What is more, over-consumption of fresh water in our toilets is combined with a waste of yet another potential resource for our self-sufficient sustainable future: human excrement. Human excrement is a valuable renewable resource for our future sustainable society (Korčulanin and Ferreira 2015; Korčulanin, Ferreira and Barbosa 2016). With the help of already existing technologies, human excrement can be transformed into clean energy. We can convert it into fertilizer and biochar; extract from it biofuel and biogas; transform it into electricity and bioplastic; use it as a construction material; and, believe it or not, we can already extract fine metals out of our excrement. According to the US Geological Survey, human excrement is worth millions; for a community of 1 million people, metals in biosolids were valued at up to US$13 million annually (Westerhof 2015).

From both an economic and an ecological point of view, with every new flush, we are not only spending enormous amount of money while consuming scarce planetary resources, but also wasting our own precious resource for a greener future. Today there are more people around the world with access to a mobile phone than access to a toilet. 'According to a study by the United Nations, out of the world's estimated 7 billion people, 6 billion have access to mobile phones. Far fewer – only 4.5 billion people – have access to working toilets' (Wang 2013; WHO 2012). Simultaneously, the fact that we flush down the toilet more drinkable water than people lacking access to it have for their survival (UN-Water 2010) questions the appropriateness of existing toilet design. Through the centuries, toilets have always brought significant changes to society. Until today, they represent one of the biggest advancements of our time (Korčulanin, Ferreira and Barbosa 2015; Laporte 1993). From an anthropological and design perspective, toilets as a case study may be seen as an eloquent object, significant for our sustainable self-sufficient future and an inspiration for action.

All the gathered data and research is the base for Give a Shit's actions, incorporated within its mission and main objectives. The project's general objectives are: focusing on water as a common good (Ostrom 1990) that should be secured for future generations; advocating an urgent need for technological innovation and social change within existing urban water management practices; advocating for sustainable water management in our future cities; informing policy makers and business on real societal needs related to water based on academic research. Its specific objectives are: focusing on tangible micro-scale of fresh water use in domestic usage: evoking positive values within society about our common (fresh) water resources; promoting systemic solutions for efficient and sustainable use of drinkable water in domestic use; promoting necessary change within the existing Western system of flushing toilet design (reducing usage of drinkable water in toilets); breaking taboo on toilets and constructing a dialogue; constructing guidelines for use as operational knowledge for those included in implementation and dissemination of sustainable sanitation systems.

Understanding the complex environmental challenges we are facing in our future, I can clearly subscribe to International Water Association principles, which state that 'the first line of defense against water scarcity should be a comprehensive demand management strategy that promotes sustainable lifestyles and creates tangible incentives to conserve' (IWA 2016: 7). As such, the need to transform theoretical results into applied practice and design solution-oriented strategies becomes imperative.

The Give a Shit project: 'Redressive action' as an example of agency for change

The Give a Shit project advocates for the engagement of science, research and gathered facts in applied results, bringing them closer to society and different stakeholders. Within the project I am advocating for the creation of a combined set of strategies whereby I believe problems can be solved and innovations promoted only once they are acknowledged and shared among society in either formal or informal ways (see Ferreira 2008a). General awareness of society and individuals is important, but it is not enough to make a change or mobilize individual stakeholders for a change to happen. As such, it is essential to consider the following key tasks defined by Randy Swing:

> [Spread information] in a context that helpfully defines issues and makes understanding complex phenomena easier … Communicating data-based information that identifies and disaggregates components of complex issues … continue (from awareness building) refining the language used in defining issues … ensuring that others can articulate the timeliness of issues … communicating what is not within the scope of the issue of reference … encouraging debate and discussion of the issues.
>
> Swing 2009: 10–11

I am including within the Give a Shit project a model of different steps for paradigm change, as proposed by Randy Swing, as a 'basic framework for how a new initiative moves from concept into integration. Each step includes opportunities for the institutional researcher serving as an agent of change' (Swing 2009: 7).

Through the First Step – 'build awareness' and Second Step – 'develop focus' (Swing 2009: 8–11), we are, together with invited colleagues, primarily focusing on communication and awareness-raising strategies related to water and sanitation issues in the developed world, always based on collaborative and co-creative actions with society and different sets of interdisciplinary individuals involved.

Based on Turner's 'redressive action' (1987: 4), the crisis is being here addressed with redressive mechanisms and different steps presented with the help of different creative narratives (e.g. art performance, photography, video, installation, exhibition and social media) for the experimental/research activities focusing on artivism and education. Our artistic performative actions and interventions are always placed in the real-world context and are focused on interaction and invitation of individuals to the participatory action and engagement in the public domain to experience the proposed narrative through their personal involvement. Previously gathered scientific data about toileting, sanitation and water issues is being communicated in interesting, humoristic, ironic, interactive and stimulating ways closer to society. Visitors and observers are invited to interact and engage with the performance, exhibition or installation and are thereby invited to become active participants and the key element for the construction of final results.

So far, as part of the First Step – 'build awareness' we have organized manifold artistic interactive activities. The main principle within the First Step is to create a concrete strategy for raising awareness about previously researched issues (Swing 2009: 8). In the First Step of the project I envision to inform citizens and increase their awareness around unspoken issues, primarily about wasteful attitudes within the Western system of flushing toilet design. Altogether, we have performed in public spaces in Lisbon six interventions/performances as part of the United Nation's celebration of World Water Day (22 March) and World Toilet Day (19 November): *1st Step to Give a Proper Shit* (Rossio Square, Lisbon, November 2015), *2nd Step to Give a Proper Shit* (Porta do Sol, Lisbon, July 2016), *Give a Poopcake* (Miradouro da Graça, Lisbon, November 2017), and three different versions of *Glass of Water* performance (*Copo de Água* at Largo do Camões, Praça do Comercio and Innovative Hub Mouraria, Lisbon, March 2017). With every intervention we have engaged more individuals to become part of our initiatives and inform them to act as conscious citizens who take better care of the resources in their daily life on a visible and invisible basis (invisible water footprint creation).

All the above-mentioned interventions are based on scientifically obtained results and ethnographic research using creative artistic narrative to bridge the gap between obtained results and societal needs. The interventions are aiming to raise awareness of the value we waste – water and human excrements – every time we visit the toilet. They are also advocating for toilet innovation and social reorganization of the existing Western system of toilet design and urging for behavioural change related to the taboo subject of toilets and human excrement.

All of the interventions – *1st Step to Give a Proper Shit*, *2nd Step to Give a Proper Shit*, *Give a Poopcake* and *Glass of Water* – are composed of performance and interactive artistic installation, supported and advertised through social media campaigns. Public intervention represents the tangible sphere of toilet issues where individuals can touch, smell, see and even take with them the precious objects: Golden Poops, stickers, poopcakes and informative booklets. The installation is composed of between 130 and 150 pieces of Golden Poops replicating the actual size of human excrement (various sizes; they are all different but not bigger than 30 cm). On some occasions, the installation includes a golden toilet, the Holy Toilet, which represents the centre of the exhibition universe around which the Golden Poops are being exposed, honouring the luxury objects to which one-third of the world's population still do not have access. Golden Poops and the Holy Toilet represent a futuristic vision of what the toilet should/could represent in our future: self-sufficiency with recycling of human excrement and no waste of drinkable water. The object is seen as interventional, political, informing and disruptive, with huge potential towards a more sustainable future.

In the Second Step – 'develop focus', focus means:

> enhanced awareness that establishes a fuller context of the problem or change opportunity . . . In essence, framing is moving beyond just presenting the facts to presenting the facts in a context that helps define issues and makes understanding complex phenomena easier.
>
> Swing 2009: 10

Presenting research data and in-depth analysis within their sociocultural and real-life context became the second challenge for interventions and actions of the Give a Shit project. Although the First Step and Second Step's key tasks and missions have many crossover points, in the Second Step our actions became more focused and consistent within their physically articulated environment. To be able to 'develop focus' consistently, we have, together with awareness-raising public space actions, created an online open *2nd Step to Give a Proper Shit* call to action, promoted on social media. With help of the internet and advertisements in online and printed (social) media, the project gained a huge wave of individuals' interactions from different parts of the world. Through the call to action, under the slogan and hashtag #WeDoGiveAShit we have invited interested individuals to participate in our social media campaign. Each individual was asked to share their toilet story and/or water and sanitation concerns. Surprisingly, most of the individuals who took part in the action have

Figure 7.1 Advertisement for World Toilet Day, 19 November 2015. Photo: Pedro Carvalho Fernandes.

shared their own stories from their private bathroom space or toilet, speaking about the value we waste every time we use toilets or sharing their selfies with a piece of paper #WeDoGiveAShit in front. In addition, all the individuals visiting Give a Shit project's website or Facebook page could freely download informative and didactic water and sanitation-related stickers to disperse in public toilets of their own choice.

In the Second Step, together with the artist Xana Sousa I created the educational and informative permanent exhibition *Golden Poops in the Woods*, translated into interior design for the public toilet of collaborative and artistic space Lx Factory (Lisbon, 2016). The interior design of this toilet became an emblematic artistic space inspiring and educating hundreds of weekly users and visitors to Lx Factory. As such, the educational purpose of the exhibition around toileting and sanitation gains new focus and impact in the original context of the (public) toilet space.

Figure 7.2 Permanent installation *Golden Poops in the Woods* in the public toilet of Lx Factory, Lisbon, November 2016. Artists: Laura Korčulanin and Xana Sousa. Photo: Melita Gjergjek.

Formation of the action platform and 'reintegration'

After interviewing some of the participants and stakeholders who were directly or indirectly participating or experiencing Give a Shit actions, I realized that the project is lacking solution-oriented results and practices. Thereafter, I have moved the research objectives of the Give a Shit project from defining and understanding the problem and communicating it, towards learning and studying solution-oriented methods and practices. Acknowledging Turner's fourth phase, 'reintegration' (1987, 1974), which leads to a change, I understand that resolution of the problem and addressing the water crisis related to toileting must be negotiated with different stakeholders and integrated as a common legitimate solution for all.

As such, Give a Shit is starting to transform from project to action platform with its Third Step – 'increase knowledge' (Swing 2009: 11). Under the Third Step of the project, the awareness and focus are centred on defining issues that might be changed (ibid). Currently, I am mapping common understandings of issues between different stakeholders working in urban water management, so as to be able to prioritize those they should change first. This orientation has led me to organize different kinds of discussions and debates with the aim of finding innovative approaches towards more sustainable solutions for our future well-being. The project has been presented in formal and non-formal summits worldwide. I have given numerous lectures, talks and discussions outside and inside of academia. Within discussions and debates, the main focus is always to bring together multidisciplinary dialogue. I invite individuals and stakeholders from different fields (academia, research, business, industry, municipalities, policy agents, etc.) to discussions and lectures, where we all together think of barriers and solutions within urban water and sanitation management, towards sustainable change. Lately, one of my main activities is focusing on workshops and interdisciplinary discussions for capacity building. The last series of workshops, Aqua Labs, about the water in future cities, has been organized as part of my PhD research in design at IADE-UE and promoted together with worldwide bathroom company Roca, Roca Lisbon Gallery and Give a Shit project. In this workshop I use active design anthropology collaborative methods combined with design and system thinking to enhance the discussion and solution-oriented practice.

Within the First and Second Steps, the Give a Shit project was especially focusing on raising awareness in society about toilet and water issues and demystifying taboos. Now as part of the Third Step I have focused my project research towards sustainably oriented solutions in search of the Fourth Step – 'resolve to change'. This has led me to understand that 'individuals need resolve to continue pushing the flywheel to build momentum' (after Swing 2009: 12). Although I am aware that the solutions I research and practise within workshops, multi-stakeholder dialogue creation, artivism and education are just partial answers, they are important to be experienced as possible ways and procedures to inform holistic and systemic solutions. As a final goal I am focusing on the

Fifth Step – 'incorporate or replace' (Swing 2009: 13) the outdated paradigm of urban water management and 'reintegrate' (Turner 1987) innovative sustainable solutions for urban water management. The idea is to create an improvement over prior performance of the existing urban water paradigm. In this case the existing model becomes obsolete and is replaced with innovative urban water technology and integrated sustainable systems based on people's needs. I propose to create guidelines with design strategy which is going to bridge the lacuna between existing technologies and more appropriate sustainable toilet innovations for users based on overall systemic water need (Korčulanin, Ferreira and Muršič 2018).

In the need of social f(r)iction

> What we need today is not science fiction but social fiction, the capacity to imagine very different ways of living.
>
> Tokinwise 2015: 287

The discussion within this chapter can be summarised by the statement that the world needs more critical thinkers on existing issues and system content dialogue creators who care about our sustainable future and have the capacity for collaboration and co-creation of innovative sustainable solutions to legitimate problems (see Turner 1974). In my opinion, today's convergent crisis in which we live calls for knowledgeable insight, creation of a dialogue between academia, society and business models, to be able to devise positive outcomes and create long-lasting sustainable impact for future generations which could lead out of 'social drama'. There are several competing paths proposed by which 'a radically new, more sustainable mind-set can be installed: become more informed about self-organizing stochastic systems, pay greater heed to the ways in which your self is not a self' (Tonkinwise 2015: 283). There are many other interrogating, stimulating ways to bring us closer to make a change. And even so, according to the state of the crisis we are facing, our engagement to change is still focused on small groups of society. Since global issues are leading to even bigger unavoidable crises at every level of our well-being – climate change, unemployment, refugee crisis, individual unhappiness, among others – we should proceed toward a change more actively (Green 2015; Papanek 1995; Whiteley 1993). As discussed by Turner in his theory of social dramas and addressed on the Give a Shit platform, four phases – breach, crisis, redressive action and reintegration – are needed to instigate change. I believe that we as citizens, professors, researchers, artists, anthropologists, designers and any other professionals are being asked to become agents of change and, as such, should be mediating redressive action and reintegrative mechanisms in our daily routines. I believe we should become examples of positive change that are proposing radical steps towards collaborative sustainable change at the level of our common human existence. Although innovative radical approach to the existing situation within society absolutely questions the fundamental values of the society as a whole and interferes with our daily lives on each and every level of our existence – the food we eat, the clothes we wear, the materials and transport we use, the way we think and speak, how and what we create and design – we are aware that we need to start to make radical and fast changes towards a more sustainable future (Tonkinwise 2015).

Since I trust we are very familiar with existing problems, especially in academia, we should be the first to advocate and demonstrate examples in making change on a real scale. We should stop merely talking about problems but start discussions about changes where we present reliable solutions based on collaboration with interdisciplinary teams. The frame of interdisciplinary groups is proposed to search for potential quality solutions based on holistic perspectives and systemic solutions with the use of innovative technologies. To reach the goal, it is urgent to strive for simultaneous reorganization of our mind-sets and mind-set conversion (see Mau 2004). There is no way back or forward to the wonderful lands and equity within society without radical approaches to change and innovative frameworks.

A collaborative approach between sciences should be mandatory to contribute towards harmonic social processes which could lead out of social drama and the environmental crisis we face as a consequence of imprudent behavioural patterns and attitudes in our daily life. Typically, obscure academic language should be translated to empower society and inform innovative policies and business. Engagement of different creative narratives and a collaborative approach should lead anthropological research from the beginning to the end. Ethnography is not science fiction and should lead us, and society at large, to the social f(r)iction. Through the example of the case study of Give a Shit, I have learned that social drama can serve as an aspiration and inspiration, leading from the breach and crisis towards positive redressive action and reintegration of innovative solutions towards positive change. The Give a Shit project is one among many great societal initiatives, which establish common platforms with minds that think alike and give us positive influences towards the world where #WeDoGiveAShit leads to improvement for our nature, well-being and future generations.

Acknowledgements

I would like to dedicate this chapter in memory of beloved teachers, Nuno Neves Palmeiro and Carlos Barbosa, who taught me about the importance of sustainability in these times in which we live. I would like to sincerely thank my interdisciplinary team of supervisors for their support during my PhD, Ana Margarida Ferreira and Rajko Muršič. Especially, I would like to thank Alisse Waterston for her support and clarity given on my academic track. I would also like to thank Fiona Murphy, Emma Heffernan and Jonathan Skinner for giving me the opportunity to contribute to this special volume with the Give a Shit project, which was brought to life to create dialogue and bridges between academia, society and the problems of need. To my family, Marta Korčulanin, Miodrag Korčulanin, Lana Korčulanin and Matilda Škaper, for believing in me and to the eternal support of Five Rhythms community for flowing with me through the five rhythms of life. I give special thanks to SEYN and Lost in Lisbon and to all the individuals who brought the Give a Shit project to life; they have supported me in bringing this work closer to society.

Notes

1   To find out more about the Give a Shit project, visit giveashitnow.org.
2   For more information about the event Why the World Needs Anthropologists: Designing the Future, visit www.applied-anthropology.com.
3   For the examples of different artists and their projects who base their work on previous ethnographies, see *Contemporary Art and Anthropology* and *The Challenge of Practice* from Schneider and Wright (2006, 2010; see also Marcus 2010; Basu and Macdonald 2007).
4   Titling this section with a cardinal #WeDoGiveaShit represents a hashtag used in social media as an invitation and mobilization statement for the individuals to become active participants of the cause promoted through the Give a Shit project.

References

Basu, P. and S. Macdonald (eds) (2007), *Exhibition Experiments: New Interventions in Art History*, Oxford: Blackwell Publishing.
Battilana, J. and T. Casciaro (2012), 'Change Agents, Networks, and Institutions: A Contingency Theory of Organizational Change', *Academy of Management Journal*,

55 (2): 1–41. Available online: https://dash.harvard.edu/bitstream/handle/1/9549319/
Battilana%2BCasciaro_ChangeAgents,Networks,andInstitutions.pdf?sequence=1
(accessed 12 April 2016).

Bernarda, J., A. Ferreira and L. Neimeyer (2016), 'Collaborative Design Methodologies
Empowers Resilience of Communities', *Design Doctoral Conference '16:
TRANSversality. Proceedings of the DDC 3rd Conference*, online source. Lisbon:
Edições IADE.

Bhamra, T. and V. Lofthouse (2007), *Design for Sustainability: A Practical Approach*,
Hampshire and Burlington: Gower.

Boeijen, A van, J. Daalhuizen, R. van der Schoor and J. Zijlstra (2013), *Delft Design
Guide: Design Strategies and Methods*, Amsterdam: BIS Publishers, TU Delft.

Conti, G. (2015), 'Get Better Customer Insights: How Anthropology Can Guide Product
Design'. Available online: https://zapier.com/blog/business-anthropology/ (accessed
27 September 2016).

Denny, M. and P. Sunderland (2014), *Handbook of Anthropology in Business*, Walnut
Creek, CA: Routledge.

Dexter, B. and C. Prince (2007), 'Facilitating Change: The Role of Educators as Change
Agents', *Strategic Change*, 16 (7): 341–9.

Dias, M. and L. Gontijo (2006), 'A Interdisciplinaridade no Ensino do Design', Revista
Design em Foco, III(2), in M. Dove and D. Kammen (2015), *Science, Society and the
Environment: Applying Anthropology and Physics to Sustainability*, 49–66, New York:
Routledge.

Eriksen T. (2016), *Overheating: An Anthroplogy of Accelerated Change*, London: Pluto
Books.

Ferreira, A. (2008a), *Caracterização e Quantificação da Inovação no Processo
Evolucionista do Design: Análise de um Século da Prática Médico-cirúrgica em
Portugal*, PhD thesis, Engenharia de Produção, Universidade da Beira Interior,
Covilhã.

Ferreira, A. (2008b), 'Evolução do Conceito e da Prática do Design', Prova
Complementar à Dissertação para obtenção do Grau de Doutor em Engenharia de
Produção, Universidade da Beira Interior, Covilhã.

Fry, T. (2009), *Design Futuring*, Oxford: Berg.

Gunn, W., T. Otto and R. Smith (2013), *Design Anthropology: Theory and Practice*.
London: Bloomsbury.

Harvey, D. (2011), *The Enigma of Capital and the Crises of Capitalism*, London: Profile.

International Water Association (2016), *Water Utility Pathways in a Circular Economy
Report*, London: IWA Publishing. Available online: http://www.iwa-network.org/
wp-content/uploads/2016/07/IWA_Circular_Economy_screen.pdf (accessed 30
September 2017).

Jordan, A. (2013), *Business Anthropology*, Prospect Heights, IL: Waveland Press.

Korčulanin, L. (2013), 'Public Space Like Narrative Space – Privatization of Public Space
and Lack of Public Toilets: Alternative Solution with Project *Give a Shit* in Lisbon',

BA dissertation, Faculty of Arts, Department of Ethnology and Cultural Anthropology, University of Ljubljana, Ljubljana.

Korčulanin, L. and A. M. Ferreira (2016), 'Design and Anthropology in Collaboration: The *Give a Shit* Project', Design Doctoral Conference '16: TRANSversality – Proceedings of the 3rd DDC Conference, Lisbon: Edições IADE, 144–51.

Korčulanin, L., C. Barbosa and A. Ferreira (2015), 'Placing Toilets in Sustainable Design – The Need for Social and Technological Innovation', in Proceedings of 8th Senses & Sensibility – Design as a Trade, IADE – Creative University/Edições IADE, 204–11.

Korčulanin, L., A. Ferreira and C. Barbosa (2015), 'Toilet Innovation and Water Management – Revolutionary Steps for a Green Society and Wellbeing', Cumulus Mumbai 2015: 'In a Planet of our Own – a Vision of Sustainability with Focus on Water', Industrial Design Centre (IDC), Indian Institute of Technology Bombay (IITBombay), 4–6 December 2015, Mumbai, India.

Korčulanin, L., A. Ferreira and R. Muršič (2018), 'Active Design Method for Sustainable Urban Water Management', Design Doctoral Conference '18: TRANScendency – Proceedings of the 5th DDC Conference, online source (forthcoming), Lisbon: Edições IADE.

Kuhn, S. T. (1970 [1962]), *The Structure of Scientific Revolutions*, Chicago, IL: University of Chicago Press.

Laporte, D. (1993), *History of Shit*, London: The MIT Press.

Malhi, Y. (2017), 'The Concept of the Anthropocene', *Annual Review of Environment and Resources*. Available online: https://www.annualreviews.org/doi/pdf/10.1146/annurev-environ-102016-060854 (accessed 10 February 2018).

Manzini, E. (2011), 'Design Labs for an Open Design Program: Design Schools as Agents of (Sustainable) Change', in Z. Haoming, P. Korvenmaa and L. Xin (eds), *The Tao of Sustainability: An International Conference on Sustainable Design Strategies in a Globalization Context*, 356–60, Beijing: AUT University.

Manzini, E. (2015), *Design, When Everybody Designs: An Introduction to Design for Social Innovation*. Cambridge, MA: The MIT Press.

Marcus, G. (2010), 'Affinities: Fieldwork in Anthropology Today and the Ethnographic in Artwork', in A. Schneider and C. Wright (eds), *Between Art and Anthropology: Contemporary Ethnographic Practice*, 83–95, Oxford and New York: Berg.

Mau, B., J. Leonard and Institute Without Boundaries (2004), *Massive Change*, Phaidon Press.

Olsson, P., M. Moore, F. Westley and D. McCarthy (2017), 'The Concept of the Anthropocene as a Game-changer: A New Context for Social Innovation and Transformations to Sustainability', *Ecology and Society*, 22 (2): 31. Available online: https://doi.org/10.5751/ES-09310-220231 (accessed 15 March 2018).

Ostrom, E. (1990), 'Governing the Commons: The Evolution of Institutions for Collective Action', *Natural Resources Journal*, 32: 415–17.

Pink, S., E. Ardèvol and D. Lanzeni (eds) (2016), *Digital Materialities: Design and Anthropology*, London: Bloomsbury Academic.

Podjed, D. and M. Gorup (2014), 'What Comes Next in European Applied Anthropology?', *Anthropology in Action*, 21(1): 45–6.

Podjed, D., M. Gorup and A. Mlakar (2016), 'Applied Anthropology in Europe Historical Obstacles: Current Situation, Future Challenges', *Anthropology in Action*, 23 (2): 53–63.

Rabinow, P. and A. Stavrianakis (2013), *Demands of the Day: On the Logic of Anthropological Inquiry*, Chicago, IL: University of Chicago Press.

Rabinow, P., M. George, J. Faubion and T. Rees (2008), *Designs for an Anthropology of the Contemporary*, Durham, NC: Duke University Press.

Schneider, A. and C. Wright (2005), *Contemporary Art and Anthropology*, Oxford and New York: Berg.

Schneider, A. and C. Wright (2006), 'The Challenge of Practice', in A. Schneider and C. Wright (eds), *Contemporary Art and Anthropology*, 1–29, Oxford: Berg.

Smith N. (2011), 'Locating Design Anthropology in Research and Practice: PhD Workshops Provoke Expansion of Cross-disciplinary Horizons', in L. Justice and K. Friedmann (eds), Pre-conference Proceedings, The Doctoral Education in Design Conference, Hong Kong Polytechnic University and Swinburne Universtiy, 23–25 May 2011. Available online: http://www.academia.edu/895695/Locating_Design_Anthropology_in_research_and_practice (accessed 3 April 2016).

Ståhlbröst, A. and M. Holst (2012), *The Living Lab Methodology Handbook*, Copenhagen: Danish Agency for Science Technology and Innovation.

Stebbing, P. and U. Tischner (2015), *Changing Paradigms: Designing for a Sustainable Future*, Mumbai: Vedanta Art.

Swing, R. (2009), 'Institutional Researchers as Change Agents', *New Directions for Institutional Research*, 2009: 5–16.

Tonkinwise, C. (2015), 'Radical Sustainable Innovation', in P. Stebbing and U. Tischner (eds), *Changing Paradigms: Designing for a Sustainable Future,* 284–96, Mumbai: Vedanta Arts.

Turner, V. (1974), *Dramas, Fields, and Metaphors: Symbolic Action in Human Society*, Ithaca and London: Cornell University Press.

Turner, V. (1987), *The Anthropology of Performance*, New York: PAJ Publications.

Yuqiong L, H. Gupta, E. Springer and T. Wagener (2008), 'Linking Science with Environmental Decision Making: Experiences from an Integrated Modeling Approach to Supporting Sustainable Water Resources Management', *Environmental Modelling and Software,* 23 (7): 846–58.

UN-Water, FAO (2007), 'Coping with Water Scarcity: Challenge of the Twenty-first Century. Available online: http://www.un.org/waterforlifedecade/scarcity.shtml (accessed 3 April 2016).

United Nations (2010), 'The Human Right to Water and Sanitation' (Declaration of Human Rights, media brief). Available online: http://www.un.org/waterforlifedecade/pdf/human_right_to_water_and_sanitation_media_brief.pdf (accessed 3 April 2016).

Wang, T. (2013), 'Why Big Data Needs Thick Data?', *Ethnography Matters* (May 2013). Available online: https://medium.com/ethnography-matters/why-big-data-needs-thick-data-b4b3e75e3d7#.pqr3q6ibr (accessed 9 April 2016).

Westerhoff, P. (2015), 'Characterization, Recovery Opportunities, and Valuation of Metals in Municipal Sludges from U.S. Wastewater Treatment Plants Nationwide'. Available online: http://pubs.acs.org/doi/abs/10.1021/es505329q (accessed 13 October 2015).

World Health Organization and UNICEF (2012), 'Fast Facts WHO/UNICEF: Joint Monitoring Report 2012'. Available online: http://www.who.int/water_sanitation_health/monitoring/jmp2012/fast_facts/en/ (accessed 5 April 2016).

8

Anthropology and Architecture: Motives and Ethics in Creating Knowledge

Anne Sigfrid Grønseth and Eli Støa

Introduction

This chapter was born from an interdisciplinary research project,[1] which aimed to document and explore the effects of the physical surroundings on belonging and well-being among asylum seekers in Norway. Among other approaches, the project combined anthropological and architectural perspectives in exploring materiality and the housing qualities offered at asylum seeker reception centres. While the overall motive was to undestand the relation between humans and the physical surroundings, we also came to discuss the motives, merits and ethics in the mutual process of learning. We will argue that by the two disciplines collaborating, the result was a holistic, nuanced and in-depth insight and a shared awareness of an ethical direction of care for humanity and self as it is intervowen in its physical surroundings.

While our analytical approach contains little new, the research presents original empirical material feeding into a controversial and heated political debate concerning immigration policy, housing quality, integration and well-being. Furthermore, the anthropological as well as architectural disciplines' calls for responsibility and commitment in terms of a need to 'study up', 'speak for' and uphold human rights for our research subjects, gives opportunity for an enriched voice to asylum seekers' everyday lived life in Norway. The main contribution of this chapter is to document and reflect on the research process, as it negotiates anthropological and architectural approaches and perspectives, and discuss the contributions in the knowledge created, thereby emphasizing the important role of collaboration in both anthropological and architectural endeavours.

In the following, we first introduce the theoretical perspectives that address complexities in the creation of knowledge and our approaches to dwelling and materiality. Second, we present a brief historical context for asylum seeker reception centres in Norway followed by a short overview of methods employed. Third, we present a case study of an asylum seeker reception centre called Open River Reception Centre. Then, we discuss the case material in light of place and practices of housing[2] (as it includes dwelling) followed by a section relating to ethics in the knowledge creation. By way of concluding we call for a policy that attends to a care of self and humanity.

Views on creating knowledge: Relations of persons, relations of materiality

Theoretically, we are concerned with the interdisciplinary creation of knowledge as we deal with the complex relations between housing, belonging and well-being in a particular context of asylum seekers, while also being crucial to all human lives. As part of this process, we highlight how an anthropologically inspired attention to the relations of knowledge creation also stimulates an ethical concern that may encourage respect for human equality and diversity (see also Grønseth and Josephides 2017). The creation of knowledge is always embedded in a complex web of relations between people distinctly positioned within wider social and material structures, cultural values and meanings, while we highlight distinct disciplinary positions. How such disciplinary relations and positions interact in the creation and employment of knowledge is always an (often implicit) ethical issue, while also affecting what is 'valuable knowledge' in a given context (see also Grønseth and Josephides 2017; Rabinow 2003; Strathern 2005). As international and national state-regulated conventions, laws and agreements increasingly tend to reach into, define and shape asylum seekers' life trajectories and day-to-day lives, issues of modes and content of knowledge and how it is created and employed are of crucial ethical concern and vital for asylum seekers' power to voice concerns of their own that affect important areas of their lives, such as material and social security, health, belonging and well-being.

While acknowledging a vast complexity related to the purposes of how knowledge is created and to whom it is or is not imparted, this chapter explores interdisciplinary views on materiality, social positions and persons. How we treat each other, here with a particular concern for the physical environment wherein asylum seekers' lives take place, lies at the very heart of our belonging and well-being in everyday life, and speaks directly to the anthropological quest for knowledge about human lives. Exploring asylum seeker reception centres as architecture, while including an anthropological approach of belonging and well-being, we furthermore see the study as shedding light on the social and political ruptures and disputes, which make the often implicit ethical concerns explicit (see also Lambek 2010).

With a focus on anthropological perspectives in the overall study, we include a brief note on anthropological views on materiality, housing and architecture. Until quite recently, materiality and forms have not been a focused issue in anthropological inquiries. Rather than exploring the materiality of built forms and wider architectonic contexts, anthropologists have concentrated on immaterial abstracted social and cultural processes. Images and built forms have become increasingly difficult to separate from the anthropological analysis as visual representations and new technologies have become central in theory building (see also Buchli 2013). However, recent work on materiality and architecture have still tended to focus on the discursive, semiotic or mental aspects.

In line with Tim Ingold (2007) we rather see material qualities as having an inherently relational quality, not reducible to some empirical material quality such as building material of mental constructs, but existing within what Ingold describes as relational context of action, material and environment, reminiscent in certain ways of the philosopher of science Karen Barad's (2007) notion of 'intra-action' (see also Latour 1979; Gell 1998). More so, we draw on the growing attention to bodily and sensoric perceptions that opens up an anthropological interest in the physical environment and the aesthetics that embed and direct our everyday social lives. Together, the different approaches can be seen to make up a multiplicity of entries or registers attending to the 'house' (Ingold 2007), all as vital in negotiations of competing social claims and their value in conflicting assertions feeding social life.

Herein, we draw attention to how houses and their surroundings affect belonging and well-being as these are deeply interwoven with experiences of identity, personhood and self. Through this perspective, houses are seen not only as places or 'cases' of symbolism, but more as interplaying subjects (see also Humphry 1988). This refers to how materiality, such as buildings and outdoor spaces, can be seen to take on a certain agency in reinforcing and shaping social relations and senses of belonging and well-being.

Architects share anthropologists' interest in understanding people, their needs and aspirations, as well as the role architecture may play in order to reach goals such as social inclusion, dignity and mental health (Stender 2017). It is further acknowledged within architectural theory that buildings and places inevitably both create and symbolize socially constructed identities and differences between people: 'The politics of identity in built form mediates who we are and where we belong' (Dovey [1998] 2009: 18). The architecture of reception centres therefore not only affects asylum seekers' own situation and self-understanding, it also influences other people's perception of them. At the same time, meanings related to the built environment are continuously reframed due to changing practices. An important starting point for the research presented in this chapter is thus that architecture in itself may bring about change (Awan et al. 2011).

The theoretical basis for understanding the dynamic and mutual relationship between humans and material objects within architecture has developed from actor network theory, and has led to a growing interest in spatial and architectural agency within the discipline (see e.g. Yavena and Guy 2008; Latour and Yavena 2009; Schneider and Till 2009; Awan et al. 2011). Agency in this context reflects an approach to architectural and physical spaces as not only autonomous products and objects, but also continously changing entities entangled in and dependent on social, cultural, economic and political contexts. Within this understanding, architecture has the ability to make changes and even 'lead to other possible futures' (Doucet and Cupers 2009: 1).

In our research on receptions centres, we are looking for other and better ways to house asylum seekers than what is currently offered them in order to affect their belonging and well-being and, as part of this, to change how we as a hosting society perceive and relate to newcomers. And here, the architect's approach tends to differ slightly from the anthropologist's. In order to transgress the present situation in reception centres, architects will challenge the housing qualities offered to asylum seekers and search for other solutions. In order to do this, normative judgements are made. This implies the need to distinguish between 'good' and 'bad' housing quality, something that might be rather problematic among anthropologists being 'trained in a paradigm of cultural relativism' (Stender 2017: 35).

Within architectural practice, quality is understood as an essential dimension of the built environment, although continuously up for debate both within the discipline as well as in society at large. Housing quality is thus understood as characteristics related to housing which are given value at a certain time (Guttu 2003), and it is regarded as an important task for architects not only to add value to society (Stender 2017) but also to take part in the public debate of what housing quality is, or could be, for various situations and residential groups. Related to the research on housing qualities for asylum seekers, it becomes even clearer that there is a need to contextualize judgements of quality based on knowledge and awareness of the specific situation of this specific group. This we will return to later.

As we can see from the above, the anthropological and architectural theoretical approaches drawn on here, although diverse, share an understanding of dwellings and materiality as holding a relational and agentive force that feeds into social life. However, the architectural concern for knowledge about the residents is given depth and emphasis by the anthropological hallmark and call for knowledge deriving from ethnographic and engaged explorations of 'face-to-face' encounters and the 'natives' points of view', accompanied by ethics of solidarity and responsibility for our fellow human beings. Later on we will further explore how anthropology and architecture feed into each other. Before this, we introduce a brief context of asylum seeker reception centres in Norway.

Context: Asylum seeker reception centres in Norway

In Norway, asylum seekers are the responsibility of the government. While waiting for their case to be concluded, they live in special asylum seeker reception centres, which are spread around the country. Those asylum seekers who are either granted refugee status or residency on humanitarian grounds are relocated to municipalities where they are offered settlement, often in public rental housing. The time spent in reception centres may vary from a few months to more than a year, and sometimes several years (Strumse et al. 2016; Lauritzen and Berg 1999). The number of UN refugees is a quota, which is negotiated every three years. The UN refugees are commonly transmitted from the reception centre to the municipal authorities during the first month, or directly settled in municipalities.

Today's Norwegian state and government reception system is a consequence of the increasing numbers of asylum seekers during the 1980s. Until 1987 the reception of refugees and asylum seekers was rather random and improvised. The system of asylum seeker reception of today has existed approximately since the early 1990s (Berg 2012). The debate concerning the housing conditions of asylum seekers was then, as today, directed and focused on not being too generous, although not too simple. In policy documents the asylum centres are described to offer a 'simple, but reasonable' (*nøktern, men forsvarlig*) standard.[3] The reception centres are commonly established within already existing buildings (NOU 2011: 10; Strumse et al. 2016). Many centres have building-related problems such as damp, draughts, worn-down surfaces, poor indoor climate and poor accessibility for disabled residents (Strumse et al. 2016). Overcrowding is also a problem, since single residents most often must share a room with one or more others (Strumse et al. 2016).

The housing standard can be seen as a response to the policy demands of 'reasonable standard' and fluctuations in the number of asylum seekers. The state sets a minimum coverage of the reception centres' housing capacity to be utilized at all times, which implies frequent openings and closings of centres. The limited economic resources and variations in the number of asylum seekers in Norway make planning and managing reception centres challenging. The contracts to run centres are tendered for open competitions in the private market, while the Norwegian Directorate of Immigration (UDI) keeps agreements with municipalities, voluntary organizations and private operators (Larsen 2014). The employment of short-term contracts and the risk of losing the contract on three months' notice may contribute to low housing standards and simple solutions, as well as instability in staff and a general perception of such work to be of lower status.

The original function of buildings utilized for reception centres varies, although the most common original function is found to be ordinary housing (this is due to a large number of the centres being organized as fully or partly decentralized), followed by former health institutions, hotels, educational institutions and military barracks (Strumse et al. 2016). Other categories are reported to be bedsits, dormitories, small lodging places, workmanship barracks, camping cabins and others. The fully or partly decentralized centres offer dwelling in detached houses or multifamily houses such as terraced housing and apartment buildings (Hauge et al. 2017). Generally, the reception centres are located in low-status areas keeping a low housing standard in terms of being worn down, and some not suitable as accommodation for people (Berg 2012; Strumse et al. 2016; Hauge et al. 2015, 2017). More so, they are often placed on the outskirts and in less inhabited areas, which implies that the residents have little opportunity for interaction with locals in public meeting places. Many of the centres make use of former hotels high in the mountains or health institutions in the countryside. If the reception centre is close to a town centre, these are often deserted after business hours.

The housing standard is based on short-term residence, while, as already mentioned, in fact many asylum seekers stay for several years. The time waiting for a final assessment of asylum application in Norway has steadily increased until 2014 (Larsen 2014). In December 2014,[4] at the time of our study, 36 per cent of asylum seekers stayed more than one-and-a-half years, and 25 per cent more than three years at a reception centre (UDI 2014a). The most numerous groups came from Somalia, Eritrea, Ethiopia, Syria and Afghanistan. At the time of our fieldwork, about one-third of residents had a resident permit and were waiting for settlement in a municipality, one-third were waiting for an answer to their application, and one-third had received a negative assessment and were waiting to be deported out of Norway (UDI 2014b).

Considering the study's concern with asylum seekers who seek refuge from war, prosecution and/or discrimination, we see a need to recognize these populations' and individuals' specific life conditions. Some central features of relevance for such refugee populations' situation often include: a) not choosing or understanding their destination; b) migration marked by trauma and persecution; c) vulnerable mental and physical health; d) separation from family members whose safety may be at risk; e) arrival without identity document or with false documents; f) arrival without evidence of qualifications; g) arrival under the stress of deportation or detention; h) temporary admittance under the fear of return (Kissoon 2010). In particular, the forced transitional and temporary condition and experience need special attention, as these are crucial for the perception and reception from the host society, authorities and community, the decisions for placing and shaping of reception centres, as well as arriving families and individuals who are at different ages and life phases.

In the following, we present a brief overview of methods employed, while highlighting the ethnographic approach.

Methodological approaches and doing ethnography

The methods chosen for the project were anchored in an architectural approach that sought to document the material environment offered asylum seekers, with concern for access to and quality of spaces for privacy, sleep and rest, socializing, food storage, cooking, enjoying a meal, cleaning and washing of clothing, children's play and school work, religious practices, sanitary facilities, light, air, greenery, outdoor recreation, and location in relation to local community, neighbourhoods, town centres and more. Such documentation was sought by developing a quantitative web survey sent to the total number of reception centres (105 ordinary centres) in 2013 (Strumse et al. 2016). To gain first-hand information, researchers in the project carried out various one-day visits at seven different reception centres, interviewing employees and having informal conversations with asylum seekers. Shorter visits were conducted by student groups at four centres, where the architectural features were documented. In addition, ethnographic fieldwork was conducted at four centres, one of which was used as the empiric basis for this chapter.[5] Furthermore, interviews were carried out with actors employed in institutions (public and private) who regulate and administer the reception centres according to political demands and guidelines. In the last phases of the research, information on built examples of temporary housing was gathered in order to discuss alternative and more future-oriented architectural solutions to the housing needs of newly arrived asylum seekers identified through the survey and fieldwork.

Anne (the anthropologist) conducted ethnographic fieldwork at the Open River Asylum Seeker Reception Centre over a five-month period (August–December 2014), focusing on being there and engaging in the everyday life of asylum seekers and employees of the centre. At the time of fieldwork there were about eighty asylum seekers at the centre. While the Open River Reception Centre was a semi-centralized centre, most asylum seekers lived in the central building – a former hotel with reception and office area. Others lived in more or less worn-down but ordinary flats and houses in nearby vicinities. The most numerous groups of asylum seekers came from Eritrea, Somalia, Ethiopia, Afghanistan, Syria, Iran and Iraq. The residents had lived there for various lengths of time (from two months to nine years), and some had previously lived in another reception centre that was now closed down. Some of the residents were waiting for the result of their application, others had a positive resolution and were waiting for settlement in a municipality, while others again had a negative resolution and were waiting for return to their country of origin.

Conducting fieldwork at Open River Asylum Seeker Reception Centre, Anne emphasized an approach of engaging with the ongoing activities and people present, with a special concern for the asylum seekers' experience of everyday life and the housing conditions. This implied visits and talks with the residents in their private rooms, cooking and sharing meals, going shopping in the nearby town, hanging around in the hallways, television room and outdoor benches, as well as entering the employees' office area to do interviews, share lunch breaks and have informal conversations. Speaking with the asylum seekers was a challenge in terms of language issues. Some asylum seekers spoke fluent English or sufficient Norwegian to make conversation, others spoke very little Norwegian or English and often included a third person, sometimes a friend on the phone, to help out as interpreter.

The employees were commonly busy with administrative tasks, planning activities for the residents such as information meetings, various courses about topics such as Norwegian ways of child upbringing and the legal prohibition of (parental) physical violence against children, meetings with individual residents to prompt them to make a voluntary return their country of origin, discussing residents' wishes and needs such as a change of room (often a wish for single room or change of roommates), access to fitness centres, health consultations, or visits to friends or relatives in other parts of Norway. These and other matters were discussed and dealt with on the basis that the employees, as explained to Anne, in principle knew nothing about and had no access to formal information concerning the individual residents' asylum application, their reasons for seeking asylum, family background or actual network outside the reception centre, health status or sickness story. As Anne approached the employees, it was often difficult for them to make appointments for interviews or discussions as their time was generally heavily booked, and they often needed to rearrange their schedule to meet the most urgent tasks and needs of the day. Most employees had scarce or no specific education or work experience related to their actual line of work. Several of the staff said that they were on the lookout for more 'respectable', 'steady' and 'less strenuous' work, while some thought they would

Figure 8.1 Former hotel converted into a reception centre. Photo: Stine Glennås.

Figure 8.2 Entrance. Photo: Karine Denizou.

Figure 8.3 Bedroom. Photo: Karine Denizou.

Figure 8.4 Kitchen. Photo: Ragne Ø. Thorshaug.

gradually professionalize by long-term engagement and experience, making themselves eligible for other work positions within the management of asylum seekers and refugees, or other (often municipal) jobs concerning integration and multiculturalism.

Together, the combined methods of web survey, one-day visits and ethnographic fieldwork produced data which enlightened distinct and overlapping themes and levels of concern. In the following section, we present case material followed by two sections of discussion: first, concerning views on housing, and second, views on knowledge creation.

Case: Open River Asylum Seeker Reception Centre

Leaving the train station, Anne entered the small town's main street and centre with bakery, hairdresser, shops and stores, cafes, banks, health centre and several municipal offices of different kinds. Ten metres down the main road, the shopping area came to an end and the road met a roundabout, giving options to turn to the left for schools and kindergarten, straight ahead and leading south to the next town, or turning right passing some warehouses, outdoors stocking of agricultural and labour machinery, while leading down to the riverside. Along this road was also the old brick-built hotel, which today serves as an asylum seeker reception centre.

Just outside the building, there were some wooden benches on the grass between the road and the parking area in front. Surrounding the reception centre was a rather large green lawn with a few trees here and there, before small bits of cultivated lands led the eye to new roads leading in between new lands and woods. In the parking and benching area there were a few old-looking bicycles parked; some old shoes and plastic bags lay along the building walls. The many windows indicated each one to be a 'hotel room' and appeared in regularly distanced neat rows both horizontally and vertically. A variety of textile curtains hung in different lengths, mixed with other kinds of materials closing up the windows, which together gave a messy appearance in the otherwise regular pattern.

In front of the main entrance there was a small outbuild roof with a bench beneath. This bench was used as a meeting and waiting point. Most times there would be a few people around having a cigarette, a soda drink, or just hanging out. It was mostly men who occupied the area. Already at this entry point, one was introduced to the most common attire for both men and women: cheap kinds of 'gym clothing', loose trousers, runners or slippers, and sweaters or T-shirts, depending on the season and weather. The staff told Anne that most outside visitors did not dare to enter the reception centre before someone from the staff came out to meet them and accompany them into the staff office area. Being a first-time visitor, the residents would commonly just watch you pass by, not knowing the purpose of your visit and supposing it was to meet with staff, not themselves. As Anne came to be well known, they greeted her and smiled and the opportunity could be used for small talk and making later appointments.

Passing through the double doors at the main entrance was a small hall from which a door to the left led into the staff area. Just passing the main entrance door there was a staircase leading up to long corridors between the former hotel rooms, now private rooms for the asylum seekers. Going down, right ahead there was a large kitchen with about ten cooking stoves and a long kitchen bench with several sinks. Turning right, there was a sanitary room with about five toilets and showers. Turning left, there were a few larger rooms used as billiard room and staff meeting room, and washroom facilities for staff only. In addition, passing the sanitary room, the downstairs contained an area with a few larger and smaller rooms for female residents only, inhabited by women from various African countries. Together they made a group of some of the most vulnerable women in terms of pregnancy, various illnesses and non-literacy, who, according to the staff, helped and supported each other.

Staying on the ground floor and turning right led to a long corridor with private rooms for asylum seekers on each side. As in the corridors above and below, this corridor was dimly lit and there were no windows. In front of each room were different pairs of shoes and a few other items. Behind the doors lived the asylum seekers in rooms for two, three and four people; a few rooms housed six people. Most of the inhabitants of the corridors were single men from both African and Asian countries, but also some women from Asian countries such as Iran and Afghanistan, and two married couples. The rooms contained one bed and a small wardrobe per person (the couples put their beds together making it into one), one or two refrigerators shared between the room residents, and a small bathroom with a toilet and shower for shared use. In most of the rooms, one or more of the residents had bought themselves a private television set and/or personal computer. The residents struggled to find places to stash and keep their few belongings, using every inch under beds, on top of wardrobes, underneath small coffee tables and/or bookshelves. Having little space, many complained about the unpleasantness of keeping clothing and shoes next to food and cutlery. Many would mark an individual private space in the room by, for instance, hanging a textile from the top bed down, making a 'wall' down to the bed below, or setting a chair or large pillow so as to draw a line between the private bed and the shared space in the room. Generally, the bed was the only area for one individual, although many said it did not feel sufficiently personal or private. As many pointed out, they did not approve when someone sat down on their bed. On the other hand, there was often not much other space to sit on, so it had to be allowed for.

Being with and speaking with the asylum seekers, they generally expressed a concern that they were 'treated like animals, not as humans'. Ammaan, a woman in her late twenties from Somalia, said:

> The camp is our transition to Norway. It is our doorstep. What we experience at the camp give us the image of Norway. If the person who works here is good with me, I get a positive image of Norway. If the person who works here is bad with me, I get a bad image of Norway. The same is about the building we live in, our rooms and environment. If the place is nice, we have a positive feeling for Norway. If the place is bad we have a negative feeling. We have only a small room shared with one, two, or three others. There is no place to keep our things, no place to dry our clothings. My shoes and garbage are kept next to my food-storage and kitchen utensils. It is not right. It makes me feel uncomfortable. It is not to complain, as we have many good things. But it is not what we had hoped for. I come for humanity, not to be spoken to and treated like animals. Humanity is in Norway, but not for us. Sometimes I feel like not to make the effort. I am tired. I tell myself I need to try. We live outside society. We are not so different;

we are humans first. It is not war outside. Here we have peace, bed, and clothing. But, we have lack of consideration of humanity. This makes us hate Norway. We go out and feel not welcome. It is not possible to feel good. I feel sick and dizzy. I shiver in my bed, and cannot sleep.

Another asylum seeker, Akram from Iraq, also in his late twenties, said:

Here is like a prison. But it is worse than a prison, because we do not know when we are finished. I am a mechanic. I want to work, but I am not allowed. My bedroom is very small and I share with one more. I do not like to make food in the kitchen. It is often dirty. We live like in a hole. See for yourself, you do not want to live here. It is not for human beings to live here. People get tired and sick. I have constant headaches and cannot sleep. The most important I have is my religion, my faith. It keeps me going.

Speaking with the staff, they generally agreed that the asylum seekers live 'on top of each other' and that the facilities are poor for long-time residency. One of the reasons for not finding better accommodation was, according to the centre leader, related to the local community's reluctance to include the asylum seekers in their neighbourhood. He explained:

It is difficult to find autonomous housing for our residents. The owners prefer other residents for their houses. The locals complain that the neighbourhood degrades and falls on the market, they get lesser price if they want to sell. We have one house with six housing-units. It is a lot of trouble there. They are too many together, living kind of on top of each other. The standards are low. The electric capacity is too low, since it is not measured for six units. It is also too little warm water for six units.

Another male employee, aged in his forties, who worked part-time as a custodian and sometimes helped out with transport to the local doctor and suchlike, spoke about local people's reaction to asylum seekers in their neighbourhood. He said:

Our centre had managed to get three autonomous houses on a row in one neighbourhood. When we took over the third house, we received a concerned phone from one of the neighbours saying:

– *Is one more of the houses turning into a house for such?*
– *Who such you mean?*
– *Such, you know . . . .*
– *But, has there been any problems?*
– *To be honest, not really, I was just wondering how many houses you are taking?*

Clearly, the phone call indicated that our renting of the houses was not to his liking. It never is.

The place and practice of housing: Belonging and well-being

From the above descriptions and interview citations, we can see how housing cannot be assessed simply on its own terms. It is always linked and related to the surroundings as well as to the people who engage with the buildings and outdoor areas with different aims and viewpoints. What was previously a hotel accommodating guests was transformed into an asylum seeker reception centre accommodating persons with a status of being 'in between' and 'Other' of 'us'. Thus, both the social and the environmental contexts in which housing is situated are important. The location and setting of the buildings affect the asylum seekers' experiences of belonging and well-being (Potter et al. 2005), while also expressing and shaping how the local community and wider society perceive asylum seekers. While it is reasonable to assume that the earlier hotel guests experienced their stay as agreeable for their purposes, the dwelling experience of an asylum seeker becomes something totally different. As Akram says, 'We live like in a hole. See for yourself. You do not want to live here. It is not for human beings to live here. People get tired and sick. I have constant headaches and cannot sleep.'

As already mentioned, the different perspectives and perceptions of the buildings can be seen to make up a multiplicity of entries or registers to the 'house' (Ingold 2007). By shifting between the different entries, the house, as architectural object, can be seen not as a lasting and fixed material entity, but as a process with moments of stoppage that both illustrate and enable social life. Such a view highlights how materiality and architecture hold a relational quality as it is formed by relations between practice, material and environment (see also Ingold 2007). Our research on asylum seeker reception centres supports the understanding of materiality as holding a relational quality and highlights how the human practice of dwelling includes senses of belonging, well-being, illness and emotions.

From the illustrative photographs, ethnographic descriptions and interviews, we see how the buildings, locations and aesthetics affect and shape not only what the residents can do, how they organize things, possessions and activities, but also inform and shape the residents' senses of illness, belonging and well-being. Recognizing the generally poor aesthetic, technical and functional standard of the asylum seeker reception centres, it appears that how we organize space, and place people in distinct localities, expresses certain forms of power (Foucault 2000). Foucault (1974) argues how something that is institutionalized and constructed for one purpose can be turned and altered into another meaning and effect. Understanding power as exercised by organizing of space and material structures, reception centres may be seen as examples of creating distinctions and defining 'Others' from us.

Simultaneously, the same organization and structures are by their political creators said to uphold immigration justice, social security, and a minimum of local integration. We recognize how such processes of Othering are not only mental processes, but also spatial processes. By placing the asylum seekers in buildings and houses of low standard, on the outskirts of society, and originally meant for other purposes, they become places of 'in-between-ness'. The reception centres can be seen to offer a zone in between – neither fully inside nor outside – and as such as 'non-places' (Augè 1995) or 'empty spaces' (Agamben 1998). Living in such places, the asylum seekers can come to experience being 'treated as animals', as 'not human', as 'not welcome', and simply as 'such … that degrade the neighbourhood'. Experiencing these dehumanizing processes, the asylum seekers, such as Ammaan and Akram, generally feel 'tired', 'not feeling like making the effort', and suffer from headaches, sleeplessness, dizziness and much more.

From such a spatial and material dehumanizing process, we call for a housing practice within the asylum seeker reception system based on an acknowledgement of how the built environment and its qualities may play specific roles in transformation processes. Furthermore, we encourage architects and planners to be even better informed by studies that recognize knowledge as it is always linked to materiality as well as social relations, positions and persons (see Grønseth and Josephides 2017).

Creating ethical knowledge on housing qualities: Care for self and humanity

Traditionally, anthropology has sought to ensure social progress (in the West) by means of knowledge, which implies that the creation of knowledge and social reform were seen as harmonious tasks (see Stoczkowski 2008). This interwoven ambition was present in the 'colonial anthropology' of the 1920s, in the 'applied anthropology' of the 1940s and 1950s, and later in the 'critical anthropology' from the 1970s onwards, in terms of reflectively taking on blame and responsibility for Western traditions of imperialism, colonialism, capitalism, racism, nationalism and more (Stoczkowski 2008: 348). In a similar vein, some anthropologists call for moral commitment by empathizing and defending the rights of the oppressed (see for instance Scheper-Hughes 1995), whereas others term such a call as 'moral anxiety' (Faubion 2003). Common for all these approaches is a belief that the fundamentals for knowledge creation match the fundamentals of ethics, and that the epistemology for social studies is similar and accommodates the moral values that guide social reform for the benefit and well-being of populations. Rather than going into discussions of the moral agenda in social sciences, or knowledge as a means for 'doing good', we suggest that when 'doing ethnography' and creating knowledge in face-to-face relations it makes us recognize, beyond the verbal and factual, that the tacit, imaginative, emotional and empathic aspects are crucial to the creation of knowledge (see Grønseth and Josephides 2017; Grønseth and Davis 2010; Josephides 2008). In line with this, we propose that knowledge creation takes place in the process of the knowledge seeker becoming a knower (Josephides 2017; Daston and Galison 2010), thus stressing the link between not only the local and the non-local, but knowledge and person. Highlighting how knowledge is created in relations between persons relates to an ethical view of quality or care for self and humanity (Grønseth and Josephides 2017). This approach is in line with the Foucauldian and Aristotelian view in which an action is assessed by the virtuous disposition that underlies the agent's psychology (Fassin 2012: 7). Thus, we understand ethics as a process of inner states encouraged by virtue and care, while also encouraging action.

When knowledge on housing qualities is created in an ethnographic approach of 'being there' and 'sharing experiences', it adds not only a depth and complexity in our understanding, but we suggest it also can draw attention to an ethic of knowledge creation that goes beyond an already prepared checklist of 'to-do's' and 'not-to-do's'. It is an ethic that underlines the perceptions, experiences and relations between persons as they take place in various social, cultural, material and environmental contexts. Moreover, we suggest a need to explore how architecture, aesthetics and politics are not only rational interests, but include sensual and emotional dynamics in how individuals and groups struggle to have their voices heard and recognized as legitimate and equal partners in debate and everyday social life.

Combining anthropological and architectural perspectives in this research has not only strengthened the ethnographic insights of life in receptions centres. Just as importantly, it has shown how negotiations between the two approaches during the explorations have led to a shared acknowledgement of the normative dimensions of architecture. Creating knowledge within architecture is not only about gaining understanding of the effect of buildings or what shapes them. It is just as much about the knowledge embedded in the buildings themselves, how they speak to us, make us feel safe or 'at home', how they strengthen our dignity or sense of belonging, how they support our control over our daily routines, and so on. Therefore, among the outcomes of the research were not only scientific publications, but also a handbook with guidelines directed towards stakeholders involved in the planning and operation of reception centres (Støa et al. 2016). The guidelines are meant to improve conditions in Norwegian reception centres by describing housing qualities that should be aimed at for this specific residential group. The handbook does not define minimum standards or specific solutions but is intended to provide a basis in order to make better judgements when establishing and assessing reception centres or other kinds of accommodation for asylum seekers. It includes presentations and discussions of relevant built examples that both inspire to innovation and show possibilities. As there are few high-quality reception centres worth showing, most examples are other kinds of institution-like or temporary housing such as student housing, homes for elderly, mental patients, etc. The book highlights topics that are relevant for all kinds of housing, but that are particularly valid for asylum seekers: identity and participation, spaces for meaningful activities, and architectural solutions that provide privacy, safety and health.

We see ethnography as a way to help create a body of theory that recognises that knowing is 'understanding in practice', entangled with 'making' as an active engagement with the material world (Ingold 2013: 5). Participant observation, Ingold argues, is a way of knowing 'from the inside', 'because we are already *of* the world' (2013: 5; see also Faubion and Marcus 2009). When we extract 'data' from this existential mode of knowing – which includes the tacit, empathic and imaginative – and present it as knowledge reconstructed from the outside, we set up participant observation as a paradox, when it is simply part of dwelling in the world. Arguing otherwise removes us from the world in which we dwell and 'leaves us strangers to ourselves' (Ingold 2013: 5). Understanding fieldwork and ethnography as part of world-dwelling liberates us from 'descriptive fidelity' and opens up 'transformational engagements' with people beyond the settings of fieldwork. This openness acknowledges that the theorist 'makes through thinking' and thus that fieldwork is part of that process (Ingold 2013: 6).

Taking such a view, we suggest that by including ethnographic methods and anthropological perspectives in a research on housing qualities, our study creates a mode of knowledge that reaches beyond the factual and visual and adds an approach that can open up an ethic of mutual respect and cosmopolitan solidarity (see Grønseth 2014), so crucial when dealing with sensitive and political issues of belonging and well-being in everyday life and the shaping of a new future in radical new environments.

Concluding remarks: Towards a policy of care for humanity

By way of conclusion, we highlight how asylum seekers as a group are not treated as equal to other vulnerable and marginal groups in Norway. The facilities they are offered are of a lower standard than those offered to other Norwegian groups of residents. Asylum seekers are not Norwegian citizens, and as such do not have the same rights in Norwegian society. However, they have a legitimate right to be in the country while their asylum application is under review and the Declaration of Human Rights sets all people as equal. Recognizing how politics, largely governed by economic and marked interests, directs political decisions towards increasing differences in people's and individuals' socio-economic position, together with belonging and well-being, we call to challenge these mechanisms.

In this perspective, we see a need for new ideas, perspectives, concepts and architectural solutions when developing models for reception centres in which the physical environment may positively affect individual and group belonging and well-being processes. We suggest that combining anthropological and architectural theoretical perspectives and methodological approaches may be helpful in developing knowledge, perspectives and concepts for future reception centres, based on values that rest in respect for humanity across cultural and social differences, and which recognize a need for compassion and solidarity founded on a shared humanity. Rather than understanding a betterment of housing standards and quality as a threat to Norwegian society and identity, we see a need to underline the social benefits of acknowledging equal humanity as well as providing secure housing that will ensure, at a minimum, a positive sense of belonging and well-being among asylum seekers in Norway. In this endeavour, we argue for the value of ethnographically based knowledge from the sphere of everyday life as it is lived and felt, and thus adding crucial knowledge for policymakers who govern processes of migration and integration, and in turn shape our views on self and humanity.

Notes

1 The project 'What Buildings Do – The Effect of the Physical Environment on Quality of Life of Asylum Seekers' was funded by the Norwegian Research Council and the Norwegian Directorate of Immigration (UDI) for the period 2012–17. It was led by the Faculty of Architecture and Fine Arts, NTNU. Other partners were SINTEF Building and Infrastructure and Inland Norway University College. It consisted of the following work packages: WP1: 'State of the art'; WP2: Case studies; and WP3: Architectural solutions for time-based dwellings.

2 The term 'housing' is here understood in line with the interdisciplinary field of housing studies, encompassing the built environment (the architectural dimensions), the social and economic structures (tenure, finances, policies, etc.) and residential or dwelling practices (how people dwell).

3 In Norwegian the term '*Nøkternt men forsvarlig*' is used. We have chosen to translate *forsvarlig* with 'reasonable' although this is not a fully adequate term. *Forsvarlig* means not only *reasonable*, understood as *proper*, *sound* and *safe*, but has also connotations of *dignity* and *decency*.

4 In 2015, one million refugees and asylum seekers came to Europe, thousands drowned in the Mediterranean Sea, and about 30,000 asylum seekers came to Norway (Østby 2016). At its peak, more than 8,000 asylum seekers came each month, most of them crossing the border from Russia entering Storskog, South Varanger, in the arctic north of Norway during the months of September to November. The situation created great concern for future devolpment, and a series of strict political interventions was introduced so as to reduce the number of asylum seekers and secure integration of those who were granted residence. More than half of the asylum seekers in 2015 came from Afghanistan and Syria, while Eritreans were the most numerous during the years 2008–14 (Østby 2016). Previously, the largest number of asylum seekers was 17,480 in 2002 (number for the whole year) (Østby 2016).

5 The three other fieldworks are part of the PhD project 'Housing quality, home-making and dwelling in reception centres for asylum seekers' carried out by Ragne Øwre Thorshaug.

References

Agamben, G. (1998), *Homo Sacer: Sovereign Power and Bare Life*, Stanford, CA: Stanford University Press.

Augè, M. (1995) *Non-places: Introduction to An Anthropology of Supermodernity*, London: Verso.

Awan N., T. Schneider and J. Till (2011), *Spatial Agency: Other Ways of Doing Architecture*, London: Routledge

Barad, K. (2007), *Meeting the Universe Half Way: Quantum Physics and the Entanglement of Matter and Meaning*, Washington DC: Duke University Press.

Berg, B. (2012), 'Mottakssystemet: Historikk og Utviklingstrender', in M. Valenta and B. Berg (eds), *Asylsøker i Velferdsstatens Venterom*, 17–32, Oslo: Universitetsforlaget.

Bourdieu, P. (1977), *Outline of a Theory of Practice*, Cambridge: Cambridge University Press.

Buchli, V. (2013), *An Anthropology of Architecture*, London: Bloomsbury.

Doucet, I. and K. Cupers (2009), 'Agency in Architecture: Rethinking Criticality in Theory and Practice', editorial in *Footprint* 04 (Delft School of Design, 2009): 1–6: 1.

Daston, L. and P. Galison (2010), *Objectivity*, Brooklyn, New York: Zone Books.

Dovey, K. (2008 [1999]), *Framing Places: Mediating Power in Built Form*, Routledge, London.

Fassin, D. (2012), *A Companion to Moral Anthropology*, Oxford: Wiley-Blackwell.

Faubion, J. (2003), 'Toward an Anthropology of Ethics: Foucault and the Pedagogies of Autopoiesis', in E. Wyschogrod and G. McKenny (eds), *The Ethical*, 146–65. Malden, MA: Blackwell Publishing.

Faubion, J. and G. Marcus (eds) (2009), *Fieldwork is Not What It Used to Be: Learning Anthropology's Method in a Time of Transition*, London: Cornell University Press.

Foucault, M. (1974), *The Order of Things: An Archaeology of the Human Sciences*, London: Tavistock Publications.

Foucault, M. (2000), *Power: Essential Works of Foucault 1954–1984*, 3, London: Penguin Press.

Gell, A. (1998), *Art and Agency: An Anthropological Theory*, Oxford: Clarendon Press.

Grønseth, A. (2014), 'Experiences of Pain: A Gateway to Cosmopolitan Subjectivity', in L. Josephides and A. Hall (eds), *We the Cosmopolitans: Moral and Existential Conditions of Being Human*, London: Berghahn.

Grønseth, A. and L. Josephides (2017), 'Introduction: The Ethics of Knowledge Creation: Transactions, Relations and Persons', in L. Josephides and A. Grønseth (eds), *The Ethics of Knowledge Creation: Transactions, Relations and Persons*, London: Berghahn.

Guttu, J. (2003), *'Den God Boligen': Fagfolks Oppfatninger av Boligkvalitet Gjennom 50 år*, PhD thesis, Oslo: AHO.

Hauge, Å. L., E. Støa, and K. Denizou (2017), 'Framing Outsidedness – Aspects of Housing Quality in Decentralized Reception Centres for Asylum Seekers in Norway', in *Housing, Theory and Society*, 34 (1): 1–20.

Hauge, Å. L., K. Denizou and E. Støa (2015), *Bokvalitet på Norske Asylmottak*, SINTEF Fag 29, Oslo: SINTEF Akademisk Forlag.

Humphrey, C. (1988), 'No Place Like Home: The Neglect of Architecture', *Anthropology Today*, 4 (1).

Ingold, T. (2007), *Lines*, New York: Routledge.

Ingold, T. (2013), *Making*, New York: Routledge.

Josephides, L. (2008), *Melanesian Odysseys: Negotiating the Self, Narrative and Modernity*, New York and Oxford: Berghahn.

Josephides, L. (2017), 'Towards an Epistemology of Ethical Knowledge', in L. Josephides and A. Grønseth (eds), *The Ethics of Knowledge Creation: Transactions, Relations and Persons*, London: Berghahn.

Kissoon, P. (2010), 'From Persecution to Destitution: A Snapshot of Asylum Seekers' Housing and Settlement Experiences in Canada and the United Kingdom', *Journal of Immigrant and Refugee Sudies*, 8: 4–31.

Lambek, M. (ed.) (2010), *Ordinary Ethics: Anthropology, Language and Action*, New York: Fordham University Press.

Larsen, H. (2014), *The Organisation of Reception Facilities for Asylum Seekers in Norway*, Oslo: EMN/ UDI.

Latour, B. (1979), *Laboratory Life: The Construction of Scientific Facts*, Beverly Hills, CA: Sage Publications.

Latour, B. and A. Yavena, (2009), '"Give Me a Gun and I Will Make All Buildings Move": An ANT's View of Architecture', in R. Geiser (ed.), *Explorations in Architecture: Teaching, Design, Research*, 80–9, Basel: Birkhauser.

Lauritsen, K. and B. Berg (1999), *Mellom Håp og Lengsel – å Leve i Asylmottak*, Trondheim: SINTEF.

Østby, L. (2016) 'From Asylum-seeker to Refugee: Before and After the Year of Crises 2015' [Fra Asylsøker til Flyktning – Før og Etter Kriseåret 2015], *Samfunnsspeilet* 4, Statistics Norway: SSB.

Potter, J., R. Canterero, X. Yan, S. Larrick, H. Keele and B. Ramirez (2005), 'How Does Immigration Impact on the Quality of Life in a Small Town?' in R. García-Mira, D. Uzzell, J. Real and J. Romay (eds), *Housing, Space and Quality of Life*, 81–97, Aldershot: Ashgate.

Rabinow, P. (2003), *Anthropos Today*, Princeton, NJ: Princeton University Press.

Scheper-Hughes, N. (1995), 'The Primacy of the Ethical: Propositions for a Militant Anthropology', *Current Anthropology*, 15: 227–83.

Schneider, T. and J. Till (2009), 'Beyond Discourse: Notes on Spatial Agency', *Footprint* 04: 97–111.

Stender, M (2017), 'Towards an Architectural Anthropology – What Architects can Learn from Anthropology and Vice Versa', in *Architectural Theory Review*, 21 (1): 27–43.

Stoczkowski, W. (2008), 'The "Fourth Aim" of Anthropology: Between Knowledge and Ethics', *Anthropological Theory*, 8 (4): 345–56.

Strathern, M. (2005), 'Robust Knowledge and Fragile Futures', in A. Ong and S. Collier (eds), *Global Assemblages: Technology, Politics, and Ethics as Anthropological Problems*, 464–81, Malden, MA: Blackwell Publishing.

Strumse, E., A. S. Grønseth and E. Støa (2016), 'The Effects of Physical Environment on Well-Being and Level of Conflict: Websurvey on Housing Quality of Asylum Seeker Reception Centres in Norway [Fysiske Vmgivelsers virkning på Trivsel og

Konfliktnivå: Spørreundersøkelse om Bofholhold på Asylmottak i Norge], Research Report no. 170/2016, Lillehammer: Lillehammer University College.

Støa, E., Å. L. Hauge, K. Denizou, R. Ø. Thorshaug and A. S. Grønseth (2016), *Bokvalitet i Asylmottak – En Veileder.* NTNU, Trondheim. Available online: https://www.ntnu. no/documents/10310/1269826659/Asyl-veileder-web_redusert_220616. pdf/409e7511-0cac-46d9-90b2-3eb549288173.

UDI (2014a), *Botid på Norske Mottak* [time spent at Norwegian reception centres], mail correspondance with employee at The Norwegian Directorate for Immigration, UDI, 8 December 2014.

UDI (2014b), *Kort Tilbakeblikk på Mottakssystemet* [a brief looking back at the reception system], document handout at The Norwegian Directorate for Immigration, UDI, Spring Conference, 15 May 2014.

Yavena, A. and S. Guy (2008), 'Understanding Architecture, Accounting Society', guest editorial in *Science Studies*, 21 (1): 3–7.

9

Collaboration in Crisis: Towards a Holistic Approach to Health and Social Care Supports for Vulnerable Populations[1]

Emma Heffernan

Sitting at a large round table with a group of prisoners and prison guards, I reluctantly tucked into my plate of stew. The younger, more exuberant prisoners dominated the dinner table conversation, arguing about a scene in last night's episode of EastEnders *and loudly complaining about having to eat custard again for pudding. Amid the din, my eyes were drawn to the brown-haired, sullen-looking woman, sitting across from me, slightly hunched at the edge of her seat and avoiding all eye contact. She seemed a million miles away, playing with her food, pushing the grey meat to the edge of her plate while at the same time making a small potato mountain in the centre, forcing the gravy into a watery moat. She didn't speak at all during dinner, so I was surprised she agreed to talk with me. Later, in private, it seemed like she could talk forever. In a tiny airless room reserved for prison visits, as tears and snot ran down her lined face, her story poured out. Sally spoke for almost twenty minutes, barely pausing to catch her breath, detailing her poverty-stricken childhood in inner-city Dublin, moving to her teenage years when she started drinking vodka and taking Valium at thirteen. 'I grew up quicker than what I should have', she said quietly. I wondered what she meant. I passed her a tissue, which quickly became sodden. Are you ok?, I asked. Do you need to take a break?, I asked, passing her another tissue, 'No, no, thanks, I'm sorry', she said, looking directly at me for the first time. 'I'm sorry, I'm so emotional, it's the benzos, I'm on a benzo detox. I want to tell you my story.'*

Field notes, Women's Prison, Dublin

Following a period of high unemployment and emigration that defined the 1980s and early 1990s, the birth of the 'Celtic Tiger' was a time of huge social and economic change. Ireland progressed from a closed, insular economy to one that eagerly embraced the global capitalist system (Inglis 2008). In this transition, the country went from being one of the poorest states in Europe to one of the richest (Sweeney 2005). One of the most remarkable developments during this time was rapid social mobility and the expansion of the middle classes (McWilliams 2006). However, even though the expanding middle classes saw a dramatic increase in their standard of living, there were still major gaps between these new globally oriented 'cosmopolitan elite' and a 'local underclass' reliant on the social welfare system (Inglis 2008: 19). While the poverty gap fell from 20 per cent in 2004 to 17 per cent in 2007 (Russell et al. 2007), the EU Survey on Income and Living Conditions (EU SILC) estimates that in 2006, at the height of the economic boom, 6.9 per cent of the population were living in consistent poverty, with 8.8 per cent of people experiencing debt paying for everyday expenses, such as food, clothing and heat (CSO 2007).

In 2008, Ireland experienced its worst economic and labour market crisis since the foundation of the state, deeply impacting the standard of living in Irish households (CSO 2013; Maître et al. 2014; Whelan 2013; Nolan et al. 2012; CSO 2013a; Savage et al. 2015; Whelan and Nolan 2017). Following the financial crash, austerity policies pushed people deeper into poverty and reduced access to essential public services and supports. The Irish state's focus on cutting funding to public services had severe social impacts, disproportionately affecting the poor and those most in need, as well as reducing the ability of the state to function in critical areas of poverty, health, education, social services, housing and homelessness (Harvey 2012; Burke 2010; IMO 2012; Burke et al. 2014; Community Platform 2014; Healy et al. 2015; Irish Human Rights and Equality Commission 2015, Heffernan 2017). Due to multiple forms of entrenched discrimination, women were particularly vulnerable to the detrimental effects of austerity policies (ESRI 2014). Access to public services such as health, education and training, and social housing are critical to the functioning of any society, with social structures and institutions playing a critical role in alleviating the impact of economic shocks, reducing vulnerability and supporting coping mechanisms to prevent and provide pathways out of poverty. This is especially so in times of crisis when people, particularly those with fewest resources and least ability to cope, become even more dependent on these services and supports (NESC 2005, 2013). The voluntary and community sector plays a crucial role, working in collaboration with public agencies to provide services especially to the poorest and most disadvantaged. It is estimated that between 2008 and 2012, the reduction in government spending across all sectors was 2.8 per cent, while cuts to the community and voluntary sector amounted to 35 per cent, leading to a loss of employment in the sector, as well as drastic cuts to service provision (Harvey 2012). This coincided with a reduction in disposable incomes and public charitable donations, and an increase in demand for the same services and supports, as the recession began to bite, deprivation rates increased, and more people sought support (CSO 2015). One of the most shocking and widely publicized outcomes of the financial crash has been an unprecedented increase in homelessness, especially in Dublin. Recent figures from the Dublin Region Homeless Executive (2017) indicate that almost 4,710 individual adults accessed emergency homeless shelters in Dublin in 2017. Nationally, there was an increase of 81 per cent in the number of people recorded as homeless between December 2011 and December 2016 (Simon Communities 2017). Cuts to funding for housing support, health services, probation and welfare services, as well as to education and training services, contribute to homelessness, but also prevent people from escaping homelessness – again, impacting some of the most vulnerable sections of society (Simon Communities 2014).

This chapter examines the experiences of one of the most vulnerable populations in Irish society, who even at the height of the boom were struggling to survive: homeless, drug-using women involved in street-based sex work in Dublin's inner city. The research presented here comes from my PhD work – an in-depth analysis of female sexual labour in Dublin from 2005 to 2011, which coincided with the peak of the economic boom and the early years of the economic crisis. Sex workers are one of the most marginalized, criminalized and stigmatized populations in the world, and the criminalization not only stigmatizes the work sex workers do, but also acts as a barrier, preventing sex workers from accessing health and social care services and supports. Further, it increases violence and abuse from clients, those posing as clients, other sex workers, their partners, and the public (Krüsi 2015; Lancet 2015, Shannon et al. 2015, among others).

Sex work is a human rights issue. Like other marginalized and socially excluded groups, homeless, drug-using sex workers bear a disproportionate burden of health inequalities (WHO 2000, 2008; Marmot 2005; Whitehead and Dahlgren 2006). By using narratives of women engaged in street-based sex work, such as Sally in the opening piece, I argue that we need to adopt a human rights-based approach to sex work, grounded in public health principles, that prioritizes the health and safety of sex workers, while at the same time tackles the underlying causes of poverty, inequality and structural violence – the social and structural forces that constrain the choices people make in their everyday lives (Farmer 1996; Marmot 2004; Wilkinson 2005). Reducing harm and protecting the physical, mental and sexual health of sex workers should be at the core of any policy and legal framework.

Tackling these issues requires a collaborative, whole systems approach that incorporates the voices and experiences of sex workers, as well as recognizes the broader social determinants of health that shape people's lives. The World Health Organization (2015) defines these social determinants of health as:

> the conditions in which people are born, grow, work, live, and age, and the wider set of forces and systems shaping the conditions of daily life. These forces and systems include economic policies and systems, development agendas, social norms, social policies and political systems. [Furthermore] factors such as poverty, food insecurity, social exclusion and discrimination, poor housing, unhealthy early childhood conditions and low occupational status are important determinants of most of disease, death and health inequalities between and within countries.
>
> WHO 2004: 1

Wider political action is needed to tackle the inequalities, stigma and social exclusion that some sex workers , particularly homeless, street based sex workers face, across a whole host of sectors including health, housing, criminal justice, social policy, social protection, education and training, and employment. Policies that address the complex health and social care needs of sex workers, as well as those that tackle the broader structural causes of ill health, must be developed and implemented across these various sectors, and involve government departments, community and voluntary organization, academics and activists, and, of course, sex workers themselves (Platt 2013). Support is needed to ensure those experiencing poverty and health inequalities are empowered to participate in the planning and implementation of these policies (Farrell et al. 2008). It is essential that the voices of sex workers are central to policies that impact their daily lives.

Stigma, sex work and risk

Modern Western societies assess sex acts according to 'a hierarchical system of sexual value' (Rubin 1999: 153). According to Rubin, individuals whose behaviour ranks highly on the scale, such as heterosexual, reproductive, married couples, are rewarded with legality, respectability, social and physical mobility, institutional support and material benefits. Those with occupations and behaviours lower down on this scale, such as sex workers, often suffer loss of social and physical mobility, loss of institutional support and economic sanctions. Stigma, asserts Rubin, keeps some sexual behaviours as low status and effectively punishes those who engage in them. Miller and Vance (2004) argue that the concept of a sexual hierarchy provides a useful analytical device for identifying and interrogating how societies evaluate sexual practices, relationships and expressions, its value in the way it exposes rules for evaluating 'legitimate' and 'illegitimate' sexuality. Furthermore, they contend that while the organizing principles that various members of a culture use for ranking standards of sexual legitimacy may vary across cultures, they are deeply implicated in all sexuality and rights-based questions, since people lower down in the hierarchy are often subject to discrimination and abuse. Furthermore, they argue that the sexual hierarchy 'metes out rewards and deprivations with material as well as symbolic resources' and a sexual hierarchy intersects with other social hierarchies and inequalities including class, race and gender, allowing different types of stigma to reinforce each another (Miller and Vance 2004: 7). They add that the greatest influence – and harm – of the sexual hierarchy is in the way it 'animates and is embodied in a range of state interventions, especially criminal law'. The state, then, by criminalizing and disenfranchising certain sexual behaviours and identities, reinforces this sexual hierarchy. Those engaging in transgressive behaviours deemed immoral or dangerous to society, such as sex workers, often become the target of social control, criminalization, violence, harassment and marginalization (Seidman, 2005).

The issue of sex work is a deeply divisive issue among feminists. While it is beyond the scope of this chapter to interrogate this highly polemical debate in detail, in simple terms, some feminists view sex work as the ultimate expression of patriarchy, arguing that prostitution is inherently a violence against women, and call for the abolition of prostitution. Others view sex work as a form of work, and advocate for a human rights approach, usually arguing for legalization or decriminalization of sex work (for a more nuanced discussion see Chapkis 1997; Doezema 1998, 2005; Kempadoo 1998; Outshoorn 2005; Vanwesenbeeck 2017). Mounting evidence suggests that abolitionist regimes, such as the 'Nordic' or the 'Swedish' models, which criminalize sex work, harm those working in the industry by pushing sex work underground, thereby forcing sex workers into more dangerous working environments (Shannon et al. 2015; Bekker et al. 2015). Recent changes to the law in Ireland (Criminal Law Sexual Offences Act 2017), which moves to criminalize the purchase of sex, represents a worrying development in progressing social justice for sex workers, as this new law only serves to deepen existing inequalities and reinforce the stigma associated with sex work, putting sex workers at increased risk of human rights abuses (WHO 2014; Amnesty International 2016). Stigma is implicit in the laws governing the sale of sex, and criminalization of sex work not only stigmatizes the work sex workers do, but also acts as a barrier, preventing sex workers from accessing health and social care, as well as increasing violence and abuse from clients, other sex workers, police, domestic partners, and the public. For workers in certain sections of the industry, their social exclusion and vulnerability is further exacerbated in that they also belong to other stigmatized populations, such as drug users, the homeless, the poor, prisoners – those who, based on prevailing social attitudes, are seen 'as not quite human' (Goffman 1963: 5), and therefore not deserving of social protection.

Sexual services markets are generally highly stratified and often comprise a mixture of outdoor (street-based) and indoor work venues, such as brothels, massage parlours and escort agencies. The last few years have seen a shift away from traditional red light districts, as the industry constantly adapts and reinvents itself, absorbing innovations and modern technologies (Plachy and Ridgeway 1996). Internet and mobile phone technologies, in particular, have transformed all sectors of the market and are implicated in the expansion of indoor sexual service markets. In Dublin, this has resulted in a decrease in the visibility of street-based sex workers, with some former street-based workers working indoors and accessing clients via their phones and only occasionally accessing clients from street-based work. However, women who remain in street-based work, like Sally in the opening piece, are often the most vulnerable, selling sex under highly constrained social and structural circumstances.

Like other industries, the sex industry has relatively privileged and exploitative positions for its workers, and those working in different sectors of the market encounter different types of risk and operate within different 'risk environments' (Rhodes 2002). Many of the risks associated with sex work can be attributed to a variety of factors, including the legal frameworks that govern the sale of sexual services, the stigma attached to sex work and, to some extent, societal ambivalence to the welfare of sex workers. Sex work can be dangerous and workers face multiple occupational health risks in their daily lives, including risk of disease, violence, discrimination, exploitation and criminalization, depending on the social location of the worker and the social context of where the work takes place (Chapkis 1997; Ward et al. 1999; Potterat et al. 2004; Sanders 2004; Rekart 2005; Canter et al. 2009; Sanders et al. 2009; Das and Horton 2015). The social location of workers largely determines how sex is sold, how much control workers have over their working environment and the risks they are likely to encounter in their everyday working lives. More visible forms of sex work, such as street-based sex work, are often associated with higher risks (Brookes-Gordon 2006; Church et al. 2001; Kinnell 2006). Testimonies from street-based sex workers I met during my fieldwork reveal a litany of physical, sexual and verbal abuse and violence, perpetrated by clients, those posing as clients, other sex workers, their partners and the public. The majority of these attacks were not reported to the police. Women described feeling afraid to report assaults to the police for fear that they would not be believed, that they may be arrested for drug use or having outstanding bench warrants, or that they would blamed for engaging in 'risky' activities. Many of their narratives, suggested an acceptance and normalization of violence as part of 'the game', with many viewing it as something that cannot be entirely avoided, but instead must be managed. Sally articulates the risks and dangers inherent in her everyday experiences of selling sex in Dublin's inner city:

> It's a dangerous game, do you know what I mean? It is very, very dangerous. You don't know who you're dealing with, you don't know this, that, and the other, do you know what I mean? You could be murdered, you could be, and all that. It frightens me a lot, you know. I still take the risk though, do you know what I mean?

It is not only the violence itself that my research participants found very difficult to cope with, but the constant threat of violence. The constant fear of being murdered, raped, robbed or arrested caused a huge amount of distress and worry. Many attributed issues with their emotional well-being to the stigma associated with sex work, the stress of concealing their occupation from family and friends, as well as the constant worry for their safety. Louise, who was brutally raped by a client several years ago, describes how she lives in constant fear, worrying that each night she works will be her last:

> The worst is the fear, yeah the fear of being raped or attacked, it's constant like. You know, every time you get into a car, every time. Like when I got raped, it wasn't in a car, I was on foot, yeah, so every time I get into a car I think, is this me last one? Will I see my kids again?

Sex workers reported using a variety of strategies for managing risks associated with their work, including assessing potential clients, categorizing and discriminating between clients, maintaining good relationships with regular clients, working with other sex workers, exchanging information about 'dodgy' clients, working in a familiar geographical location, attempting to control their drug use, and trusting their intuition. Being able to manage occupational risks is crucial for sex workers to maintain their personal health and safety (Williamson and Folaron 2001; Krüsi et al. 2012). However, attempts at reducing risk may be compromised by local and contextual factors (NACD 2009; Maher et al. 2011). For example, as well as changes to the social and economic landscape, the Celtic Tiger brought huge change to the built environment. As former dilapidated parts of Dublin city were regenerated, one such area north of the River Liffey emerged as a highly contested space among sex workers, local residents, the police and politicians (Heffernan 2013). Central to this conflict was the commissioning of a new tramline and its subsequent works, which illuminated a previously dark and largely derelict part of the city frequented by street-based sex workers. This forced sex workers from their usual working patches, along these secluded alleyways, back into residential areas and into direct conflict with local residents, who mounted nightly protests. These protests, coupled with an increased police presence in the area, meant that clients were scared away, and women were forced to move into more dark and dangerous spaces, further down the quays and towards the Phoenix Park, in order to attract this dwindling client population. Increased competition for clients meant that women were often forced to work alone, to drop prices, to engage with clients they would rather reject or offer more risky services, such as unprotected sex.

The laws governing prostitution (and drug use) and how they are enforced through policing and the judicial system have a detrimental effect on the health and safety of sex workers, particularly street-based workers. There is little evidence that criminalization of sex work has reduced the numbers of sex workers, but instead has pushed it underground and increased the stigma associated with it. This in turn means that sex workers have less control over their working environment and working conditions (Daniel 2010). In many instances, sex workers are forced to choose between their own health and welfare and providing an income for themselves and their families.

Stigma and access to health and social care services

Homeless, street-based, drug-using sex workers often have multiple, complex intersecting health and social care needs. Many of the women I met during my fieldwork reported extremely poor mental and physical health and felt their health deteriorated as a result of their drug use, being homeless and engaging in sex work. Issues reported included problem drug (heroin, cocaine, benzodiazepines, anti-depressants, ecstasy, cannabis) and alcohol use; mental health issues, including depression and anxiety; and physical problems, including HIV, hepatitis, respiratory and gastrointestinal problems, abscesses, dental problems, frequent coughs and colds, various STIs including chlamydia, gonorrhoea, HPV and genital herpes.

Despite their multiple health issues, many women reported being haphazardly connected to public services and supports, such as drug and alcohol treatment services, GPs, mental health services, homeless services, hospitals, social welfare, and other health and social care services. They described facing substantial barriers when attempting to access health and social care and supports, as well as a broad range of public services such as housing, education and training, largely because of stigma, discrimination and criminalization associated with their sex work and drug use. Those that did engage found service provision to be fragmented, incoherent and sometimes overly complicated, reporting that it required significant social capital to navigate the health and social care landscape. Others felt that there was a duplication of some services, while mental health service provision and sex worker-specific sexual health services were found to be non-existent or severely lacking. While some indicated positive experiences with individual services, it was felt that the majority of services and supports were unable to cater for their complex needs, with women reporting a lack of integration and poor communication between existing services, and a lack of a coordinated approach to their care.

Likewise, discussions with community-based health and social care workers revealed that many felt they were poorly equipped to provide holistic person-centred care to people with complex needs, such as homeless, drug-using sex workers. Some workers reported feeling stressed by their inability to provide the level of service appropriate to the needs of their service users and blamed chronic underfunding, particularly for addiction and homeless services, a lack of capital investment in purpose-built facilities, poor planning and policy development and poor integration of existing services. Services providers were often forced to work in badly maintained and dilapidated buildings, sometimes without adequate heat and lighting. Service managers found it difficult to recruit and retain staff due to low salaries and poor working conditions in the sector. Indeed, some questioned the government's commitment to reducing poverty, inequality and social exclusion, even during the economic boom. Much of this work was carried out under even more difficult circumstances for many organizations during the recession, as cuts to drugs services had a catastrophic impact on staffing and service provision. Between 2008 and 2014 the Drugs Initiative Budget was cut by 37 per cent, affecting a wide range of services including treatment and rehabilitation (Citywide 2016). Services that previously acted as a safety net for vulnerable people, such as availability of a key worker or outreach services – often a vital interface between vulnerable women and the wider health and social care system – were forced to reduce their services and lay off staff. Sally was distraught when her key worker was let go from the community drug project where she worked with vulnerable drug-using women: 'there's nothing now, no one, no fucking support at all. I've nowhere else to go, no one to talk to and I've all this stuff going on in me head.'

Perceptions of poor service provision were compounded by a reluctance of sex workers to engage with health and social care services due to the stigma associated with sex work, which was exacerbated by belonging to other stigmatized populations, such as being 'an addict', being homeless, having a history of incarceration, mental health issues, or being HIV-positive. Sex workers reported feeling ashamed and embarrassed to admit their involvement in sex work, fearing that they would be looked down on or would not get the care they needed from service providers, as Sally attests:

> The thoughts of telling someone that I stood on Benburb Street or fuckin' Baggott Street I'd deny it down to the ground . . . I'd deny it down to the ground, I would, I'd deny it down to the ground, sure even in the clinic I wouldn't even give them me name or me proper date of birth. Going to a clinic where they are helping you and I still lie because of the shame.

Some women felt they could not trust healthcare workers and other service providers to keep their information confidential, and that it could somehow be used against them. Sex workers who were also mothers lived in fear that if they disclosed the nature of their work to service providers, they would be deemed 'unfit mothers' and reported to social services, and their children would be taken away from them and placed in care. Sally, for instance, is afraid to disclose her involvement in sex work to her GP in case it means she will not be able to get her children back from care:

> I don't want them to find out anything more about me, in case they won't give me my kids back, they don't care anyway, once they get paid . . .

The stigma associated with sex work, and other stigmatizing identities such as being a problem drug user or having a history of incarceration, can have serious implications for the health and well-being of sex workers, meaning that they are unable to access appropriate healthcare and are unable to have open and frank discussion with providers about their needs, further increasing their vulnerability and exclusion.

Sally's experience

In the opening piece, I spoke of my first encounter with Sally in the Women's Prison, where she was serving a nine-month sentence for soliciting, stealing and outstanding bench warrants. I met Sally several times over the course of my research, following her release from prison. On the first day I met her, Sally was very emotional as she was on a 'benzo detox' (benzodiazepine detoxification) and spent most of the time talking to me while crying into a sodden tissue. Sally had a traumatic childhood and started drinking and taking Valium as a teenager, when introduced to it by her older brother and his friends. She left school without any qualifications and eventually managed to get part-time work in a cafe to supplement her inadequate social welfare. Things went well for a few years and Sally was able to rent a house for herself and her children. After she was let go from the cafe and was struggling to make ends meet on social welfare, she became involved with sex work when introduced to it by a friend, became addicted to heroin and eventually became homeless: 'I was only getting me benefit, which is hard to live on when you're living on the streets . . . so a lot of the women that lived in the hostel were on the game . . .'

This took a toll on her mental and physical health and when she became unable to cope, her children were taken into care. This was a devastating loss for Sally and what she describes as the catalyst for her life 'spiralling out of control'; as she says:

> I ended up in that hostel, it should be shut down, it's a fucking drugs den. Since living there I have just spiralled: it wasn't a spiral it was a straight slope back down, straight back down to the gutter. I ended up back using heroin, cocaine, Valium: you name it, I used it.

She eventually began sleeping rough after she started getting into fights in the homeless hostel, and as her drug use worsened she resorted to begging and stealing. Soon afterwards she was arrested for stealing clothes from a large department store in the city centre and was sent to prison. Sally dreamed of getting 'off the drugs' permanently, and most of all she dreamed of one day getting her children back and sharing a home with them:

I'd love to change me life, and get off the drugs for good and get a little part-time job, you know what I mean? I'd love to get my babies back, the whole lot, you know what I mean? All I ever wanted was to have a home for me kids, that kind of thing, you know. That's all I dream of . . .

After spending almost seven months in prison, Sally was released late on a Friday evening due to overcrowding, with no advance notice. Following her release she spent the night walking the streets, looking for a place to stay. The homeless hostels were full and she had no choice but to sleep rough in an abandoned building near the Liffey. By the following week Sally had overdosed on heroin and was admitted to intensive care when she was found unresponsive in a train station lavatory. For women like Sally, getting out of the poverty trap felt next to impossible, leading to increased feelings of hopelessness, desperation and suicidal ideation, as she commented on one of my last encounters with her:

I need support, I've no support, I need support to get me back on my feet. I just felt so lost, I didn't know up from down, which direction for my life to go in, I was starting to have suicidal thoughts, my life is a mess, it's a complete and utter mess.

Conclusion: Towards a collaborative approach

Paul Farmer argues that individual narratives can only be understood with the 'larger matrix of culture, history and political economy' (2003: 286). Similarly, Bourgeois writes: 'individualistic psychological determinist approaches misses the larger political economic and cultural context. It ignores historical processes and the effects of unequal power relations around class, ethnic, or gender and sexual categories' (2003: 296). Individual narratives, such as those of Sally, not only underline the multiplicity of interconnected historical, socio-economic, political and structural processes that shape people's lives, but also highlight the complexity of the challenge ahead if we are to break cycles of intergenerational poverty, inequality and marginalization.

Following the financial crisis, austerity policies have pushed people further into poverty, as well as significantly reducing access to vital public services and supports. Many of my research participants lived chaotic lives. Their life choices were curtailed by multiple intersecting health, social and economic issues, including poverty, homelessness, problem drug and alcohol use, poor physical and mental health, being haphazardly connected to health and social care services, adverse childhood events, poor educational attainment, a poor social support network, and a lack of any real opportunities to improve their lives. Many described the barriers they faced when accessing health and social care, housing and employment, often in an incoherent and disjointed health and social care landscape. Their vulnerability was further complicated by the criminalization of sex work, which only serves to deepen existing inequalities and reinforce the stigma associated with sex work, putting them at increased risk of human rights abuses.

Wider political action is needed to address the inequalities, stigma and social exclusion that homeless, street- based, drug- using sex workers face across a whole host of sectors, including health, housing, criminal justice, social policy, social protection, education and training, and employment. Reducing harm and protecting the physical, mental and sexual health of sex workers needs to be central to any policy and legal framework. Policies that address the complex health and social care needs of homeless drug using sex workers, as well as those that tackle the broader structural causes of ill health, must be developed and implemented across multiple sectors and in collaboration with all relevant stakeholders, and, especially, incorporate the voices and experiences of sex workers.

Acknowledgements

This research was funded by a Government of Ireland Irish Research Council Postgraduate Scholarship and a John and Pat Hume Doctoral Award from Maynooth University.

Note

1   I have been given permission to reproduce some of the data and analysis from E. Heffernan, N. Moore-Cherry and J. McHale (eds) (2017), *Debating Austerity in Ireland: Crisis, Experience and Recovery*. Dublin: Royal Irish Academy.

References

Amnesty International (2016), 'Amnesty International Policy on State Obligations to Respect, Protect and Fulfil the Human Rights of Sex Workers'. Available online: https://www.amnesty.org/en/documents/pol30/4062/2016/en/ (accessed 16 September 2017).

Bourgois, P. (2003), *In Search of Respect: Selling Crack in El Barrio,* Cambridge: Cambridge University Press.

Burke, S. (2010), 'Boom to Bust: Its Impact on Irish Health Policy and Health Services', *Irish Journal of Public Policy,* 2 (1). Available online: http://publish.ucc.ie/ ijpp/2010/01/burke/08/en (accessed 12 November 2017).

Burke, S., S. Thomas, S. Barry and C. Keegan (2014), 'Measuring, Mapping and Making Sense of Irish Health System Performance in the Recession', Working Paper from the Resilience Project in the Centre for Health Policy and Management, School of Medicine, Trinity College Dublin. Available online: http://www.medicine.tcd.ie/ health-systems-research/assets/pdf/pubs/Resilience-working-paper-March-2014.pdf (accessed 12 December 2017).

Brooks-Gordon, B. (2006) *The Price of Sex: Prostitution, Policy and Society,* Devon: Willan Publishing.

Canter, D., M. Ioannou and D. Youngs (2009), *Safer Sex in the City: The Experience and Management of Street Prostitution,* Surrey: Ashgate.

Chapkis, W. (1997), *Live Sex Acts: Women Performing Erotic Labour,* London: Cassell.

Church, S., M. Henderson and M. Barnard (2001), 'Violence by Clients Towards Female Prostitutes in Different Work Settings: Questionnaire Survey', *British Medical Journal,* 322 (7285): 524–5.

Citywide (2016), 'Citywide Drugs Crisis Campaign: Manifesto for Election 2016, Tackling Ireland's Drug Problem'. Available online: https://www.citywide.ie/download/pdf/ general_election_2016_manifesto_citywide.pdf (accessed 23 September 2017)

Comiskey, C., K. O'Sullivan and J. Cronly (2006), 'Hazardous Journeys to Better Places: Positive Outcomes and Negative Risks Associated with Care Pathway Before During and After an Admittance to the Dochas Centre, Mountjoy Prison, Dublin, Ireland', Dublin: Health Service Executive: Dublin.

Community Platform (2014), 'Now You See Us: The Human Stories Behind Poverty in Ireland'. Available online: http://communityplatform.ie/wpcontent/uploads/2016/10/ nowyouseeus.pdf (accessed 23 September 2017).

CSO (2007), 'EU Survey on Income and Living Conditions' (EU-SILC), Dublin: Central Statistics Office.

CSO (2013a), 'Quarterly National Household Survey: Effect on Households of the Economic Downturn Quarter 3 2012', Dublin: Central Statistics Office.

CSO (2013b), 'Survey of Income and Living Conditions (SILC) 2011 and Revised 2010 Results', Dublin: Central Statistics Office.

CSO (2015), 'Survey on Income and Living Conditions (SILC) 2013 Results', Dublin: Central Statistics Office.

Daniel, A. (2010), The Sexual Health of Sex Workers: No Bad Whores, Just Bad Laws, *Social Research Briefs,* 19.

Decker, M., A. Crago, S. Chu, S. Sherman, M. Seshu, K. Buthelezi, M. Dhaliwal and C. Beyrer (2015), 'Human Rights Violations Against Sex Workers: Burden and Effect on HIV', *Lancet,* 385 (9963): 186–99.

Doezema, J. (1998), 'Forced to Choose: Beyond the Voluntary v. Forced Prostitution Dichotomy', in K. Kempadoo and J. Doezema (eds), *Global Sex Workers: Rights, Resistance and Redefinition*, London: Routledge.

Doezema, J. (2005), 'Now You See Her, Now You Don't: Sex Workers at the UN Trafficking Protocol Negotiations', *Social and Legal Studies*, 14 (1): 61–89.

Dublin Region Homeless Executive (2017), 'Dublin Region Families who are Homeless (Q3 July to September 2017)', Infographic, Dublin: Dublin Region Homeless Executive.

Epele, M. (2002), 'Gender, Violence and HIV: Women's Survival in the Streets', *Culture, Medicine and Psychiatry*, 26: 33–54.

ESRI (2014), 'The Gender Impact of Tax and Benefit Change: A Microsimulation Approach', Dublin: ESRI.

Farmer, P. (2003), 'On Suffering and Structural Violence: A View from Below', in N. Scheper-Hughes and P. Bourgois (eds), *Violence in War and Peace: An Anthology*, Oxford: Blackwell.

Farrell, C., H. McAvoy, J. Wilde and Combat Poverty Agency (2008), 'Tackling Health Inequalities – An All-Ireland Approach to Social Determinants', Dublin: Combat Poverty Agency/Institute of Public Health in Ireland.

Goffman, E. (1963), *Stigma: Notes on the Management of Spoiled Identity*, New York: Prentice Hall.

Harvey, B. (2012), 'Downsizing the Community Sector: Changes in Employment and Services in the Voluntary and Community Sector in Ireland, 2008–2012', Dublin: Irish Congress of Trade Unions Community Sector Committee.

Healy, S., A. Delaney, A. Leahy, M. Murphy, B. Reynolds and J. Robinson (2015), 'Health – Towards a Just Society: Securing Economic Development, Social Equality and Sustainability', Socio-economic Review 2015, Social Justice Ireland, Dublin, 1–344.

Heffernan, E. (2013), '"I Live Here Too": Sex Work, Contested Space and the State', Paper, Session Panel: Urban Renewal over the Globe: The Spatial Dimensions of Citizenship, International Union of Anthropological and Ethnological Sciences, Manchester, UK.

Heffernan, E. (2017) 'Poverty and Risk: The Impact of Austerity on Vulnerable Females in Dublin's Inner City', in Heffernan, E., N. Moore-Cherry and J. McHale (eds) *Debating Austerity: Ireland's Response to the Global Economic Crisis*, Dublin: Royal Irish Academy.

Inglis, T. (2008), *Global Ireland: Same Difference*, London: Routledge.

Irish Human Rights and Equality Commission (2015), 'Ireland and the International Covenant on Economic, Social and Cultural Rights', Dublin: Irish Human Rights and Equality Commission.

Irish Medical Organization (IMO) (2012), 'Position Paper on Health Inequalities', Dublin: Irish Medical Organization.

Kempadoo, K. (1998), 'Introduction: Globalizing Sex Workers' Rights', in K. Kempadoo and J. Doezema (eds), *Global Sex Workers: Rights, Resistance and Redefinition*, London: Routledge.

Kerrigan D., C. Kennedy, R. Morgan-Thomas, S. Reza-Paul, P. Mwangi, K. Win,
    A. McFall, V. Fonner and J. Butler (2015), 'A Community Empowerment Approach to
    the HIV Response Among Sex Workers: Effectiveness, Challenges, and
    Considerations for Implementation and Scale-up', *Lancet.* 385 (9963): 172–85.
Kinnell, H. (2006), 'Murder Made Easy: The Final Solution to Prostitution', in
    R. Campbell and M. O' Neill (eds), *Sex Work Now,* Devon: Willan Publishing.
Krüsi, A., J. Chettiar, A. Ridgway, J. Abbott, S. Strathdee and K. Shannon (2012),
    'Negotiating Safety and Sexual Risk Reduction with Clients in Unsanctioned Safer
    Indoor Sex Work Environments: A Qualitative Study', *American Journal of Public
    Health*, 102 (6): 1154–9.
Maher, L., J. Mooney-Somers, P. Phlong, M. Couture, E. Stein, J. Evans, M. Cockroft,
    N. Sanothy, T. Nemoto and K. Page (2011), 'Selling Sex in Unsafe Spaces: Sex Work
    Risk Environments in Phnom Penh, Cambodia', *Harm Reduction Journal*, 8 (1):
    30–40.
Maître, B., H. Russell and C. Whelan (2014), 'Trends in Economic Stress and the Great
    Recession in Ireland: An Analysis of the CSO Survey of Income and Living
    Conditions (SILC)', Technical Paper no. 5, Dublin: Department of Social Protection.
Marmot, M. (2005), 'Social Determinants of Health Inequalities', *Lancet,* 365: 1099–104.
McWilliams, D. (2005), 'The Pope's Children: Ireland's New Elite', Dublin: Gill and
    Macmillan.
Miller, A. and C. Vance (2004), 'Sexuality, Human Rights and Health', *Health and Human
    Rights*, 5–15.
National Economic and Social Council (2005), 'The Developmental Welfare State',
    no. 113, Dublin: National Economic and Social Council Office.
National Economic and Social Council (2013), 'The Social Dimensions of the Crisis',
    no. 134, Dublin: National Economic and Social Council Office.
NACD (2009), 'Drug Use, Sex Work and the Risk Environment in Dublin', National
    Advisory Committee on Drugs, Dublin: Stationery Office.
Nolan, B., B. Maître, S. Voitchovsky and C. Whelan (2012), 'Inequality and Poverty in
    Boom and Bust: Ireland as a Case Study', GINI Discussion Papers, 70, AIAS
    (Amsterdam Institute for Advanced Labour Studies).
Outshoorn, J. (2005), 'The Political Debates on Prostitution and Trafficking of Women',
    Social Politics, Spring: 141–55.
Potterat J., D. Brewer, S. Muth, R. Rothenberg, D. Woodhouse, J. Muth, H. Stites and
    S. Brody (2014), 'Mortality in a Long-term Open Cohort of Prostitute Women',
    American Journal of Epidemiology, 159 (8): 778–85.
Plachy, S. and J. Ridgeway (1996), *Red Light: Inside the Sex Industry*. New York:
    Powerhouse Books.
Platt, L. (2013), 'Sex Workers Need More Than Condoms and Shelters', *The Conversation*.
    Available online: https://theconversation.com/sex-workers-need-more-than-
    condoms-and-shelters-21140.
Rekart, M. (2005), 'Sex-work Harm Reduction', *Lancet.* 366: 2123–34.

Rhodes, T. (1997), 'Risk Theory in Epidemic Times: Sex, Drugs and the Social Organization of "Risk Behaviour"', *Sociology of Health and Illness*, 19 (2): 208–27.

Rhodes, T. (2002), 'The "Risk Environment": A Framework for Understanding and Reducing Drug-related Harm', *International Journal of Drug Policy*, 13: 85–94.

Rubin, G. (1999), 'Thinking Sex: Notes for a Radical Theory of the Politics of Sexuality', in R. Parker and P. Aggleton (eds), *Culture, Society and Sexuality: A Reader*, London: UCL Press.

Russell, H., B. Maître and B. Nolan (2010), 'Monitoring Poverty Trends in Ireland 2004–2007: Key Issues for Children, People of Working Age and Older People', *Research Series*, 17.

Sanders, T. (2004), 'A Continuum of Risk? The Management of Health, Physical and Emotional Risks by Female Sex Workers', *Sociology of Health and Illness*, 26 (5): 557–74.

Sanders, T., M. O'Neill and J. Pitcher (2009), *Prostitution: Sex Work, Policy and Politics*, London: Sage Publications.

Shannon K., S. Strathdee, S. Goldenberg, P. Duff., P. Mwangi, M. Rusakova, S. Reza-Paul, J. Lau, K. Deering, M. Pickles and M. Boily (2015), 'Global Epidemiology of HIV Among Female Sex Workers: Influence of Structural Determinants', *Lancet*, 385 (9962): 55–71.

Savage, M., T, Callan, B. Nolan and B. Colgan (2015), 'The Great Recession, Austerity and Inequality: Evidence from Ireland', ESRI Working Paper no. 499, Dublin: Economic and Social Research Institute.

Shewan, D., R. Hammersley, J. Oliver and S. Macpherson (2000), 'Fatal Drug Overdose after Liberation from Prison: A Retrospective Study of Female Ex-prisoners from Strathclyde Region (Scotland)', *Addiction Research*, 8; 267–78.

Simon Communities (2014), 'Making the Right Choices – Simon Communities in Ireland Pre-Budget Submission 2015'. Available online: http://www.simon.ie/ Portals/1/Simon%20Communities%20in%20Ireland%20Pre%20Budget%20 Submission%202015123.pdf (accessed 23 September 2017).

Simon Communities (2017), 'Simon Communities Respond to Census Data on People who are Homeless', press release. Available online: https://www.simon.ie/ MediaCentre/MediaReleases/TabId/206/ArtMID/851/ArticleID/170/Simon-Communities-respond-to-Census-data-on-people-who-are-homeless.aspx (accessed 12 December 2017).

Stardust, Z. (2017), 'The Stigma of Sex Work Comes with a High Cost'. Available online: https://theconversation.com/the-stigma-of-sex-work-comes-with-a-high-cost-79657 (accessed December 2017).

Steinman, S. (2005), *From Outsider to Citizen. In Regulating Sex: The Politics of Intimacy and Identity*, New York: Routledge.

Sweeney, E. (2005), 'Ireland's Economic Environment: The SCM Context. Technical Focus in Logistical Solutions', *The Journal of the National Institute for Transport and Logistics*, 8(4): 9–10.

The Lancet (2015), 'Editorial: Keeping Sex Workers Safe' *Lancet*, 386 (9993): 504.

Vanwesenbeeck, I. (2017), 'Sex Work Criminalization Is Barking Up the Wrong Tree', *Archives of Sexual Behaviour*, 46: 1631–40.

Ward H., S. Day and J. Weber (1999), 'Risky Business: Health and Safety in the Sex Industry Over a 9-year Period', *Sexually Transmitted Infections*, 75 (5): 340–3.

Watson, D., B. Maître, C. Whelan and J. Williams (2017), 'Child Poverty in a Period of Austerity', in E. Heffernan, N. Moore-Cherry and J. McHale (eds), *Debating Austerity in Ireland: Crisis, Experience and Recovery*, 157–74, Dublin: Royal Irish Academy.

Whelan, C. and B. Nolan (2017), 'Austerity and Inequality in Ireland', in E. Heffernan, N. Moore-Cherry and J. McHale (eds), *Debating Austerity in Ireland: Crisis, Experience and Recovery*, 100–14, Dublin: Royal Irish Academy.

World Health Organization (2004), Commission on the Social Determinants of Health: note by the Secretariat, no. EB115/35, Geneva: WHO.

World Health Organization (2008), 'Health Equity Through Action on the Social Determinants of Health', Geneva: WHO.

World Health Organization (2014), 'Consolidated Guidelines on HIV Prevention, Diagnosis, Treatment and Care for Key Populations', Geneva: WHO.

Williamson, C. and G. Folaron (2001), 'Violence Risk and Survival Strategies of Street Prostitution', *Western Journal of Nursing Research*, 23 (5): 463–75.

10

Anthropology and Peace Making

Colin Irwin

Introduction

Can anthropology help us to resolve some of the most pressing problems of our age or is it just an anachronism of a colonial past? That is the question posed by this book. Total war, as an industrial enterprise, and war as terrorism in an age of globalization are undoubtedly two of the most pressing problems of our age – in one form or another perhaps they always were. So can the insights of anthropology help us to reach a better understanding of this most destructive of human behaviours and in so doing resolve them?

Anthropology, in the American tradition, is divided into four sub-disciplines: biological anthropology, cultural anthropology, linguistics and archaeology. I have used the first three to better understand the nature of deadly group conflict in humans and how war might be prevented. Critically, if humans have developed a society based on a culture that excludes the deadly behaviour of war, can we learn from that example and apply such lessons to our contemporary circumstances?

The answer to the first part of this question is a definite 'yes'. The Inuit in the Canadian Arctic developed a culture without war, but my application of their various cultural adaptations to our modern circumstances has only met with mixed success. The effort worked very well in Northern Ireland where it assisted in the successful negotiation of the Belfast Agreement (Irwin 1999, 2002a) and helped to sustain a slightly fragile peace following the Troubles of the 1970s and 1980s. Elsewhere the application has not been so successful – Israel, Palestine and most recently Syria. In this chapter I will explain why, but first, I should work through the subdisciplines of anthropology and what they have told me about human group conflict from my various researches, starting with human socio-biology.

The socio-biology and evolutionary psychology of human group conflict: *The critical lesson of human socio-biology made here is that group conflict in humans does have a genetic component and, as such, humans, in the absence of effective genetic engineering (not advisable or presently possible), have to be vigilant to prevent such conflict.*

Prior to pursuing academic interests I had lived with the Inuit of the Canadian Arctic for about ten years, having crossed Arctic North America by dog team from Hudson Bay to Alaska in 1973 (Irwin 1974) fifty years after the famed Arctic explorer and ethnographer Knud Rasmussen (1927) made the same journey. At that time the Inuit were still organized into tribes of about 500 individuals, as had nearly all so-called 'primitive' hunter-gatherers of our evolutionary past (Boas 1907, Lee and DeVore 1968, Tindale 1974). Critically, from Rasmussen's (1930a, 1930b, 1931) detailed ethnography it was possible to calculate the extent to which individuals were related (coefficient of consanguinity) to each other both within and between these tribal units as a result of in-group and out-group marriage (Wright 1922, 1931, 1951). Using a computer program that could model the genetics of these natural human populations, the results clearly demonstrated that the differences in the degree of relatedness between these groups could account for differences in in-group cooperation in contrast to, relatively speaking, out-group competition (Irwin 1985, 1987).

The significant term here is 'relative', as West Eberhard (1975) pointed out that it was the relative differences in relatedness that determined social behaviour and not absolute differences in relatedness (Hamilton 1964). It followed that small differences in relatedness between groups could precipitate competitive behaviour, although in mega-population terms the Inuit from Alaska to Greenland had a lot in common. However, in order for such group behaviours, including mate choice, cooperation, competition and out-group violence, it is absolutely necessary that individuals can identify the members of the group they belong to and those that they do not.

Culturally learnt behaviours, referred to as 'badges' for dialects of bird songs (Nottebohm 1969, 1972), can do this, and it seemed very likely that any cultural 'badge' could do the same in human populations. To this end I then mapped differences in tribal dialect onto my Arctic model of Inuit tribes coefficients of consanguinity and got a positive correlation with a boundary effect between tribes (see Figure 10.1). It also followed as dialect, mate choice, cooperation and competition were tied together in the same evolutionary imperatives (Shields

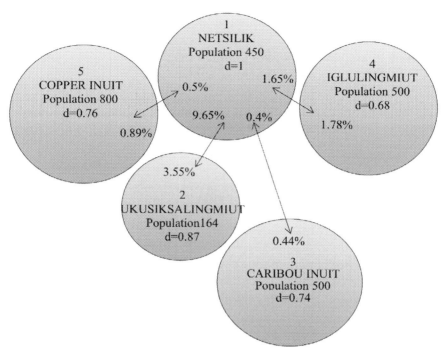

Figure 10.1 Inuit tribes of the Central Canadian Arctic, where the rates of migration (in-group and out-group marriage) are: 1 to 2 – 3.55%, 1 to 3 – 0.44%, 1 to 4 – 1.78%, 1 to 5 – 0.89%, 2 to 1 – 9.65%, 3 to 1 – 0.4%, 4 to 1 – 1.6%, 5 to 1 – 0.5% and d = dialect coefficient (Irwin 1985, 1987).

1982), then dialect as a matter of evolutionary and developmental psychology should be largely set by puberty. For the most part this seems to be the case.

Of course, we do not live in tribal groups of 500 any more, but we do live in groups bound by common elements of culture. Learnt, for the most part, through enculturation in schools, and by puberty we know who we are, who our in-group is and most probably who our out-groups are. Our dominant preferences for mate choice are set, as is the potential for violence towards out-groups given the right circumstances.

But the differences are relative, not absolute, so when I got to Northern Ireland and found two populations of ethnic Europeans who both spoke English with quite similar accents, the fact that they went to different schools – both Christian, but with different denominations, Catholic and Protestant – was enough to create, in this case, a sectarian divide. To all intents and purposes they belonged to two different tribes. But the Inuit are the exception to this apparently universal law of human nature. They created a world without war. How did they do that and why?

The ecology, linguistics and cultural anthropology of Inuit non-war: *The critical lesson here is that humans can create societies underpinned by a culture that excludes war as an inevitable behaviour. Having done it at least once, we should be able to do it again.*

I will begin with the why? In socio-biology it is important to differentiate between ultimate cause and proximate mechanism. In evolutionary terms, the ultimate cause of in-group/out-group behaviour is the genetics of such groups in our evolutionary past while the proximate mechanism, the levers and buttons of pro-social and anti-social behaviour are, among other factors, the group 'badges' we acquire through enculturation. So what, first, then, is the evolutionary ultimate cause of Inuit non-war? Or, putting it another way, what are the factors that make the behaviour of war so maladaptive that it threatens their very survival?

Quite simply, the harshness of the Arctic environment (Irwin 1985, 1989) to which the Inuit adapted through a wide range of material culture inventions, including hunting techniques, the igloo made of snow blocks, dog teams and sledge, kayaks and very sophisticated Arctic clothing. The clothing was made by the women, while the hunting was dominated by the energy, persistence and bravery of young men often risking their lives to bring meat home to their families or dying in the attempt. This division of labour by gender required a manipulation of the sex ratio and a certain flexibility in sexual relations. As young males were so essential for the harvesting of Arctic game and as they so frequently met an early death in doing so, males were always kept at birth while females were frequently considered surplus to requirements and disposed of. Thus the post-birth sex ratio in the central Canadian Arctic was about 2 to 1 in favour of boys to girls. By mid-age, due to male deaths, the sex ratio was balanced 1 to 1 and in old age there were more women than men (Weyer 1932). Males most certainly could not be wasted on war. The challenges of Arctic survival were challenges enough. From an evolutionary perspective it might have been thought better if the birth sex ratio could have been manipulated genetically, thus saving unwanted female pregnancies, but this is not possible in mammals. Additionally there may have also been some advantage in manipulating the ratio rationally by design to fine-tune the sex ratio to the precise degrees of Arctic harshness of the Inuit habitat from Alaska to Greenland. A strong positive correlation between the post-birth sex ratio and annual mean temperature across the Arctic would seem to prove the veracity of this hypothesis (see Figure 10.2).

So much for the ultimate cause, but what then is the proximate mechanism? First and foremost, humans determine right and wrong behaviour through

Figure 10.2 Annual mean temperature plotted against the index of female infanticide – ratio of girls/100 boys – for Alaska, Canada and Greenland.

their moral codes and central to all moral codes are discriminations between right and wrong killing of humans. Table 10.1 lists the cognates for killing humans in Inuktitut (Inuit language). Significantly the abandonment or freezing of a baby does not constitute the taking of human life if the baby does not have a name associated with a person's spirit or soul. In Inuit metaphysics the ethical benefits of personhood are only achieved with the giving of a name/ soul associated with the reincarnation of a deceased relative (Irwin 1981). Suicide can be right or wrong, murder is wrong, and revenge killing or execution is acceptable when necessary in order to prevent a blood feud. 'Fighting' and 'many people fighting' is descriptive and 'many people fighting and killing' is also descriptive, but in Inuktitut this cognate is achieved by adding *murder* to *many people fighting*, so 'war' can never be a praiseworthy act – it is always murder (Irwin 1989).

Other elements of what can be characterized as co-adaptive culture types for pro-social behaviour in general included pseudo-kinship, wife exchange, systematic adoption, sharing partnerships, a common language, common ownership of resources, and a very rich mythology that emphasized right and

Table 10.1 Netsilingmiut cognates for taking human life

English	Inuktitut and literal translation
Baby abandonment	*Nutaraarluk* Iksingnaoktauyoq*
	Baby Leave it – he or she – doing it
Baby freezing	*Nutaraarluk Qiqititauyoq*
	Baby Freeze it – he or she – doing it
Suicide	*Inminik Pitariok*
	Self He or she took life
Murder	*Inuaktok*
	Human – he or she took life
Revenge killing or execution	*Akeyauok*
	Back – he or she – to him or her
Two people fight	*Unatuktook*
	Fight – them (two)
Many people fight	*Unatuktoon*
	Fight – them (many)
War**	None
Many people fighting and killing each other	*Unatuktoon Inuakgrotioon*
	Fight – them (many) – human – they took life (many)

*A baby that is not a person can be discriminated by the qualification that the baby does not have a name/soul, *Nutaraarluk Atikungitok*: Baby – Name – he or she – without.

**With a holoplastic language like Inuktitut it is possible to generate almost any meaning. However, 'war' as an organized activity that does not entail the blameworthy taking of life (murder) cannot be given an adequate translation. Revenge killing or execution, *Akeyauok*, can only be used with respect to specific acts of murder and the associated murderer(s).

wrong behaviour. With regard to decision making, this mostly followed the lines of authority laid down in kinship. A younger brother would be expected to be guided by the decisions of an older brother and then by their father, and he by his older brother or father, and so on. But when a difficult decision had to be made among peers, then the decision had to be by consensus. To avoid conflict everyone had to agree. There were no tribal chiefs to make a decision one way or another (Steenhoven 1959). I first came across this political decision-making process when I had occasion to look over the minutes of the council meetings in the Arctic village of Chesterfield Inlet and noticed that all issues voted on were carried unanimously. Later, when I worked for Inuit organizations as an adviser and attended their board meetings, an agenda would sometimes take a day or two to work through, with all voting decisions left to the last hours of business on the last day only after, through extensive informal discussions, consensus decisions had been arrived at outside the formal meetings of the board.

Over a period of several years I got the hang of this very different kind of decision making that required listening to the different points of view, searching out common ground, and if necessary the best possible compromise, and anyone who was good at doing this was rewarded with a position of leadership. Subsequently, following my academic training and my first appointment in the Department of Sociology and Anthropology at Dalhousie University in Halifax, Nova Scotia, I was invited to join the departmental meetings that also followed an agenda. But after what sometimes seemed to me to be the briefest of discussions, a vote was taken and the majority decision prevailed. I was horrified. Some colleagues had been overruled and left the meeting quite disappointed with the outcome – and then I remembered that that is how the 'white man' made their decisions. Quite shocking!

From enculturation to 'peace polls' and the application of consensus decision making to the Northern Ireland conflict: *The critical lesson here is that some lessons from pre-industrial societies that have moved beyond war can be applied to modern societies and help them to peace.*

With the benefit of a postdoctoral fellowship from the Social Science and Humanities Research Council of Canada (SSHRC), which had also supported my Master's and doctoral research, I based myself at Queen's University Belfast to make a comparative study of the education systems in Northern Ireland, Israel and Palestine. The schools were segregated and always had been, ensuring the separate enculturation of Catholics and Protestants, Jews and Palestinians (Akenson 1970, 1973; Secretary of State for the Colonies 1937, 1946). But in Northern Ireland, against the wishes of the established church hierarchy, there was significant grass-roots support for integrated education. Depending on how the question was asked, between 30 and 70 per cent wanted their children to go to schools together as long ago as 1968 (*Belfast Telegraph* 1968ab). But the UK Government had only made provision for 2 per cent of children to attend integrated school by 1990 at the height of the Troubles. Armed with this polling evidence and signed affidavits from parents who had been forced to send their children to segregated schools against their wishes, I was able to take a human rights case to the UN Committee on the Rights of the Child in 1994, which ruled that the UK Government should put more resources into integrated education (UN Committee on the Rights of the Child 1995).

The 'silent majority' were given a voice through polling and they had won, and by giving this silent majority a 'seat at the negotiating table' through public opinion polls, peace was achieved in 1998 with the signing of the Belfast Agreement. To this end, I conducted nine surveys of public opinion in support of the Northern Ireland peace process between April 1996 and February 2003. Critically, the questions for eight of these polls were drafted and agreed with the co-operation of party negotiators to enhance the peace process by increasing party inclusiveness, developing issues and language, testing party policies, helping to set deadlines, and increasing the overall transparency of negotiations through the publication of technical analysis and media reports (Irwin 1999, 2002a).

Most importantly, *all* the parties to the conflict were included in this process and *all* the policies that they wanted in a peace agreement were fairly tested against public opinion, using a method that would find common ground where it existed and what the best possible compromise was where it did not. This was done by not only identifying an informant's first choice but also the rank order of all their other choices by asking them which policies, over a range of policies, they considered to be 'essential', 'desirable', 'acceptable', 'tolerable' or 'unacceptable' for peace (see Figure 10.3). In so doing it was possible to apply the Inuit methodology of compromise and consensus discourse to a modern population using a combination of one-to-one private discussions with the representatives of the conflicting parties, public opinion polls that covered all sections of the Northern Ireland population, and a public diplomacy campaign to disseminate the results of the research to everyone who had a right to vote in a referendum (Irwin 2002a).

Significantly this process encompassed some additional aspects of research methodology central to the discipline of cultural anthropology. First, the use of

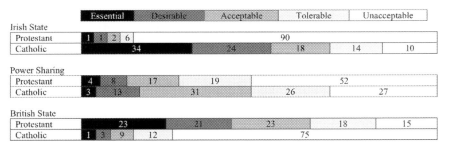

Figure 10.3 The incorporation of Northern Ireland into the Irish state is 'unacceptable' to 90 per cent of Protestants and incorporation into the British state is 'unacceptable' to 75 per cent of Catholics, with 'power sharing' the only acceptable compromise.

Table 10.2 Protestant and Catholic priorities for peace in Northern Ireland

	Protestant per cent	**Essential**	**Catholic per cent**	**Essential**
1st	Disband all paramilitary groups.	70	A Bill of Rights that guarantees equality for all.	78
2nd	Stronger and effective anti-terrorist measures.	70	Completely reform the police service.	70
3rd	The Republic ends their claim on Northern Ireland.	62	A Bill of Rights that protects the culture of each community.	67
4th	A Bill of Rights that guarantees equality for all.	37	Disband all paramilitary groups.	67
5th	End the Anglo-Irish Agreement.	36	Return the army to their barracks.	61
6th	A Bill of Rights that protects the culture of each community.	36	Politics without a sectarian division.	59
7th	Integrate Northern Ireland into the UK.	35	A right to choose integrated education.	53
8th	A right to choose integrated education.	35	A right to choose integrated housing.	51
9th	Politics without a sectarian division.	32	British withdrawal from Northern Ireland.	46
10th	Separate politics and religion in Northern Ireland.	31	Open government and Freedom of Information Act.	46
11th	A right to choose integrated housing.	30	Stronger and effective anti-terrorist measures.	40
12th	Separate politics and religion in the Republic.	30	Reformed and shared government.	32
13th	Open government and Freedom of Information Act.	24	Separate politics and religion in Northern Ireland.	20
14th	Reformed and shared government.	12	Separate politics and religion in the Republic.	15
15th	Return the army to their barracks.	8	End the Anglo-Irish Agreement.	10
16th	Completely reform the police service.	7	The Republic ends their claim on Northern Ireland.	7
17th	British withdrawal from Northern Ireland.	1	Integrate Northern Ireland into the UK.	4

in-depth interviews with all the parties to the conflict to both understand and then test *their* proposals from *their* perspective against public opinion in *their* communities to reveal the central concerns through *their* world view, *their* emic perspective. Secondly, testing their proposals in other communities and in turn testing the 'others'' proposals in their communities and publishing the full results to create a reflexive public discourse in which each party to the conflict had an opportunity to 'see' the conflict from the perspective of the 'other' (see Table 10.2). Through this process in Northern Ireland the peace agreement, when it arrived, was not a surprise to anyone and it easily passed a referendum, as predicted by the polls. Facilitated by an inclusive discourse, a consensus had been achieved.

Beyond Northern Ireland and the politics of peace making: *The critical lesson here – fortunately for me and those caught up in the Irish wars – is that Northern Ireland in the 1990s was 'the exception that proves the rule'.*

Following on from Northern Ireland, the first opportunity I had to apply the peace poll methods elsewhere was Macedonia. The Balkan wars had taken their toll in Serbia, Bosnia Herzegovina, Croatia and Kosovo and it was thought that rebels from Kosovo were about to take their armed struggle into Macedonia, which in 2002 had managed to stay out of the war. I was asked to conduct a peace poll that was expected to expose this clear and present danger, but what it revealed was a desire for both Serb Macedonians and Albanian Macedonians to have free and fair elections (Irwin 2002b). With support from the European Union and the Organization for Security and Co-operation in Europe (OSCE), this was done and a war was avoided. Peace polls were then run in Bosnia Herzegovina, Kosovo and Serbia, but for them it was too late and the polls could only show what needed to be done to help secure a peace following the devastation – and in some cases, genocide (Irwin 2005ab).

With colleagues from India and Pakistan I was able to run peace polls in Kashmir and tease out compromises acceptable to the Buddhist, Hindu and Muslim communities, but then another poll undertaken by Ipsos-MORI for the Royal Institute of International Affairs (RIIA), which only identified the informants' first choice, suggested a peace agreement was not possible – a serious mistake (Irwin 2012). With support from the Norwegian Government I then moved on to Sri Lanka and building on polling work done by others, it was not difficult to demonstrate that the people of Sri Lanka would be very content with a modest degree of devolution. They did not require a separate Tamil state (Irwin 2008, 2009a, 2010).

But the Rajapaksa brothers who ran the country would have none of it. Following their defeat of the Tamil Tigers in 2009, they could have easily entered into a magnanimous agreement that would have settled the ethnic and sectarian disputes on the island for generations to come. But they preferred to play the ethnic card in elections and pit one community against the other to hold on to power. Fortunately, the Rajapaksa brothers were repalced in 2015 and the prospects for the people of Sri Lanka were much improved. Significantly, the civil wars in Sri Lanka could have been avoided if they had not torn up their original constitution that protected all communities before the law in favour of ethnic electoral politics that briefly entrenched the power of a ruling elite (Irwin 2012).

In Sri Lanka I had been allowed to run my polls with the support of their Minister of Science, Professor Tissa Viterana, who tabled my reports in his Parliament and in so doing made a contribution to the democratic process. The Tamils would be satisfied with powers devolved to the Provinces in the North and East in accordance with their constitution and the president could no longer deny that fact. In time this truth – and rampant corruption – caught up with him. This was arguably a small success, although delayed.[1] In Israel, Palestine, Sudan, Egypt, Syria and more generally in terms of relations between the West and the Muslim world, I have been less successful (Irwin 2012).

I had been working with Senator George Mitchell in Northern Ireland for several years, so when Barack Obama became US President and George Mitchell became his Special Envoy to the Middle East, I was given an opportunity to run a peace poll in Israel and Palestine. In addition to confirming what many other polls had shown, namely that a two-state solution was acceptable to the people of Israel and Palestine, I was also able to demonstrate that the peace process itself was not acceptable and that both Israelis and Palestinians wanted it reformed to produce a result (Irwin 2009b). Secret negotiations behind closed doors were not enough. International involvement and a timetable would be welcome. But the president of Israel, Benjamin Netanyahu had no such interest, so the talks continued to fail and George Mitchell resigned his post. Netanyahu, who had grown up in America, understood Washington politics and could manipulate US policy towards Israel to meet his interests of no peace deal with the Palestinians (Irwin 2012).

In Syria I thought, and was advised by colleagues, that peace polls might work better there, but again the interests of nation states got in the way –this time Washington, Turkey and the Gulf States on one side of the equation and Iran and Moscow on the other (Irwin 2015a). In Darfur, Sudan and Egypt the situation was less complex and quite cut-and-dried. In Sudan the government put an end to a peace-polling project when they were not allowed to edit the questionnaire to meet their interests and in Egypt, at the time of the Arab Spring uprising, the Central Agency for Public Mobilization and Statistics (CAPMAS) would not give permission to run polls at all. Finally, with regard to relations between the West and the Muslim world, Michael Traugott brought me to America for a seminar to explore this issue following the publication of a report from their Council on Foreign Relations (2003) that highlighted this problem. Subsequently, following the '7/7' London bombings in 2005 I was able to conduct a peace poll-style research programme among the UK Muslim community in 2006 (Irwin 2006). But following the recent wars in the Middle East and the '7/7' London bombings, the results of that research were not welcome; attempts were made to silence the report and ten years on the problem remained unaddressed with the Taliban and al-Qaeda transformed into the Islamic State.

My efforts in this regard are not unique. Negotiators involved in the Northern Ireland peace process such as Jonathan Powell (2014) also advocate *Talking to Terrorists,* as does the anthropologist Scott Atran (2010) in *Talking to the Enemy.* The approach I take in reporting my research has a lot in common with peace journalism, which advocates balanced analysis from all sides to a conflict as well as the applied methodologies of Donald Campbell (1984) with its emphasis on the inclusion of adversarial stakeholders. Critically the interviews lead to public opinion polls, which are published to create a discourse designed to facilitate a process of consensus decision making. Telhami and Kull (2013) made another effort in this regard during the Israel/Palestine round of negotiations when John Kerry became US Secretary of State in 2013, but with no more success than myself given the same Washington politics.

Worlds without war: *The critical lesson here is that worlds without war and an objective social science devoid of political interests are the exception rather than the rule – but does it always have to be so?*

The Inuit created a world without war as a matter of ecological necessity. They could only survive in the high Arctic if they ended war, and they did. In Northern Ireland the fragile peace only came about when all the other players shared a common interest in peace and the rest of the world does not seem to have reached that point quite yet. Can we hurry them along by understanding the situation we are in, as we now surely do, and change things for the better? Evolution theory – biological, cultural or otherwise – is neither optimistic nor pessimistic on this point. Quite simply, those worlds of sentient beings that come to terms with the dangers that face them – principally, competition for finite resources on a finite planet – will survive and those that do not will not. With this point in mind, I have tried a number of options for the mainstreaming of consensus decision making as an essential aid to conflict resolution and peace making globally, but so far without the hoped-for result.

First, as an academic, I did what academics do and applied for grants, undertook peace polls whenever funding became available, gave international conference papers and published. My colleagues in the World Association of Public Opinion Research (WAPOR) recognized the value of the work and with the encouragement of their then president, Professor Michael Traugott, we drafted new research standards for polls that deal with violent conflict (Irwin 2012). But these standards that emphasized transparency and working with all sides to a conflict were incompatible with the interests of the multi-million-dollar polling industry that was collecting this data globally for the intelligence services of national clients and consequently the new standards were never approved.

So then I tried the UN. Their Department of Peace Keeping Operations (UNDPKO) had come to the conclusion that their country missions would be far more successful if they took on board the views of local people and what they wanted instead of focusing solely on the agenda of political elites and third-party donor states (UN 2009, 2011). Through a series of workshops, consultations and publications, a UN (2013) manual was produced for best practice in this regard. It was very well researched and illustrated with numerous examples of local successes to set a new international standard for such work and peace polls were a part of it. This was in 2013 and I thought these new best practices would necessarily become a central feature of the activities of the UN Special Envoy to Syria in his efforts to bring that war to an end. But the views of the local people were only given lip service in favour of a grand bargain that would encompass the interests of the Syrian regime, regional and global powers. The UN, I quickly discovered, is the servant of the nation states that make up the UN and not the people that make up those nation states.[2]

Knowledge is power and if the power of peace making is to be given to the people, then the people must own that knowledge. The people must know what a reasonable compromise in any conflict must look like and be given an opportunity to accept or reject it. They are the people who are living and dying in the conflict, not the third parties who survey their hopes and dreams and edit them to meet their own selfish interests. Peace polling should be a right, not the last point of enquiry when all else has failed. Better still, peace polling should track and monitor potential sources of conflict globally before they become deadly (Irwin 2013, 2014, 2015b). In our age of globalization, world peace polls are now possible and in this age of information their time has surely come.

Notes

1   Unfortunately in 2019 the Rajapaksa brothers regained power when the security services failed to stop Muslim suicide bombers killing more than 200 Christian worshipers at Easter services.
2   In 2020 the UN launched their 'UN75 Conversation' on the role of global cooperation to help implement the UN Sustainable Development Goals (SDGs). Hopefully this welcome initiative will be extended to peace polls, conflict analysis and conflict resolution.

References

Akenson, D. (1973), *Education and Enmity: The Control of Schooling in Northern Ireland, 1920–1950*, Newton Abbot: David and Charles.

Akenson, D. (1970), *The Irish Education Experiment: The National System of Education in the Nineteenth Century*, London: Routledge and Kegan Paul.

Atran, S. (2010), *Talking to the Enemy: Religion, Brotherhood, and the (Un)Making of Terrorists*, New York: HarperCollins.

Belfast Telegraph (1968), 'Clear Call for End to Religious Separation in Schools', 22 October.

Belfast Telegraph (1968), 'Poll Favours Integration of Education', 22 October.

Boas, F. (1907), 'The Central Eskimo', Bureau of American Ethnography, Annual Report no. 6 (1884–1885): 399–699.

Campbell, D. (1984), 'Can We be Scientific in Applied Social Science?' in R. Conner, D. G. Altman and C. Jackson (eds), *Evaluation Studies Review Annual*, vol. 9, Newbury Park, CA: Sage Publications.

Hamilton, W. D. (1964), 'The Genetic Evolution of Social Behaviour I and II', *Journal of Theoretical Biology*, 7: 1–52.

Irwin, C. J. (2015a), 'Making Peace Through Polls', *openDemocracy.net*, 9 September.

Irwin, C. J. (2015b), 'Constructing a "World Peace Poll" in an Age of Global Conflict: Sample Designs for Monitoring and Tracking Conflict in Global, Regional, Transnational, National and Local Contexts', 68th WAPOR Annual Conference, Buenos Aires, Argentina, 16–19 June.

Irwin, C. J. (2014), 'A Critical Review of Perceptions Based and Fact Based Peace Indicators and Indexes', 67th WAPOR Annual Conference, Nice, France, 4–6 September.

Irwin, C. J. (2012), 'The People's Peace: Pax Populi, Pax Dei - How Peace Polls are Democratizing the Peace Making Process', Scotts Valley, CA: CreateSpace.

Irwin, C. J. (2010), '"War and Peace" and the APRC Proposals', *Daily Mirror*, Colombo, Part 1: 7 May, Part 2: 8 May.

Irwin, C. J. (2009a), 'The APRC Proposals and "Winning the Peace"', *Daily Mirror*, Colombo, Part 1: 13 July, Part 2: 14 July.

Irwin, C. J. (2009b), 'Israel and Palestine: Public Opinion, Public Diplomacy and Peace Making', Part 1: The Shape of an Agreement, Part 2: Process, *Peacepolls.org*, April.

Irwin, C. J. (2008), 'Peace in Sri Lanka: From Symbols to Substance', *Daily Mirror*, Colombo, Part 1: 21 June, Part 2: 23 June.

Irwin, C. J. (2006), 'The West and the Muslim World: A Conflict in Search of a Peace Process', *Peacepolls.org*.

Irwin, C. J. (2005a), 'A People's Peace Process for Bosnia and Herzegovina?' *Ethnopolitics*, 4 (3): 311–28.

Irwin, C. J. (2005b), 'Coming to Terms with the Problem of Kosovo: The Peoples' Views from Kosovo and Serbia', *Peacepolls.org*, October.

Irwin, C. J. (2002a), *The People's Peace Process in Northern Ireland*, Basingstoke and New York: Palgrave Macmillan.

Irwin, C. J. (2002b), 'Forum Macedonia: An Opinion Poll and its Implications', *The Global Review of Ethnopolitics*, 2 (1).

Irwin, C. J. (1999), 'The People's Peace Process: Northern Ireland and the Role of Public Opinion Polls in Political Negotiations', *Security Dialogue*, 30 (3): 105–17.

Irwin, C. J. (1987), 'A Study in the Evolution of Ethnocentrism', in V. Reynolds and V. Falger (eds), *The Sociobiology of Ethnocentrism*, 131–56, London: Croom Helm.

Irwin, C. J. (1989), 'The Sociocultural Biology of Netsilingmiut Female Infanticide', in A. Rassa, C. Vogel and E. Voland (eds), *Sociobiology of Sexual and Reproductive Strategies*, 234–64, London: Croom Helm.

Irwin, C. J. (1985), *Sociocultural Biology: Studies in the Evolution of Some Netsilingmiut and Other Sociocultural Behaviors*, PhD Thesis, Syracuse University, New York.

Irwin, C. J. (1981), *Inuit Ethics and the Priority of the Future Generation*, Master's Thesis, University of Manitoba, Canada.

Irwin, C. J. (1974), 'Trek Across Arctic America', *National Geographic Magazine*, March.

Irwin, C. J. and Y. Deshmukh (2013), 'The Development of a "People's Peace Index" (PPI)', 66th WAPOR Annual Conference 'Revolutions in the Measurement of World Public Opinion', Boston, 14–16 May.

Lee, R. B. and I. DeVore (1968), *Man the Hunter*, Chicago: Aldine.

Nottebohm, D. (1972), 'The Origins of Vocal Learning', *American Naturalist*, 106: 116–40.

Nottebohm, D. (1969), 'The Song of the Chingolo, *Zonotrichia capensis*, in Argentina: Description and Evolution of a System of Dialects', *Condor*, 71: 299–315.

Powell, J. (2014), *Talking to Terrorists: How to End Armed Conflicts*, London: The Bodley Head.

Rasmussen, K. (1931), *The Netsilik Eskimos: Social Life and Spiritual Culture*, vol. VIII, no. 1–2, Report of the Fifth Thule Expedition 1921–24, Copenhagen: Gyldendalske Boghandel.

Rasmussen, K. (1930a), *Observations on the Intellectual Culture of the Caribou Eskimos*, vol. VII, no. 2, Report of the Fifth Thule Expedition 1921–24, Copenhagen: Gyldendalske Boghandel.

Rasmussen, K. (1930b), *Intellectual Culture of the Hudson Bay Eskimo*, vol. VII, Report of the Fifth Thule Expedition 1921–24, Copenhagen: Gyldendalske Boghandel.

Rasmussen, K. (1927), *Across Arctic America*, London: Putnam.

Secretary of State for the Colonies (1946), *The System of Education of the Jewish Community in Palestine*, Report of the Commission of Enquiry appointed by the Secretary of State for the Colonies in 1945, London: His Majesty's Stationery Office.

Secretary of State for the Colonies (1937), *Palestine Royal Commission Report*, presented to Parliament by Command of His Majesty, July 1937. London: His Majesty's Stationery Office.

Shields, W. M. (1982), *Philopatry, Inbreeding and the Evolution of Sex*, Albany, NY: State University of New York Press.

Steenhoven, G. van den (1959), *Legal Concepts Amongst the Netsilik Eskimos of Pelly Bay, N.W.T. Canada*, Department of Northern Affairs. N.C.R.C. Report 59–3.

Telhami, S. and S. Kull (2013), *Israeli and Palestinian Public Opinion on Negotiating a Final Status Peace Agreement*, Released at the Saban Center at The Brookings Institution, Washington, DC, 6 December.

Tindle, N. B. (1974), *Aboriginal Tribes of Australia*, Berkeley, CA: University of California Press.

UN (2013), *Understanding and Integrating Local Perceptions in Multi-Dimensional UN Peacekeeping*, United Nations Departments of Peacekeeping and Field Support Policy, Evaluation and Training Division Policy and Best Practices Services, New York.

UN (2011), Letter from the Chair to the Secretary General – 'Civilian Capacity in the Aftermath of Conflict', Independent Report of the Senior Advisory Group, A/65/747 S/2011/85 February.

UN (2009), Report of the Secretary General on Peacebuilding in the Immediate Aftermath of Conflict, A/63/881-S/2009/304 June.

UN Committee on the Rights of the Child (1995), Eighth Session, Consideration of Reports Submitted by States Parties Under Article 44 of the Convention – 'Concluding Observations of the Committee on the Rights of the Child: United Kingdom of Great Britain and Northern Ireland', CRC/C/15/Add.34, 27 January.

West Eberhard, M. J. (1975), 'The Evolution of Social Behaviour by Kin Selection', *Quarterly Review of Biology*, 10: 1–33.

Weyer, E. M. (1932), *The Eskimos: Their Environment and Folkways*, New Haven, CT: Yale University Press.

Wright, S. (1951), 'The Genetical Structure of Populations', *Annals of Eugenics*, 15: 323–54.

Wright, S. (1931), 'Evolution in Mendelian Populations', *Genetics*, 16: 97–159.

Wright, S. (1922), 'Coefficients of Inbreeding and Relationship', *American Naturalist*, 56: 330–8.

11

More Than a Matter of Proportion: A Critical Consideration of Anthropology's Role in Peace and Conflict Studies

Philipp Lottholz

Introduction

The field of peace and conflict studies has seen increasingly embittered debates about the reasons for the failure of international peacebuilding and democratization interventions in post-conflict countries across the globe. Arguments that the proponents of 'liberal' and 'democratic' peace and corresponding neoliberal economic and political reforms operate on Eurocentric and culturally insensitive assumptions, and are thus detached from the realities of people in the global periphery, have gained increasing weight. The idea that Western hegemony and conditionality could be transcended in alternative, so-called 'bottom-up' and culturally sensitive forms of 'post-liberal' or 'hybrid' peace has challenged not only Western and Eurocentric conceptions of politics and society (Mac Ginty 2011; Richmond 2011; Paffenholz 2015). This strand of scholarship has also advocated the inclusion of ethnographic research approaches and an anthropological outlook into the conceptual apparatus of peace and conflict studies (Richmond 2011: 14, 146, 199 ff.; Mac Ginty 2011: 4; Richmond and Mitchell 2011; Millar 2014, 2018).

This chapter aims to assess how ethnography as a method and anthropology as a discipline have been received and constructed in peace and conflict studies and how this synthesis has evolved so far. Drawing on critiques of the 'ethnographic turn' in international relations (IR) (Vrasti 2008) and corresponding debates in peace and conflict studies (Finlay 2015; Paffenholz 2015; Sabaratnam 2013; Avruch and Black 1993), and taking inspiration from critical reflections on the contradictions of critical theory (Hobson 2007; Graef 2015), the first part of this chapter will present a critical discussion of recent applications of ethnographic methods and interpretations of the potential of anthropology in peace and conflict studies. It will specifically focus on the ethno-empiricism and positivist epistemology that is apparent both in the discussed examples and the wider literature they reflect. In the second part, a more holistic and nuanced approach will be developed by drawing on area studies and theoretical literature as well as fieldwork data analysis that illustrates the added value of two new avenues for research. These new insights suggest that the ambiguity and performativity of 'everyday forms of peace' require a critical embedding within the collective psychological, economic and social conditions that foreground them. The critical transdisciplinary research approach outlined offers a way of researching how discourses and ideologies of peace are internalized and reproduced in both 'everyday' settings of ordinary people and by practitioners of community security and order-making. These, it is shown, may give rise to forms of authoritarian governmentality and bio-politics that the ethno-empiricist and positivist approach currently prevailing in the nascent 'anthropology of peace and conflict' symbiosis risks to ignore.

Anthropology and ethnography in peace and conflict studies: A distorted imagination

The 'ethnographic turn'

Despite a relatively long history of reception of anthropological methodology in peace and conflict studies and notwithstanding long-standing debates on the meaning of culture and the positionality of the ethnographer, the imagining of ethnography prevalent in peace and conflict studies debates is one seeing it as a mere tool or 'data-collection machine' (Finlay 2015; Vrasti 2008). A partial explanation for this dissonance is the fact that peace and conflict studies are arguably dominated by political science and IR approaches, while sociology, anthropology and other disciplines have so far had little impact in challenging the prevalence of questions about conflict and peace on the global level and in universal terms (see Paffenholz 2015; Graef 2015). This global/universalist versus local/particularist ontology and the (proto-)positivist epistemology prevalent in peace and conflict studies has skewed the reception of ethnography and its construction as a methodological fix for the puzzles confronting this academic field. In short, the imagination of ethnographic methods as the missing ingredient could not but be disappointed given the general ignorance in the field vis-a-vis long-standing debates within anthropology and in light of the narrow, empiricist application of ethnographic approaches.

The recent 'turn towards anthropology and culture' (Finlay 2015: 226) in critical peace-building literature is reflective of the earlier parallel 'cultural' or 'ethnographic turn' in IR, a 'strange case' poignantly analysed and critiqued by Wanda Vrasti (2008). The claim that both students of international intervention, peace and conflict dynamics as well as practitioners and policymakers in these fields are in need of an 'anthropological sensitivity' (Mac Ginty 2008: 139; Finlay 2015: 226) reflects the idea that ethnographic methods would, in Vrasti's words, 'promise a type of knowledge ... more politically engaged than that achieved through scientific deduction and more empirically accurate than that provided by discursive theories of the political' (2008: 295). As Mac Ginty stated, '[t]o some extent, some varieties of anthropology and sociology are well placed to capture these dynamics', while peace and conflict studies would still be 'scratching the surface of what it wishes to study' (2011: 4). Another main advocate of this strand also attributes authority to ethnographic methodology, which would be required 'in order to allow an understanding of the local, locality, context and their interactions with and against the liberal peacebuilding architecture that has developed' (Richmond 2011: 14; see also 75, 146, 199 ff.). In his *Ethnographic Approach to Peacebuilding*, perhaps the most comprehensive exposition of this synthesis, Gearoid Millar states that for him, such an approach 'demands a willingness to study closely the local social and cultural context' and 'understand how international projects are experienced by people on the ground' (2014: 3, 2). These examples already indicate the ontology underlying these authors' arguments which exhibits a bifurcation between the 'local' (post-)conflict contexts and, on the other hand, the international peacebuilding projects or the international community at large (see Paffenholz 2015; Graef 2015). The consequent objectification of local populations, even though implicit, is at the root of an empiricist and positivist conception of ethnographic peace and conflict research that has arguably prevailed in the literature so far.

Millar's book further illustrates the proto-positivist epistemology and the ontology reifying categories such as 'local' and 'international', although this is not to diminish the work's meaningful contribution and significant grasp of anthropological literature in the context of his case study country Sierra Leone (Millar 2014: Chs 4, 6), and with the caveat that the same author has recently put forward more nuanced discussions on the same topic (Millar 2018). The idea that ethnography is the missing piece in critical peacebuilding studies' conceptual apparatus is most apparent in Millar's positioning of the book as filling 'a significant gap in the literature by providing a clear guidance for an ethnographic approach to evaluation that can also act as a step towards international accountability to the beneficiaries of intervention' (2014: 18). While other critical literature would not get to this level of empirical detail, the benefit of the ethnographic approach is that it enables the 'evaluation of those impacts or of local experiences of peacebuilding interventions' (16). Chapter 5 details the methodological techniques to be applied in order not to repeat the mistakes of evaluators who fail to 'fully capture the local experiences of the projects' (81). 'The key word here is representativeness', argues Millar. 'Indeed, evaluators following the ethnographic approach must recognize that there are dynamics within societies that demand purposeful sampling within a population if "local engagement" is to be achieved' (83). After dividing society in the localities of his analysis into 'elite' and 'non-elite' (according to socio-economic and educational indicators), Millar conducted and analysed interviews with subgroups from both of these strata. He found that 'elites' benefited most from international peacebuilding projects, as they had the 'social and human capital to make the most of additional resources that enter the local setting' and, in regard to language barriers and familiarity with concepts such as 'justice', 'truth' and 'reconciliation', 'understood the process far more than local non-elites' (94–5). The division foregrounding this result is not straightforward and simplistic one, however, as it needs to be 'contextualized within the anthropological knowledge developed over decades by scholars with a deep understanding of Sierra Leone's society and culture' (79). Such 'ethnographic preparation' (63 ff.) and the appraisal of cultural differences between the world views and understandings of life of the researchers and the researched, respectively (99 ff.), would enable a full understanding of local experiences of peacebuilding projects.

While this holistic view of peacebuilding processes is reflective of a critical agenda for a symbiosis between anthropology and peace and conflict studies, Millar's offer to pick and choose from this package seems too permissive:

> [A]n ethnographic approach should not be seen as an extension of anthropology but as a tool for any discipline, or, as in my own case, any interdisciplinary scholar of peace, conflict, and post-conflict peacebuilding. . . . I do believe that even non-anthropologists unwilling or unable to commit to this mode of ethnography can adopt and benefit from the evaluation process I describe.

6

Thus, rather than adopting the 'ethnographic approach' full circle, what matters most in Millar's eyes is that 'the ethnographic approach does demand a healthy "anthropological imagination"' (ibid.).

Not a matter of proportion

The contradiction of this proposal is the idea that, on the one hand, ethnography is a practical and flexible 'tool' to be used by anyone, but that, on the other hand, it also requires a 'healthy "anthropological imagination"'. It is indicative of how in the current neoliberal regime governing questions of knowledge production and epistemic authority, the desire to provide new and effective methodologies both within critical academic debates and also to a wider audience of policy makers can lead scholars to overstretch the possibilities of one approach. Hence, it can be argued the book's contribution to critical scholarship is defeated by the proposal for a piecemeal application of ethnographic methods. In fact, this appears to resonate with long-standing critiques of ethnographic research serving as the handmaiden of Western imperial and hegemonic politics (Restrepo and Escobar 2005: 105). Vrasti's critique of understandings of ethnography among IR scholars applies well to this 'ethnographic approach to peacebuilding'. The idea of ethnography as the best way to understand 'on-the-ground' experiences of peacebuilding appears to be rooted in the 'selective and often instrumental understanding of what ethnography is and does' (Vrasti 2008: 280). This mythological portrayal has arguably been sustained by the general disregard for the fundamental debates and controversies around ethnographic praxis and the discipline of anthropology, which were clearly exposed in the Writing Culture and, more indirectly, in the Third World/Women of Colour feminism debates, among others (Lottholz 2018b).

The 'realist-positivist inheritances' scrutinised in the latter debates (Vrasti 2008: 297) are implicit in Millar's Chapter 5 detailing the way in which 'local engagement' is supposed to assure the gathering of the correct data. It may be true that 'seeing peacebuilding as experiential' and engaging with how people perceive interventions in their own way is a step forward in the current impasse of culturally and socially insensitive interventions. Still, the conceptualization of ethnography as a tool to carry out this experiential data gathering is also vulnerable to Denskus' critique that '[b]y introducing managerial tools – such as the [current] focus on measuring the "effectiveness" of peacebuilding ... critical questions about the causes of violent conflict and the future outlook of societies emerging from conflict are depoliticised' (2007: 658). Furthermore, Millar's suggestion that the acquisition of accurate information is possible in case of adherence to certain scientific standards points to a positivist epistemological outlook, or at least a proto-positivist one as his general methodology remains interpretivist.

The argument that 'fully [capturing] the local experiences of ... projects' is a matter of making the right choices in studying the context, designing research and making a representative sample for the interviews seems to repeat earlier cases in which ethnography has been conceived of as 'data gathering machine' (Vrasti 2008). The underlying understanding of research appears to be one of ethno-empiricism, which 'impose[s] empirical order upon our home-made theoretical puzzles' (ibid.: 286). Lastly, the idea of making the critical contribution of research through an ethnographic approach conditional upon a 'healthy anthropological imagination' seems tautological. Rather than assuming such an imagination to exist or leaving it up to researchers' own deliberations, it is exactly the question about what constitutes such an imagination – that is, how to navigate the complicities, silences and power relations within and beyond the field in the quest for critical knowledge, which should be foregrounding the symbiosis between peace and conflict studies and anthropology. The question about critical ethnographic peace research, I would argue, can thus not be dismissed as a matter of how healthy one's anthropological imagination is, but requires a principled approach at setting and implementing a research agenda that takes full account of the 'tumultuous and controversial history' (Vrasti 2008: 281) of ethnographic praxis and anthropological theory (see Lottholz 2018b).

It may be true that a certain level of pragmatism is necessary in advancing the still young synthesis of 'ethnographic peace research'. However, calls for epistemic leniency in such an endeavour deserve critical attention as they are made in a context characterized by the objectification of anthropology as a repository of cultural knowledge, and of ethnography as the method to generate such knowledge. They furthermore need to be seen against the background of a relative persistence of what I would call an International Relations ontology that frames the 'international' and the 'national' or 'local' as relevant if not significant levels of analysis (Paffenholz 2015; Finlay 2015). The continued prevalence of this framing in debates on conflicts and peacebuilding[1] should be a reminder that calls to overcome such an ontology in favour of distinct approaches to 'international studies', 'global anthropology' or 'world anthropologies' (Sylvester 2007; Kearney 1995; Restrepo and Escobar 2005) have not received the resonance they deserve. These and other frameworks offer better ways of accounting for the role played by transnational dimensions of material and ideational exchange which are not on the radar of established approaches to studying peace and conflict (Kalb 2005; Glick Schiller 2006).

The antiquated image of anthropology understood through an ethno-empiricist scientism is also mirrored in the contribution on 'Anthropology: Implications for Peace' in the recently published *Palgrave Handbook of Disciplinary and Regional Approaches to Peace* (Souillac and Fry 2016). The authors argue that '[a]nthropology, with its vast documentation of indigenous societies ... can remind the West of the diversity of successful approaches to creating and maintaining peace' (ibid.: 75). To substantiate this point, Souillac and Fry review the debate on the antiquity of war (i.e. whether it is a relatively recent phenomenon emerging circa 10,000 years ago or it is innate to human nature) and the scientific discourse on the warlike/peaceful nature of humans' nomadic foragers ('ancestral social type'). They conclude that the evidence in both cases points to the fact that '[w]ar is neither particularly old nor inevitable' (ibid.: 77) due to a stronger proclivity towards peaceful life attested to in human nature. It is noteworthy how this deductive exercise on the basis of data with comprehensive reach throughout time and space reflects the place which anthropology, according to Restrepo and Escobar (2005), has been assigned in the division of intellectual labour within the 'modern episteme' as it was established in the Enlightenment era:

> [A]nthropology ... and psychoanalysis function as counter-sciences – that is, as forms of knowledge that present the West with its own limits by confronting it with difference and the unconscious. They nevertheless find in Western ratio – and, hence, in European dominance – their reason for being.
>
> 2005: 111

The example of this chapter and its selection as a perspective on potentials of anthropological research reflects the heuristic approach too prevalent in peace and conflict studies, which is aimed at excavating and generalizing facts from particular contexts towards other ones in the search for universally applicable concepts and models.

This ontological outlook in peace and conflict studies today has been noted as influential during the early days of the field. One case in point is the debate on the role played by culture in the analysis of peace and conflict during the 1980s and 1990s (see Avruch 1998). John Burton, for instance – considered one of the founders of the field – held that 'a generic human nature, characterized by nine ontological and probably genetic human needs, is the irreducible substrate of all human action including conflict' and that the satisfaction of these needs in a balanced way within and across groups is the prime task for the new field of inquiry (Avruch and Black 1993: 34; see also Burton 1987). Avruch and Black argue that such a 'universally valid model' is essentialist and of little practical use in analysing situations of conflict as it reduces context-specific questions of politics and culture to a secondary role (1993: 35). Thus, instead of trying to take account of the cultural and political conditions at the heart of a conflict with the help of analysis, the 'human nature' model requires the researcher to fit the data into the theoretical framework (ibid.). These and other 'human nature' approaches to theorizing peace and conflict (e.g. Pinker 2011; Fry 2006) indicate the potentially strong influence of nomological-deductive scientism and empiricism in anthropology's symbiosis with peace and conflict studies. It is reflective of the legacy of Enlightenment and the 'modern episteme', in whose imagination global processes of development and ordering are inherently – or preferably should be – dominated by the West in a 'West vs non-West' or 'West vs wild Rest' dynamic (Finlay 2015: 226). Both mainstream and critical scholarship in peacebuilding studies and more generally has been challenged for its inattention to questions and debates on culture, colour, race and racism (Sabaratnam 2013; Hobson 2007).

To summarize, peace and conflict studies have envisaged a significant role for anthropology and ethnographic methods within their field, but this significance has arguably been based on a clouded vision and a degree of ignorance as to the ambiguities and contestations that have shaped anthropology in the last decades. The two examples discussed above demonstrate that the application of ethnographic methods has been advocated from an ethno-empiricist and positivist epistemological position, according to which ethnography can be the right tool to help scholars understand the experiences and effects of peacebuilding interventions. This empiricism and the persistent objectification of 'the local' stem from the place assigned to anthropology in the 'modern episteme' – that of a functional analytical apparatus to be applied to know and thus control 'things and beings in the world' (Restrepo and Escobar 2006: 111). It also has to be seen in the context of the still dominant IR ontology and the scientific undercurrent in peace and conflict studies since its inception. The symbiosis between anthropology and peace and conflict studies thus requires a more critical and reflexive approach to analyse the dynamics of peace and conflict and the continuum of relationalities between them, which will be explored in the second part of this chapter.

Towards a reflexive anthropology of peace and conflict: Examples from the study of transitional governmentality in post-Soviet Central Asia

In order to engage constructively with the question of what a critical symbiosis between anthropology and peace and conflict studies could look like, two possible theoretical and methodological innovations will be developed by drawing on theoretical and area studies literature, and brief insights into fieldwork in Tajikistan and Kyrgyzstan, respectively. Given the limited frame of this contribution, these examples are merely indicative and taken from the author's research into the two countries (see Lottholz 2015, 2016, 2018a, 2018b). The two following sections will demonstrate the limits and pitfalls of ethnographic representation as it is perceived in the majority of critical peacebuilding literature. It will be shown how ethnographic engagement per se does not necessarily make research more insightful and deliver more 'grounded' or meaningful data. Rather, ethnographic insights can only be valuable if the interpretation of people's statements is critically embedded within the wider societal context. Triangulating ostensibly significant forms of peace and order making thus helps to understand how economic and political insecurity makes people limit their expectations, desires and claims for security and justice, which can give rise to regressive and authoritarian forms of biopolitics.

The shadow of the civil war: Post-conflict and neoliberal governmentality in Tajikistan

The first important aspect of anthropological inquiry into post-conflict settings concerns the interpretation of research against the background of historical and collective psychological imaginaries of what is possible and desirable in life after conflict.[2] In other words, it is important to investigate how experiences of conflict and its aftermath influence people's ideas of what peace could and should look like – an argument that is also made in contributions from social psychology and psychoanalytic theory (e.g. McKeown 2013; Hollander 2006). In the case of Tajikistan, it is generally argued that the civil war between 1992 and 1997 has effected a 'fatigue' with military conflict and given rise to a discourse of *tinji* or peacefulness, well-being (Heathershaw 2009: 72 ff.). Such a 'peace ideology' has depoliticizing and subordinating effects as people come to accept that, compared to the hardship experienced during the civil war, certain shortcomings in one's own life and future prospects are acceptable (ibid.; Lewis 2015: 389). This pragmatism and acquiescence is also increasingly affected by the penetration of post-Soviet societies by imaginaries of neoliberal capitalism (Collier 2011). The insertion of the local and national economy into international regimes, structures and institutions is thus being naturalized (Cameron and Palan 2004; Peshkopia 2010), and it is increasingly taken for granted that, both in Tajikistan and Kyrgyzstan, labour migration and the trans-local organization of family life according to the market are the only ways to ensure survival and sustain livelihoods (Fryer et al. 2014). The uncritical reception of narratives about development and reform in Central Asia can be explained as 'rooted in the fetishisation of capitalism by the postsocialist societies [which] reflects their deeply ingrained teleological way of perceiving the future' (Peshkopia 2010: 24). Hence, people adjust themselves to new 'market realities' and economic imperatives, but also disengage from politics or avoid it in the first place. Authority is thus 'put ... into the hands of rational political leaders who [find] themselves increasingly exposed to popular demands for better government for the sake of a better economic life' (ibid.: 27). Top-down and centralised governance is thus justified through an implicit agreement that government should have (or develop) techno-scientific competencies to do everything necessary to secure the provision of public goods and, ultimately, the fate of the nation (Makarychev and Medvedev 2015: 46; Heathershaw 2009: 66).

These aspects were found to be pertinent in a research setting in central Tajikistan where the author conducted, together with a Tajik colleague who helped with translating and transcribing, open-ended biographical interviews with rural dwellers in order to learn about their lives and understandings of their country. It is noteworthy how respondents' descriptions of how they perceive the current situation of Tajikistan and President Rahmon's role as the vanguard of peace construct a picture about a satisfied life in peace, but also point to the underlying issues discussed above. One respondent, a former collective farm (Russian: *kolkhoz*) worker in her eighties, said:

> My life was actually very good. We were young, we went to cut hay, we worked in the *kolhoz*. Sometimes we slept in the *kolhoz*. And after the *kolhoz* broke down I came here to work in a local school as a cleaner. I worked there for several years. I had a really good life. I didn't have any problems during the Soviet Union and I don't have any problems now, either. This is my daughter and this is her husband [pointing towards them]. I gave my daughter to this guy. I am grateful to God that I have four grandchildren and five great-grandchildren. Living in my son-in-law's house feels like living in my own. We're having a good life [sic]. As our president is ruling the country we are thankful to him because everything is available to us every day and night.

This small excerpt reveals the centrality that labour assumes in this respondent's life, a theme that was repeated several times. It furthermore strikes the eye how this person emphasizes the harmony and absence of problems in both her own life and in regard to her family life. Furthermore, although it could probably be interpreted as a performative speech act (see Lottholz 2018a: 104), the person praises the president for making possible the current peaceful situation and relatively good availability of all necessities of life. A comparison of this interview with the story of the woman's daughter further indicates the significance attributed to the current period of peace and prosperity. After describing how she could not afford to go to university – because of a lack of financial means and the social unacceptability of secondary education for Tajik women in the 1970s – and thus worked in the textile industry and other sectors, the respondent enumerates the educational credentials and professions of her children who live in different parts of the country, and concludes:

> And now as we have been living in the independent state for 20 years, everything is available to us. Our kids can live free. During the years of the civil war, there were some cases where I needed to go to Dushanbe at 2am to bring two bread or buns [Russian: *bulochki*] to feed my family.

Two of the stories the woman told are especially illustrative of the fears and hardship she associates with the years of the civil war. The first one is about how, while pregnant with her second child, she was threatened to be killed at a checkpoint on the way back from visiting relatives, together with a driver and her son. She concluded this story with the words:

> We are thankful to his majesty [Tajik: *Janobi Oli* – i.e. the President] that he brought peace and solidarity and we are having a good life. We can go wherever we want without any feeling of danger now. We are really thankful to our government.

The second story shows the desperation and moral dilemma people were confronting during food shortages:

> Once they brought flour to our grocery store [Russian/Tajik: *univermag*] and they set five-kilo norms to us and they said 'You are three people in your household and you get fifteen kilograms'. And I said that it wasn't enough because I had my little children. My two sons were really little; the two girls were not born yet. And [smiles], I stole two packs of flour that time from the grocery store. I cannot forget this because of hunger I stole flour, and came back to our house. And then my mum asked 'Where did you get these packs of flour from?' And then I said, 'Quiet! I stole them.' I can never forget this event.

Again, the respondent emphasizes the diametrical difference between the years of the civil war and the current situation:

> And now, dear son, we are thankful to our government that we are free and don't have any fear. Our house door is always open. People come to have a cup of tea or a loaf of bread. We are glad that we have enough of everything. We slept with danger and fear before ... We are living free now, we don't have any needs nor complaints.

The above clearly suggests that the years of the civil war, and to a lesser extent the experience of life during the Soviet Union, make the current political and economic situation in Tajikistan appear as a significant improvement. Neither needs nor complaints, danger nor fear, nor the physical hardship and moral dilemmas of making ends meet in a situation of material shortage are apparent. They are a thing of the past thanks to the peace that has been brought and kept up by 'his majesty'. It appears logical from this perspective that migration within and beyond Tajikistan is not perceived as an obstacle to a good life. The internalization and acceptance of market logics as a chance rather than a regressive mechanism becomes obvious when this respondent rationalizes the current market imperative: 'Today everything is available ... We don't have any obstacles. We work. If you don't work you cannot eat. If you work you earn money and live your life.' While this illustrates the emergence of an ideology of peace and harmony (Lewis 2016: 389; Heathershaw 2009: 75 ff.) and neoliberal governmentality (Collier 2011), the next section will show how the global discourse on Islamic radicalism and securitization is being internalized in community security practices in Kyrgyzstan.

Securitization in community security in Kyrgyzstan: Tackling 'non-traditional religion' and juvenile delinquency

The previous section has concentrated on how discourses of peace and stability are internalized by people and adopted in their justification for unconditional regime support and withdrawal into the private sphere. This section[3] will focus on how governmentality and hegemony are reproduced in community security practices in Kyrgyzstan. This transcends the classical Foucauldian understanding about the effects of discourse and combines this approach with Bourdieu's practice theory to trace how socially acknowledged categories and world views are (re-)produced (Bourdieu 1977; Henry 2012). Here, the contribution of a critical anthropology of peace and conflict can be most significant, as it could foreground an inductive inquiry into how the 'most infinitesimal forms' of knowledge and representation make up the 'regimes of truth' and practice of peace and security governance (Finlay 2015: 231; Foucault 2004: 30). Ethnography can thus help, according to Finlay (2015: 231), 'to understand how so-called communal identities and indigenous practices are produced, subsumed and reproduced in peacebuilding, i.e. how they are made useful to government'. Furthermore, by embedding the analysis within the wider semantic context, the exclusionary and marginalizing effects such governance has on people could be revealed as well.

The present example is taken from the author's research on community security projects in South Kyrgyzstan during 2015 (Lottholz 2016, 2018b) and will focus on one town at the eastern end of the Fergana valley and bordering with the Republic of Uzbekistan. The contact with the community in focus was initiated during collaborative research in which the author worked as a volunteer profiling thirteen so-called Local Crime Prevention Centres. Further participatory observation was conducted during a meeting of the local community security working group (including representatives from the local administration, law enforcement organs and civil society organizations) within the project run by the national NGO Civic Union 'For Reforms and Result' (CURR; Russian: *Grazhdanskii Soiuz 'Za reformy i rezultat'*) and supported by UN Office for Drugs and Crime (UNODC) (for further information and outputs see Saferworld 2016 and CURR 2016). During several visits and follow-up meetings, it was possible to get an insight into how building a peaceful and secure environment was a difficult task, given two major challenges that are also reflective of the major security issues identified in other communities (CURR 2016).

Of highest priority for the working group was the spread of 'non-traditional religious tendencies' (Russian: *netraditsionykh religioznykh tendencii*) and reports about young people from the town's area going to join the fighting in Syria (CURR 2016). The term 'non-traditional religion' denotes the increasingly significant role of neo-orthodox Islamic denominations and sects which are seen as a source of (violent) extremism both in public discourse and the expert community in Kyrgyzstan (Azizian 2005; Heathershaw and Montgomery 2014). One discussion on possible measures to address the issue illustrated the trade-offs of community security practices particularly well. The question preoccupying some group members was how to limit the access of missionaries whose activities were obviously at the root of the increasing radicalization. 'They should be completely prohibited from entering [the town]', posited one NGO activist during the group meeting. This visibly captured the group's general fatigue with the issue. The group leader and deputy head of the local administration (*aiyl okmotu*) agreed, but urged the members for a more modest approach: 'Our main goal is to maintain public control. I agree [that the foreign missionaries need to be controlled] but it has to be according to some rules [*na baze kakikh-to pravil*].' After a long discussion, the group found that there did not seem to be any effective means to prohibit missionaries' access and that they needed to focus on getting more information and a clearer view on the visitors' movements and activities. Furthermore, the representative of the local imams argued against the proposition of entry bans, as recruitment of supporters for radical Islamic was, according to him, mostly done via the internet. Tackling the foreign missionaries might thus not even be effective in reducing religious radicalization in the town. The group in this town and practitioners in Kyrgyzstan at large are in this sense only at the beginning of a long journey towards developing an understanding of the new trend of how violent extremism spreads – and of ways to counteract it. The choice of a framing of 'non-traditional' religion instead of the widespread 'religious' or 'Islamic radicalism' is a first step towards a more nuanced approach in this area, which has so far been dominated by an essentialist and securitizing fixation on any, and most often superficial, expression of 'non-traditional' (from a Kyrgyz point of view) Islamic interpretations, practices and apparel and understanding them in terms of security threats (Tromble 2014; Lottholz 2015).

Another core problem on which the group could not reach agreement was the frequent involvement of local youth in hooliganism, school racketeering and inter-group violence. The group members seemed to see the problem as one of lack of upbringing and moral education (*vospitanie*) in comparison with their own upbringing and the pride and dignity that had been part of their everyday lives during the late days of the Soviet Union (see DeYoung 2007). One way to re-establish the long-vanished virtues, as was proposed by the senior neighbourhood inspector of the police, was the possibility of conscribing a higher number of youth for military service, which would enhance their 'discipline'. This spurred exclamations across the meeting room and a controversial discussion. The head teacher of one of the town's schools was most outspoken against such a reinvigoration of a military-based national culture, especially given the implications of excluding different national minorities: 'Excuse me, but if Kyrgyzstan is only for the Kyrgyz, then all others will already be afraid [*to drugie uzhe boiatsa*].'

While this measure was not included in the action plan, the group decided to raise young people's spirit through strengthening their awareness about law and order (*pravosoznanie*) and organizing 'mass culture and sport events, meetings with parents', among other things (CURR 2016). It is noteworthy how this strategy appears to define and try to solve the problem *for* the youth of the town, rather than cooperating *with* them to take account of their needs and views of the problem. 'We are aware of this shortcoming and are trying to suggest such ideas to our working groups', commented the project co-coordinator of the implementing Civic Union 'For Reforms and Result' (Skype interview on 26 March 2016). But he also pointed to the fact that the head of the local youth committee (*komitet molodezhy*) is involved in the working group's efforts and that more inclusion of young people's points of view is conditional upon more long-term mobilization work, as projects such as this and local politics in general are not perceived as a way for young people to raise their voice and express concerns. This illustrates how the composition of local project working groups can be so hierarchical and patriarchal that a certain level of essentialism and 'othering' of different groups – such as followers of 'non-traditional religion' or youth in this example – seems inevitable. Thus, community security practices in Kyrgyzstan, while offering new hope for more participatory and responsive action, reproduce the categories, binaries, regimes of knowledge and practices employed by governmental and hegemonic actors elsewhere.

The two preceding sections have both shown how a critical anthropology of peace and conflict can shed light on the ambiguities and processes of normalization of hegemonic, biopolitical and authoritarian trajectories of social ordering. The framework of this contribution does not allow an in-depth study as is provided elsewhere (Heathershaw 2009; Heathershaw and Montgomery 2014; Lottholz 2018a, 2018b; CURR 2016). Still, this empirical exploration has highlighted the need to not only 'engage with' or 'listen to' people in the research setting but also to situate the data gathered within debates on the critical junctures and trajectories that will inevitably affect research participants' views and understandings. Thus, rather than fitting fieldwork data into an analytical framework for analysing a certain form of peace, research should focus on the contestation around forms of peace, as well as the ways in which peace itself becomes a vehicle for the reproduction of governmentality, hegemony and empire (Lewis 2016; Finlay 2015).

Conclusion

The symbiosis between anthropology and peace and conflict studies is happening at a time when the study of their subject matters is retaining, if not increasing, its complexity. At the same time, new and unprecedented regimes of austerity and managerialism, with corresponding expectations of justification of intellectual endeavours in terms of their 'impact' and innovative potential (see Shore's chapter in this volume), make it increasingly hard to carve out the time and space for disciplinary dialogues to occur in a depth that allows comprehensive engagement. This restricted environment is partly to blame for the distorted picture that appears to prevail in the nascent symbiosis between peace and conflict studies and anthropology. As was shown in the critical review of this literature, there is much more that the two fields can learn from each other – for instance, the long-standing debates in anthropology on positionality, power relations and the 'crisis of representation' which have had different materializations in the reflective exchanges on anthropology's 'colonial encounter', or the 'Writing Culture' and 'Third World feminism' issues (see Lottholz 2018b). To fully realize the potential of symbiosis, these significant internal critiques and renewals require much more attention in the reception of the disciplinary 'other' – as anthropology seems to be perceived in peace and conflict studies.

The overall critical commitment of this contribution notwithstanding, it is written out of a deep sympathy with the idea of combining anthropological research with inquiries into peace and conflict. New ways of identifying points of common ground and compromise through in-depth consultation within and across social groups (discussed in Irwin's chapter in this volume) is one of the end products of the critical dialogue envisaged in this chapter. That such practices are already existing and being developed in multiple places across the globe shows how much potential there is for a transfer of knowledge on peace making towards (post-)conflict settings worldwide. But in the same way as Irwin does, this chapter is trying to raise awareness that this transmission process is not straightforward, and nor is the role in it of anthropological approaches and ethnographic methods. Conceiving of peace making, or 'everyday', 'hybrid' and 'post-liberal' framings as practical tools or heuristic analytical devices to diagnose the existence or the potential of certain positive forms of peace would be to repeat the mistakes of ethno-empiricism and positivism still present in peace and conflict studies and well known in the history of anthropology.

The time has come to move on and forge a symbiosis that tackles the structural conditions, complexities and ambiguities faced by people living in (post-)conflict settings. The second part of this chapter has showcased two aspects which could possibly be part of such a symbiotic anthropology of peace and conflict: first, the role of ideological forces, imaginaries and psychological dimensions of conflict and peace; and second, the emergence of regimes of knowledge and practice determining the conduct of expert and practitioner communities. These realms and the data collection methods they require partly transcend ethnographic research as it had been classically understood. However, this also reflects the fact that ethnographic methods and anthropological theory have been and still are expanding their horizons. Keeping track of and including the evolving debates and scientific positionings of the respective research fields/disciplines thus seems to be a key ingredient for a holistic and critical symbiosis between peace and conflict studies and anthropology.

Note

1   A recent example is the *Palgrave Handbook of Disciplinary and Regional Approaches to Peace*, which acknowledges the contributions and valuable arguments in a range of disciplines but still frames the main problematics in localized and territorial terms vis-a-vis 'international' regimes and actors (Richmond, Pogodda and Ramovic 2016: 3, 4, 6, 8, 14 and 16; although more nuance is provided on pages 13–15).
2   This part has partly been adapted from Lottholz (2018a).
3   The section is partly adapted from Lottholz (2018b).

References

Avruch, K. (1998), *Culture and Conflict Resolution*, Washington, DC: US Institute of Peace Press.

Azizian, R. (2005), 'Islamic Radicalism in Kazakhstan and Kyrgyzstan: Implications for the Global War on Terrorism', Zurich: Conflict Studies Research Centre. Available online: http://mercury.ethz.ch/serviceengine/Files/ISN/44044/ichaptersection_singledocument/a46cf13f-6280-4f47-9777-49c0b1400b08/en/10.pdf (accessed 5 October 2016).

Black, P. W. and K. Avruch (1993), 'Anthropologists in Conflictland: The Role of Cultural Anthropology in an Institute for Conflict Analysis and Resolution', *PoLAR: Political and Legal Anthropology Review*, 16 (3): 29–38.

Bourdieu, P. (1977), *Outline of a Theory of Practice*, Cambridge: Cambridge University Press.

Burton, J. W. (1987), *Resolving Deep-Rooted Conflict: A Handbook*, Lanham, MD: University Press of America.

Civic Union 'For Reforms and Result' [CURR] (2016), '*Bezopasnost soobsha: Itogi programmy po razvitiu sotsialnogo partnerstva v podderzhanii pravoporiadka i profilaktike pravonarushenii finalnyi otchet* [Security Together: Results of the Programme for the Development of Social Partnership in Support of the Rule of

Law and Crime Prevention – Final Report]'. Available online: http://reforma.kg/sites/
default/files/analytics/crime-prevention-report-web.pdf (accessed 5 October 2016).

Cameron, A. and R. Palan (2004), *The Imagined Economies of Globalization*, London:
Sage.

Collier, S. J. (2011), *Post-Soviet Social: Neoliberalism, Social Modernity, Biopolitics*,
Princeton, NJ: Princeton University Press.

DeYoung, A. (2007), 'The Erosion of *Vospitanie* (Social Upbringing) in Post-Soviet
Kyrgyzstan: Voices from the Schools', *Communist and Post-Communist Studies*,
40 (2): 239–56.

Denskus, T. (2007), 'Peacebuilding Does Not Build Peace', *Development in Practice*,
17 (4–5): 656–62.

Finlay, A. (2015), 'Liberal Intervention, Anthropology and the Ethnicity Machine',
Peacebuilding, 3 (3): 224–37.

Foucault, M. (2004), *Society Must be Defended: Lectures at the Collège de France
1975–76*, London: Penguin.

Fry, D. P. (2006), *The Human Potential for Peace*, New York: Oxford University Press.

Fryer, P., E. Nazritdinov and E. Satybaldieva (2014), 'Moving Toward the Brink?
Migration in the Kyrgyz Republic', *Central Asian Affairs*, 1: 171–98.

Glick Schiller, N. (2006), 'Introduction: What Can Transnational Studies Offer the
Analysis of Localized Conflict and Protest?', *Focaal*, 47: 3–17.

Graef, J. (2015), *Practicing Post-liberal Peacebuilding: Legal Empowerment and Emergent
Hybridity in Liberia*, Basingstoke: Palgrave.

Heathershaw, J. (2009), *Post-Conflict Tajikistan: The Politics of Peacebuilding and the
Emergence of Legitimate Order*, London: Routledge.

Heathershaw, J. and D. W. Montgomery (2014), *The Myth of Post-Soviet Muslim
Radicalization in the Central Asian Republics*, London: Chatham House.

Henry, A. (2012), 'Situating Community Safety: Emergent Professional Identities in
Communities of Practice', *Criminology and Criminal Justice*, 12 (4): 413–31.

Hobson, J. M. (2007), 'Is Critical Theory Always for the White West and for Western
Imperialism? Beyond Westphilian Towards a Post-Racist Critical IR', *Review of
International Studies*, 33 (S1): 91–116.

Hollander, N. C. (2006), 'Trauma, Ideology, and the Future of Democracy', *International
Journal of Applied Psychoanalytic Studies*, 3 (2): 156–67.

Kalb, D. (2005), 'From Flows to Violence: Politics and Knowledge in the Debates on
Globalization and Empire', *Anthropological Theory*, 5 (2): 176–204.

Kearney, M. (1995), 'The Local and the Global: The Anthropology of Globalization and
Transnationalism', *Annual Review of Anthropology*, 24: 547–65.

Lewis, D. (2016), 'Central Asia: Contested Peace', in O. Richmond, S. Pogodda and
J. Ramovic (eds), *The Palgrave Handbook of Disciplinary and Regional Approaches to
Peace*, 387–96, Basingstoke: Palgrave.

Lottholz, P. (2018a), 'A *Negative* Post-Liberal Peace? Inquiring the Embeddedness
of Everyday Forms of Peace in Central Asia', in C. Owen, S. Juraev, D. Lewis,

N. Megoran and J. Heathershaw (eds), 'Interrogating Illiberal Peace in Eurasia. Critical Perspectives on Peace and Conflict', 97–119, New York: Rowman & Littlefield.

Lottholz, P. (2018b), 'Critiquing Anthropological Imagination in Peace and Conflict Studies: From Empiricist Positivism to a Dialogical Approach in Ethnographic Peace Research', *International Peacekeeping*, 25 (5): 695–720.

Lottholz, P. (2016), 'Polizeireform in Kirgistan: Mechanismen der Gemeindesicherheit als Schritt zum fundamentalen Wandel? [Police Reform in Kyrgyzstan: Community Security Mechanisms as a Step Towards Fundamental Change?]', *Zentralasien-Analysen*, no. 99. Available online: http://www.laender-analysen.de/zentralasien/pdf/ZentralasienAnalysen99.pdf (accessed 10 April 2016).

Lottholz, P. (2015), 'Reproducing the Soviet Policy Paradox? The Problem of Restrictive Approaches to Regulating Religion and Countering Violent Extremism', *Central Asian Policy Review*, 2 (1): 22–6.

Mac Ginty, R. (2011), *International Peacebuilding and Local Resistance: Hybrid Forms of Peace*, Basingstoke: Palgrave.

Mac Ginty, R. (2008), 'Indigenous Peace-Making versus the Liberal Peace', *Cooperation and Conflict*, 43 (2): 139–63.

Makarychev, A. and S. Medvedev (2015), 'Biopolitics and Power in Putin's Russia', *Problems of Post-Communism*, 62 (1): 45–54.

McKeown, S. (2013), 'Social Psychology and Peace-Building', in R. Mac Ginty (ed.), 117–31, *Routledge Handbook of Peacebuilding*, London: Routledge.

Millar, G. (ed.) (2017), *Ethnographic Peace Research: Approaches and Tensions*, Basingstoke: Palgrave.

Millar, G. (2014), *An Ethnographic Approach to Peacebuilding: Understanding Local Experiences in Transitional States*, London: Routledge.

Paffenholz, T. (2015), 'Unpacking the Local Turn in Peacebuilding: A Critical Assessment Towards an Agenda for Future Research', *Third World Quarterly*, 36 (5): 857–74.

Pinker, S. (2011), *The Better Angels of Our Nature*, New York: Viking.

Restrepo, E. and A. Escobar (2005), 'Other Anthropologies and Anthropology Otherwise: Steps to a World Anthropologies Framework', *Critique of Anthropology*, 25 (2): 99–129.

Richmond, O. P., S. Pogodda and J. Ramovic (2016), 'Introduction', in O. Richmond, S. Pogodda and J. Ramovic (eds), *The Palgrave Handbook of Disciplinary and Regional Approaches to Peace*, 1–17, Basingstoke: Palgrave.

Richmond, O. P. and A. Mitchell (eds) (2011), *Hybrid Forms of Peace: From Everyday Agency to Post-Liberalism*, Basingstoke: Palgrave.

Richmond, O. P. (2011), *A Post-Liberal Peace*, London: Routledge.

Sabaratnam, M. (2013), 'Avatars of Eurocentrism in the Critique of the Liberal Peace', *Security Dialogue*, 44 (3): 259–78.

Saferworld (2016), *Istorii uspekha: Obshestvenno-profilakticheskie tsentry Oshskoi, Zhalal-Abadskoi i Batkenskoi oblastei* [Success Stories: Local Crime Prevention Centres of Osh, Jalal-Abad and Batken Provinces], Osh: Saferworld.

Sylvester, C. (2007), 'Whither the International at the End of IR1', *Millennium: Journal of International Studies*, 35 (3): 551–73.

Souillac, G. and D. P. Fry (2016), 'Anthropology: Implications for Peace', in O. Richmond, S. Pogodda and J. Ramovic (eds), *The Palgrave Handbook of Disciplinary and Regional Approaches to Peace*, 69–81, Basinstoke: Palgrave.

Tromble, R. (2014), 'Securitising Islam, Securitising Ethnicity: The Discourse of Uzbek Radicalism in Kyrgyzstan', *East European Politics*, 30 (4): 526–47.

Vrasti, W. (2008), 'The Strange Case of Ethnography and International Relations', *Millennium: Journal of International Studies*, 37 (2): 279–301.

12

For Christ and State: Collaboration, EJK, and the Communal Subject

Scott MacLochlainn

On an afternoon in May 2017, I was in an Uber cab, on my way to the National Archives in Manila, and on the hunt for the records of an early twentieth-century court case for my research into Christians and their legal and corporate identities in the Philippines. While passing Intramuros, the old and famous administrative and economic centre in Manila, now an area of museums, Spanish colonial buildings and crumbling walls, President Rodrigo Duterte was on the radio, live from Moscow, announcing martial law in the south of the Philippines. Violence had broken out a week earlier in the city of Marawi between the Philippine army and members of the Islamic liberation and the secessionist Maute group (labelled a terrorist group by the Philippine army), which had recently aligned with ISIS. I had been sitting in the car, breezily thinking about traffic and infrastructure in Manila. It was an oddly classical, if clichéd moment. Passing Intramuros, in the very heart of the capital city, listening to a crackling radio as the president took questions regarding the state implementing military power and suspending the writ of habeas corpus. It was also very modern – in an Uber, on my smartphone, listening to talk of Islamic terror and ISIS – an engaged but distant listener.

It was not just me, of course, who was experiencing the invocation of martial law within a very particular typology of state power and historical experience in the Philippines. Having famously experienced martial law under the dictatorship of Ferdinand Marcos in the 1970s and 1980s, contemporary discourses on the subject in the Philippines are are inevitably framed within this distinct history. Thus, in discussions of martial law in Marawi in 2017 and 2018, there is no escape from a mid-1970s Ferdinand Marcos and the flitting images of his perfectly coiffed hair, mid-distance stare and upturned chin. This looping in and out of past prototypes foregrounds matters not only of similarity and, for many, a churning sense of fear of the Philippines slipping into dictatorship, but of meaning and intention. Does martial law mean the same thing now as it did before? Will it lead to similar authoritarian outcomes? Is Duterte's intention the same as Marcos'? And importantly, why are people supporting him? On what ethical basis are they lending that support? How are people collaborating with and against the Philippine state?

Amid the highly controversial presidency of Duterte (2016), with its rapid uptick in state-sponsored violence, the shifting tectonics of police and military power, the sharp undercutting of free media, and the general erosion of the inherited norms of how a liberal democracy functions, it is unsurprising that the country has been riven by the fault lines of political affiliation. Increasingly partisan, one's support for or against Duterte is now nearly always a pointed gesture. At the same time, it has been notoriously difficult to make assumptions about people's views, given how support for Duterte and his administration cuts across and around established political lines and class status. The current mode of populist nationalism engages in continuous language that demands participation and collaboration on the part of Filipinos. Inasmuch as people speak of collaborating with one another to protect rights – of speech, of judicial independence, of legal process, of life – collaboration is also spoken of in terms of complicity with the more nefarious aspects of current state forms of governance. The common experience, and the common question, of complicity in the relationship between the individual and state power, is often a common refrain: can one be complicit by standing still?

In this short piece, I want to push a little at the term 'collaboration', and frame it within the terms of affiliation – specifically religious affiliation. I do so by way of a discussion of Christian subjectivity in the Philippines, highlighting the collaborative nature of Christian affiliation, and in particular the role of partial, or nominal affiliation ('in name only'), before briefly discussing Christian responses to the nature of state governance in the Philippines since 2016. Not only does Christianity arguably form the most marked point of entry and institutional repository of ethical thinking/authority in the Philippines, the prominent role of affiliation and intention within contemporary modes of Christian discourse engages the broader remit of collaboration and the forms of subjectivity that it constitutes.

At first glance, *collaboration* and *affiliation* might seem to be conceptual cousins at best. This is arguably more so in the context of collaboration with state-sponsored forms of violence set against Christian forms of affiliation. Collaboration certainly implies a more active involvement than affiliation, which often reads more as an alignment rather than any form of action at all. But I want to suggest here that both concepts are not only more fluid, but deeper than at first glance, and speak to each other in important ways, especially amid heightened circumstances such as the Philippines is currently experiencing. In seeking to frame collaboration through the lens of religious affiliation, and religious affiliation through that of collaboration, situating affiliation in that space between those two other conceptual cousins – collaboration and complicity – is useful. For one, it complicates that which might be labelled as passive and that as active. For if affiliation appears passive, complicity is often seen to be a hugely pejorative type of passiveness. Moreover, Christianity has long emphasized notably silent acts – often those inherent in the interiority of the soul – ones that appear passive, as immensely efficacious. For example, the simple acceptance of Jesus into your life, as your saviour, for many evangelical born again Christians, is perhaps the most vital act of self possible. Thus, what are the murkier, quieter forms of collaboration that exist within contemporary neoliberal forms of subjectivity? Perhaps it is those that do not initially draw as much attention – that exist as more stance than act.

While for many, there is something of a straight line to be drawn between Christian subjectivity and neoliberalism, I am not so concerned here in replaying such a narrative. Undoubtedly, Christian ontologies are in many ways ideally suited to, and historically implicated in, neoliberal contexts. Briefly stated, this argument holds that the form of individualism constituted by Christianity – individuals, and not communities, are saved – together with a type of ethics and governance that focuses on the improvement of self, begin to look very similar to a classic neoliberal subject (Bornstein 2005, Muehlebach 2013, Werbner 2011). But my concern in this chapter is rather to highlight how within the dividing line of explicitly articulated beliefs and the lived life – being Christian – exists a space in which the individual is much more of a collaborative project than it might seem. That is, for all of the focus placed on the relationship between the Christian self and God, there are many more people and things involved in producing and maintaining that relationship (Handman 2014). Situated within the modes of interaction between anthropology and Christianity, as well as among Christians themselves, I briefly highlight then 1) how the dividing line between Christianity as a lived system of beliefs and ethics, and Christianity as an explicit and formalized (as well as ritualized) discourse on that belief and ethics results in notably partial and nominal types of affiliation, and 2) how much collaboration and communal work is invested in Christian contexts in which the individual is notably prominent.

Collaborating with Christians

If anthropology, as a discipline, has never been particularly collaborative in method, it has often been concerned with the nature of particular forms of collaboration – politically and ethically – and mostly when collaboration is framed in terms of complicity. For most contemporary anthropologists, when we think of anthropologists and collaboration, we perhaps think of the engaged anthropologist giving testimony in a lawsuit against a large petrochemical corporation, the co-authorship of a book or the shared making of a film, collaboration with the state, the donation of money and time to a cause, or the willing or unwilling lending of benefit from our work. Nearly always, collaboration within these contexts presupposes a particular set of views regarding intentionality and self-awareness of the collaborative act.

In my research on language, legality and religious corporations in Mindoro, Christians collaborated with me in a number of ways, even though it served and disserved them in different ways. For example, some of my interlocutors undoubtedly enjoyed having someone interested in their work and lives. Indeed, as is common among ethnographers, one often has a lateral expertise of institutions and communities that provides an alternative view of interest and value to those communities with whom we work. But I also occasionally disserve my interlocutors. I am engaged in a formatting of the religious into a secularized academic space. I engage in a translation of sorts, of Christian practice and subjectivities into a language I am not sure they ever want. That translation is partial, excluding in many ways what is all-important to them: the belief in the presence of Christ.

The genre of anthropological scholarship on religion, and especially Christianity, is well known for its engagement with and self-awareness regarding such complex collaborations with religious believers and practitioners. That is, as a genre, 'Anthropology of Christianity' has a somewhat ready-made commentary folded into it regarding the role of self-reflexivity within research. The reasons for this are multiple, but prominent among them are the liberal Christian-secular origins of anthropology (and many anthropologists), and the relatively late (1990s) emergence of a broad and coherent focus on Christianity as an anthropological subject. Indeed, Christianity has proven a ferocious space in which to understand the tenets, biases, borders and epistemological modes of anthropology (Cannell 2006; Chua 2012; Bialecki 2017). For all the growing literature on the closeness and distance between the anthropologist and the Christian believer, arguably the most famous of texts on this topic are some of the earliest ones, including the companion pieces, a 1991 article in *Social Research* (1991) and later *The Book of Jerry Falwell* (2000) by Susan Harding. It was these texts that gave to anthropology and the world the phrase 'the repugnant cultural other', and with it a shorthand for what it is to work with and study with those people whose views one finds morally, well, repugnant. More than a reflexive piece, Harding's work was a theoretical interjection into the peculiar dynamics of anthropological subjectivity, masterfully rounding in on issues of political, discursive and ontological closeness and distance. It is easy to find people, groups, corporations and states whose views one finds offensive. But for the Christians Harding was working with, these people were doing what she, as an anthropologist, wanted them to be doing: believing, talking about believing, enacting those beliefs, and allowing those beliefs to filter through their everyday lives. In many ways they were being the perfect anthropological subjects. It just so happened that Harding found these views – or at the least those that she was politically, socially, disciplinarily associated with – and a good deal of the habitus problematic. And thus, the question quickly arises for any anthropologist working with somewhat unsympathetic others: what exactly constitutes collaboration and complicity within research? Harding notes that in her own research with Christians, the language and omnipresence of Christian discourse and the attempts to convert her led to transformations of the self, not necessarily in terms of faith but in the sensation and stance of being in the world. As she writes of her own experience and that time leading up to full conversion, known as 'under conviction':

> The membrane between disbelief and belief is much thinner than we think . . . I began to acquire the knowledge and vision and sensibilities, to share the experience, of a believer. Believers and disbelievers assert there is no middle ground: you are either one or the other. You cannot both believe and disbelieve. But that is precisely what it means to be 'under conviction'. You do not believe in the sense of public declarations, but you gradually come to respond to, interpret and act in the world as if you were a believer.
>
> Harding 2001: 58

During my ethnographic research, I encountered, and inhabited, a different space between belief and disbelief, both in myself and in many of the people I knew. I fit the bill of the liberal-secularist, non-Christian Christian almost perfectly. Raised in Ireland in the 1980s and 1990s, I caught the last moments of an unquestioned and ubiquitous institutional Catholicism, as well as its swift collapse, when by way of a series of child abuse scandals and particular forms of modern capitalism it seemed that nearly everyone in Ireland, except for the elderly, became modernist secularists overnight. While I was an altar boy in the early 1990s, it was more habit and theatre than 'true' belief. Thus, when I found myself, two decades later, in rural Philippines, studying a range of Christian formations and denominations, I was amid scales and forms of sliding religious otherness. I was non-believing, but nevertheless long schooled in the habitus of Catholicism. In articulating my non-affiliation to any church, I occupied a particular religious role in the Philippines, and particularly in Mindoro: the nominally religious. It was not necessarily important that I was non-believing, but rather that I had been a believer at some point, or had come from a family of believers. Whether I was nominal, lapsed, or otherwise disinterested, I was categorized as potentially convertible.

In general, I was assigned the same definitional space as those people who believed in God but were unenthralled by a divine presence. For missionaries, we shared a Christian ethic, and had grown up in Christian contexts, but were either too busy, put off by institutionalized forms of religion, or disinterested in attending services and masses.

Such people, the 'nominally religious', are hugely important in the town I here call Sta. Teresita, and across the Philippines, as they are the prime focus of Christian missionaries. Similar to the Philippines overall, over 85 per cent of people living in Sta. Teresita are Catholic, and unsurprisingly, within that 85 per cent are huge differences in terms of religious identity and commitment to the Catholic Church. The majority of other Christian denominations, which are increasingly present in Mindoro, focus much of their missionary work on so-called 'lapsed Catholics'. These are the nominally Catholic, the non-practising, the believing but quasi-spiritless, or the disenchanted.

Interestingly, given that Christianity assumes certain forms of intention on the part of the believer, and the legibility of that intention to others, what then of the nominally believing? How do we read the intention of the religiously nominal, when they are often aligned and affiliated with official Christian doctrines and discourses, while simultaneously locating themselves outside of, and not responsible to, those same discourses and doctrines? The internalization of belief and faith and its relationship to the outward forms of Christianity has been well noted and has been at the forefront in understanding the nature of interiority, of language, and of the politics of representation (Keane 2007; Robbins 2004). In regard to the space between doctrine and experiences, as Webb Keane has noted, it is the 'concrete practices' of Christianity – the hymns, prayers, scripture, masses and funerals – that 'articulate public doctrine and subjective experiences', and it is the semiotic forms inherent in these practices that 'can circulate across an indefinitely wide range of contexts, and that make doctrine believable, impressive, morally commanding, and above all, part of an inhabitable world' (Keane 2007: 68). And yet that inhabitability, of Christianity, of doctrine, is varying (ibid.). Doctrine articulated is not the same as doctrine inhabited, except, perhaps, for the missionary in mid-mission. The practices of missionary work – the discursive attempt to merge textual and divine authority with the proselyte's own subjectivity and personal history – is an attempt to overcome that 'membrane' of which Harding speaks, that distance between belief and non-belief, between doctrine and experience, and, indeed, between text and practice. For in the missionary's terms, success is when the word of God becomes the experience of God.

In my work, I engage with a particular religious context – one in which formerly default religious identities, for example Catholic and Muslim ones, have increasingly become spaces that are open to interpretation and choice. This is particularly true of Christian identities – that is, to be born of Catholic parents in the Philippines no longer secures that you will be. To call this circumstance religious plurality is not necessarily to describe it, for one can find religiously plural contexts in which religious lines are drawn hard and fast. While statistically, the Philippines has remained over recent decades more or less stable with regard to religious affiliation (Catholicism), there is more movement and fluidity between and among faiths than perhaps ever before. The shifts in how religious affiliation is enacted, I would argue, influences the discursive space of doctrine and its relationship to living as a Christian. Affiliation, while arguably complex and heterogeneous, is often simultaneously and publicly reduced to more minimal sets of doctrinal difference. And it is within this space that the *nominally religious* slip away from sight – less publicly present, but nevertheless there, and importantly, the focus of missionary work.

About midway through my fieldwork, two Mormon missionaries knocked on my door. As surprised as I was to see them, they were evidently more surprised, finding themselves face-to-face with an Irish man and his cat living in a small apartment in rural Philippines. I had actually known quite a bit about Mormonism in the town. Immediately after beginning my research, I had approached their church, which stood out in the town for its newness and Americanized architecture. Disliking the idea of approaching churches and congregations during Sunday services, I had always tried to meet the pastor or church worker during quiet weekdays. But I never managed to make contact with their church and having left numerous letters of introduction in their letterbox and receiving no response, I moved on, and continued my work with other churches. But I would see Mormon missionaries on the streets from time to time, two by two, with their crisp white shirts and slacks, ties and backpacks, standing out as only Mormons and anthropologists seem to do. I invited my visitors in, and immediately jumped into an enthusiastic – and, by that stage, rehearsed – description of my research, interest in new churches and missionary work, and a statement of my own personal non-/ir-religious stance. The latter was partly habit and partly as a way of putting them at ease, given the tremendous intra-Christian competition in town. They were disinterested, a little uncomfortable, but clearly committed to their project at hand in introducing me to Mormonism and followed through with their equally rehearsed conversation on the mistaken biblical and faith interpretations made by other Christians, and the truer nature of the Book of Mormon. After an hour or so, and my own uncomfortable supplication to kneeling and praying together, I agreed to have them visit me later in the week. After two further, very similar, visits, we came to a deal of sorts: 1) they would come each week to my apartment as I read the Book of Mormon; 2) I would pray every day and open myself up to the possibility of the presence of God; 3) in return, I could accompany them on their daily house visits and missionary work. Thus began a limited three-week window in which I was able to see up close the missionary work of Mormons.

On an afternoon the following week, as we set off, it was clear we were not going door-to-door, cold calling people. Instead, the two American missionaries were visiting those church members, and possible converts, who had stopped attending services. One of the first houses we approached was typical of Sta. Teresita: three-quarters wood (bamboo and nipa), with one concrete wall, a corrugated iron roof, and an open yard of patted-down earth with clothes drying and chickens running around. The woman we were visiting was asleep. They repeatedly knocked on her door, although it was open and they could see her sleeping in the corner. Where I would have retreated and called in another time, they knocked and called to her until she awoke and came to the door. They waited patiently until she welcomed us in. What I understood as an invasive act was rather for them simply their work. While this woman was slightly groggy after an afternoon nap, the ensuing conversation was somewhat intense, maybe fifteen minutes in length, concerning her belief and her commitment, but equally concerning the amount of work she had done, and the work they had done in achieving her membership, her affiliation, to the Church of Latter Day Saints. The focus was entirely on her, and her salvation, and yet it was presented as thoroughly collaborative. They emphasized the communal nature of her hearing

God's voice, how she was surrounded and her actions situated within a community. The constant slippage between the individual and collective act was essential to how these missionaries framed the nature of affiliation, hers as well as those of other Mormons.

A lapsed Catholic and having found her way into the Mormon church through her brother, this woman clearly would have preferred to have been left alone. Seemingly regretful that she had become involved with the church, the space between Mormon doctrine and her affiliation to the church began to open up over the course of the conversation. They asked her basic questions on Mormon, and mostly general Christian, tenets: whether she believed in God (answer: yes); whether it was important to live her life in accordance with God's wishes (answer: yes); whether consistent prayer was essential to letting God into your heart (answer: yes). Throughout my research, this aspect of work and collaboration – and the discomfort, unwillingness, or willingness born of politeness or resignation – was regularly evident when accompanying missionaries and outreach workers from many, but by no means all, of the Christian groups with whom I worked. For missionaries, such was the regular engagement with the nominally religious. For many Christians, the forcefulness of the missionary endeavour, the lack of politeness to it – they would never speak of anything that would fall under the term 'coercion' – was worth it if they saved a soul. Furthermore, although across the spectrum of Christian practice the responsibility and process of proselytizing is centred on the individual and their internal state, a number of Christians I knew, including these Mormon missionaries, were not so concerned as to the present internal state of a person's faith. This would come later, they noted. What was most important in regard to their work with these nominally religious was to have them in contact and surrounded by Christians full of faith. Across denominations, conversion entailed similar forms of work as described above. The willingness or unwillingness of proselytes differed, but conversion was nearly always a collaborative effort, as we see even in Harding's description of the ubiquity of Christian language and stances. Rarely during my research did I encounter a person who had turned to a Christian church alone and outside an immediate sphere of an active proselytizing community, which is not to say that conversion is presented as such.

In evangelical circles, inasmuch as individuals are likely to articulate their acceptance/finding of Jesus, verbally marked with a statement of date, and presented very much as their own one-to-one relationship to Jesus and God, such statements are nearly always followed by another statement related to the community through which they first engaged with that particular form of

Christianity, or the person or pastor who helped them find their way. This is not so much the elision of other people's labour as it is the desired focus on self as the receptacle of living faith. And yet it does obscure the concerted efforts – the work – of proselytizers and missionaries, and more generally the Christian communities looking to expand their membership with fellow followers of Jesus.

But what of the willingness and unwillingness, or rather, the intention of the proselyte? What of those people who have an affiliation with a church or faith, are counted as members, and will at times voice support for particular doctrines, but who for most of the time do not locate themselves as individually engaged with the doctrine and ethics of a church? Their ethical lives, I would argue, are rather located within broader collaborative and collective modes of being. Thus, even in the individual's act of affiliation to a faith, a denomination, or a church, lays a complex relationship of collaboration and outward fealty to doctrine. Anthropology has long examined the concept of the individual, for example, with important strands of thinking aggregating around Marilyn Strathern's use of the concept of 'dividual', an incorporation of Charles Taylor's differentiation between porous and buffered selves, as well as a discipline-wide engagement with cross-cultural and context-bounded forms, limits and histories of personhood. Within these Christian contexts, while the concept of the individual is reified as the receptor of God's love, there is nevertheless much communal work that is invested into the stance of individualism (for an important engagement with the individual within Christianity, see Bialecki and Daswani 2015)

The term 'Rice Christian', a common, pejorative and somewhat derogatory term for people who convert, or affiliate to a particular church for financial and material benefits, rather than on the basis of belief, is widely used in Mindoro. It is not unusual and makes sense. Much of the time, missionaries will offer food assistance, or perhaps the promise of communal aid, not in direct exchange for conversion, but as an act of charity and engagement. Further, normally within church building or church planting, across denominations, a minister or leader of the new congregation is appointed, with some form of small salary. During my research I regularly witnessed the giving of material goods during Christian outreach work. This included the weekly giving of soap to prisoners in desperate need of it. It included the offer of food for people who attended worshipping services, and the giving of toys to children. It included the building of schools and the giving of school scholarships, the lending of money, the offer of labour, and – although I never saw it – apparently the direct giving of money. These are all embedded in the practices of church building, and contrasts with the financial flow of established or mother churches, in which the congregation give offerings of money and tithes to the church, thus maintaining the different facets of a living congregation. Some of these acts inevitably appear ethical to some and unethical to others, inasmuch as speaking of 'Rice Christians' places the onus of intention on the individual and the sincerity of their faith, and not on the mechanics and intentionality involved in missionary work. Beyond this, of course, exists the massive grey area of the hope for a better future, in the next life as well as in this one. While famously, televangelists and prosperity gospel promise financial reward, there are much more subtle promises of reward. For example, in Sta. Teresita, the Church of Latter Day Saints is attractive to many people, having as it does an American and middle-class sheen to it. More than once in Sta. Teresita, I heard the oft-repeated joke that people only went to the Mormon church because it had air conditioning. While that may or may not actually be true, there is undoubtedly an aspirational aspect of becoming a Mormon in Mindoro. Often set against a backdrop of poverty, the formal dress, American faces, modern architecture and display of wealth exist as a promissory note of sorts, of the life one lives as a Mormon.

But the concept of 'Rice Christian' itself raises an issue beyond the ethics of mingling money with faith – that is, the match and mismatch of intention and belief with the outward structures of public affiliation; the space between doctrine and self; and importantly, the nominally religious. Compare this with, for example, the experience of intensification, presence, and sensuously religious overload of speaking in tongues (Harkness 2017), which merges divinity and self within a single act. If we momentarily strip the term 'Rice Christian' of its flippant and derogatory uses, it points to those people who are not opposed to the performance of particular religious stances in relation to the world, but at the same time do not wholly inhabit them either: people whose relationship to doctrine and official tenets of a church are entirely shot through with the complexities of their lived experience; people whose religious intention is not clear-cut and fully aligned with doctrine, and yet who are open to forms of membership and appropriation. The woman the Mormon missionaries approached was one such person. She was clearly not as dedicated to the Church of Latter Day Saints as these two young men, but neither was she atheistic nor antagonistic to Christianity.

EJK and death

When I returned to Mindoro in May 2017, a year after the new government came into power, I was interested in Christian responses to the massive shifts in the politics of the country. Not only Duterte, but the increasingly partisan state of politics, and most importantly Oplan Tokhang (the 'war on drugs') and the ensuing violence that has dominated the Philippines since 2016, was a topic of continual discussion. Mindoro, and especially the western side of the island, Occidental Mindoro, is classically provincial, at once implicated in and outside the political machinations of Manila. The extrajudicial killings (EJK) had not occurred in Sta. Teresita, nor it seemed generally across the island (there are approximately 1.3 million people in all of Mindoro, spread across two provinces, as well as large tracts of indigenous people's ancestral lands). At the same time, Sta. Teresita has both experienced problems with drugs and has been fully immersed in the discourse on the war on drugs. But the extrajudicial killings that had swept through Manila were not present here, because, as I was repeatedly told by old friends and interlocutors, local drug users had surrendered to the regional police rather than risk violence.

While Occidental Mindoro had not, overall, voted for Duterte in the 2016 election, I found the majority of evangelical, or born again, Christians I worked with were in fact supportive of the Duterte administration and its policies. Among Catholics, opinions differed widely – some supporting and some not. But significantly, the interlocutors I found most prominently opposed to EJK located that opposition in terms of their Catholic belief. Their reasons, of course, were multiple, different, fragmented and, importantly, emerged from a different relationship to political discourses than many would assume of the Duterte administration's supporters. Despite the minority Catholic opposition, with Catholics, including clergy working among the communities affected most strongly opposed, and broad but somewhat weak institutional opposition to the state-sponsored violence, support for Duterte was, as mentioned, becoming common sense. The desire for a 'strong man' type of president, sweeping into power and sweeping up the country, has long been palpable, and understandable amid oppressive inequality, chronic corruption and a generally shared sense of entropy of government and social infrastructures. And yet the Duterte-type answer to such inequality and entropy – he has repeatedly and openly spoken of the need for violence and cleansing and defended the anonymous and extrajudicial killing of Filipinos – was not necessarily aligned with a Christian ethic, a reality with which my interlocutors were also grappling.

There is an obvious temptation to ask of Christians, across denominations: 'How can you, as a Christian, support the violence of the government?' This question, albeit one of seductive clarity, relies on reductive understandings of affiliation to doctrine, intention, and likewise erases not only the work of others, but of the nominally affiliated. In my conversations, both with Christian friends I have known for many years and with people whom I had only recently met, the topic of Duterte and the government inevitably came up. But his election and subsequent actions did not necessarily provoke the sharp partisan line of difference among the Christians with whom I worked, as it did for other communities across the country. Personal and familial rifts had occurred. There had been divisions in some congregations. And within larger denominational communities (including evangelical and Catholic communities), some pastors were strongly supportive of Duterte, while others found his government and actions so morally reprehensible that they spoke from the pulpit each Sunday on the sins of the government and implored their congregation to stand against it. But such contention was much less evident than was the phenomenon of *nominal* support or critique. People spoke of how they supported Duterte because one should support the president; how although violence was terrible it might lead to better lives for most Filipinos; how they thought the media was likely exaggerating the violence, and so forth.

Interestingly, the main national Christian organizations, including the National Council of Churches in the Philippines (NCCP), Philippine Council of Evangelical Churches (PCEC) and the Catholic Bishops' Conference of the Philippines (CBCP), have all come out against the policies of the government regarding EJK as well as recent attempts to reintroduce capital punishment. However, their engagements with the state have often been partial and limited. Outside of individual Christians working within the affected communities, and some smaller activist groups, Christian organizations have arguably been flatfooted in their response to Duterte. This might be usefully compared to, for example, the contexts of Christian engagements with violence as described by Kevin Lewis O'Neill in relation to Pentecostal work in gang violence-affected communities in Guatemala (O'Neill 2015). And yet the majority of Duterte's supporters are Christians. How do we explain this apparent disconnect between the organization and its affiliates? As I have tried to show, the nature of affiliation is a difficult thing to apprehend, existing as it does in and between spaces of explicit and unspoken meaning. We often want Christians to be their fullest Christian selves, aligned with their affiliation and doctrine; likewise, with Duterte supporters. We are far less adept, even ethnographically, at engaging with the religiously and politically nominal, especially when they align with our notion of 'repugnant other'. But I would argue that this form of nominalism – somewhere between 'in name only' and fully lived but under-determined – is inherent in how communities and collaboration are enacted. Given how Christianity, and notably the explicitness of its belief system, is ever present, articulated and performed every Sunday during masses and services and throughout the week during prayer worship, as well as in conversations, it is difficult to avoid reading articulations of faith *as* faith. Christianity, like politics, lends itself to statements of and about the world. At the same time, the Christian subject, as with the neoliberal one, is viewed within standardized forms of the individual. And yet, while Christian discourses emphasize, celebrate and often fetishize the concept of the 'individual', this is rarely ethnographically present. Instead we find continuous communal and collaborative acts. The ethical work of the individual is rarely done alone.

References

Bialecki, J. (2017), *A Diagram for Fire: Miracles and Variation in an American Charismatic Movement*, Berkeley and Los Angeles: University of California Press.

Bialecki, J. and G. Daswani (2015), 'What Is an Individual? The View from Christianity', *HAU: Journal of Ethnographic Theory,* 5 (1): 271–94.

Bornstein, E. (2005), *The Spirit of Development: Protestant NGOs, Morality, and Economics in Zimbabwe*, Palo Alto, CA: Stanford University Press.

Cannell, F. (2006), *The Anthropology of Christianity*, Durham and London: Duke University Press.

Chua, L. (2012), *The Christianity of Culture: Conversion, Ethnic Citizenship, and the Matter of Religion in Malaysian Borneo*, New York: Palgrave.

Handman, C. (2014), *Critical Christianity: Translation and Denominational Conflict in Papua New Guinea*. Berkeley and Los Angeles: University of California Press.

Harding, S. (1991), 'Representing Fundamentalism: The Problem of the Repugnant Cultural Other', *Social Research,* 58 (2): 373–93.

Harding, S. (2000), 'The Book of Jerry Falwell: Fundamentalist Language and Politics', Princeton University Press.

Harkness, N. (2017), 'Glossolalia and Cacophony in South Korea: Cultural Semiosis at the Limits of Language', *American Ethnologist,* 44 (3): 476–89.

Keane, W. (2007), *Christian Moderns: Freedom and Fetish in the Mission Encounter*, Berkeley and Los Angeles: University of California Press.

Muehlebach, A. (2013), 'The Catholicization of Neoliberalism: On Love and Welfare in Lombardy, Italy', *American Anthropologist,* 115 (3): 452–65.

O'Neill, K. L. (2015), *Secure the Soul: Christian Piety and Gang Prevention in Guatemala*, Berkeley and Los Angeles: University of California Press.

Robbins, J. (2001), 'God Is Nothing but Talk: Modernity, Language, and Prayer in a Papua New Guinea Society', *American Anthropologist* 103 (4): 901–12.

Robbins, J. (2014), 'The Anthropology of Christianity: Unity, Diversity, New Directions: An Introduction to Supplement 10', *Current Anthropology,* 55 (S10): S157–71.

Werbner, R. (2011), *Holy Hustlers, Schism, and Prophecy: Apostolic Reformation in Botswana*, Berkeley and Los Angeles: University of California Press.

Index

The letter *f* following an entry indicates a page that includes a figure.
The letter *t* following an entry indicates a page that includes a table.